An Undivided Heart

~ God's gift to his children ~

International Standard Book Number (ISBN)
978-0-9804172-7-2

NATIONAL
LIBRARY
OF AUSTRALIA
A catalogue record for this
book is available from the
National Library of Australia

Published by Cypress Project, 2019
Melbourne, Australia
https://cypressproject.com.au

REVIEWS

Do you want your foundation for faith to go deeper? *An Undivided Heart* will simultaneously stretch and strengthen you. I have found it to be a "popularly" written (though rigorous) theology of holiness, strong on historical context and theological nuance and a valuable resource for those with an interest in a stronger intellectual foundation for their faith?

Revd Dr Wayne Schmidt
General Superintendent, The Wesleyan Church of North America

-----------------I-----------------

An Undivided Heart, God's Plan for His Children presents a clear and thought-provoking understanding of holiness doctrine. Questions like: "Are justification and new birth simultaneous?" "Is there a second event in the lives of Christians, a filling with the Holy Spirit subsequent to conversion?" "What happens to inbred sin within the convert and sanctified believer?" are clarified and clearly answered by the author. His explanations of the doctrinal essentials in our experience and an on-going life of holiness is biblically sound, theologically solid and intensely practical. Dr. Cameron simply defines holiness as loving God with a whole heart.

This book is a must-read and I highly recommend it for all believers and theological students whose desire is to love God with undivided heart, and to all Christian leaders, seminary and Bible College teachers, and local church pastors whose desire is to grow in their understanding of how God works in our salvation and in our relationship with Him as we grow in grace and in the knowledge of our Savior and Lord Jesus Christ.

Revd Dr Johnny R. Guillermo
General Superintendent, The Wesleyan Church of the Philippines, Inc.

----

*A*n *Undivided Heart* covers a wide range of issues relevant to the new believer and the mature Christian. Teachers and students alike should find the historical, theological and practical insights to be of immense educational value. With respect to the historical, a wholesome description of the context in which Pietism and Evangelicalism emerged and developed in the seventeenth and eighteenth centuries is advanced. The author also skillfully deals with some of the practical and theological issues which have confronted Christians in the Wesleyan tradition over the years. In some instances, he brings an 'outside of the box' perspective to bear on these issues. One such issue has to do with the drinking of alcohol by Christians. Similarly, there is an interesting submission in relation to the concomitants in the salvation process. The suggestions that justification and the new birth do not necessarily occur at the same time, as well as the idea of Christians turning to Christ in faith but not being born again, are quite provocative, and should therefore stimulate much discussion among the clergy and laity alike.

This instructive and informative tool is a prime resource which is highly recommended reading for all Christians, persons of other faiths, the unchurched and even those who are not part of any religious persuasion. It also provides meaningful guidelines for those persons who need clarity on some of the niggling issues that confront them as they act out their faith on a daily basis. Essentially, 'An Undivided Heart' reflects the passion of the author with respect to holiness—one of the distinctives of the Wesleyan tradition.

Revd Dr Joel Cumberbatch
General Superintendent, The Wesleyan Holiness Church in the Caribbean

----

*A*n *Undivided Heart* helps individuals to identify their spiritual struggles and creates the desire for a deeper transforming relationship with the living God. It gives biblical answers to heart quest and provides ways on how to overcome daily spiritual struggles. It is simple to read, relevant to any culture and demonstrates the biblical truth that sets individuals free to serve the living God with a sincere heart full of the Holy Spirit. Reading your book has stirred my heart to think seriously about helping leaders to experience a changed heart. My prayer is that every copy of this book will lead individuals to overcome spiritual struggles and experience the fullness of God.

Revd Julius Galela
Regional Superintendent, The Wesleyan Church of Southern Africa.

The preaching on holiness in most pulpits of the Wesleyan Church in Africa, and Zambia in particular, is not heard as much as it should. And yet, the revival of Scriptural holiness was what gave birth to the Wesleyan Church. There is a great need to help pastors to experience and teach holiness in our time. Lindsay Cameron has authentically written on the subject of holiness in the book *An Undivided Heart*.

Having served as a Church leader in Africa and in his homeland, Australia, Lindsay Cameron's passion for God's people to have undivided hearts is extremely relevant and challenging. The book helps us appreciate the historical aspect of those who have gone before us and an encouragement that we too can experience what they experienced. This is so because there is never an end to spiritual growth in Christ because He is infinite. Therefore, we must go deeper and deeper in surrendering to God until we do not see ourselves any longer but Him in us. This will not happen automatically, but one has to intentionally take the step of seeking the deeper experience. I am personally looking forward to the publication of this book for my personal growth and I believe it will be a blessing for the Church in Africa.

Revd Dr Alfred Kalembo
Bishop – Pilgrim Wesleyan Church in Zambia, Former President of the Council of Churches in Zambia

----

TABLE OF CONTENTS

INTRODUCTION

For three decades I have sought to better understand the holiness teaching. At times I have seen holiness doctrine lead to legalism and at other times I have been frustrated by shallow answers to my questions. As a young Christian I sought the counsel of an older man in our church, asking why we do not drink alcohol. (I came from a decidedly unchurched background where alcohol consumption was a way a life.) The elder church member said to me, "I really don't know why we don't drink. We just never have." As a young pastor I was told of a group at a restaurant who responded to the waiter's offer of a drinks' menu, loudly announcing, "No thanks. We're Christians. We don't drink." Even as a young man, I knew these could not be holiness statements, but rather blind responses flowing from church culture. I am not comfortable to be one who follows, or leads, the blind.

Holiness is the most God-honoring concept that I have ever heard. I have been infatuated by it and yet struggled to understand it. For something so simple, holiness is quite difficult to articulate. One breakthrough came in my thinking when I realized that holiness was centered on perfect love, not on victory over sin. The more I pondered this, the more I was convinced that repentance should be primarily a matter of salvation, not of the deeper work of holiness. But there are so many complexities to it all. I know that I have both overstated and understated the teaching from the pulpit many times as I have tried to be faithful to the Scriptures. The conclusions that form the content of this book have been developing in my head for many years, and even in putting the text on the page, I have continued to learn. I have been astonished at how clearly and radically John Wesley and the early Evangelicals taught, and how far we have drifted from their teachings. This work has been a source of spiritual refreshing for me. I hope it helps you too as you seek to walk closely with God in this broken world.

I have adopted the term *An Undivided Heart* to break free from some of the older, often-abused, holiness terms. Overcoming a divided heart is a well-known biblical reference that gives focus to the attitude of the heart rather than the repentance component of holiness. Of course, holiness hugely impacts repentance but, in its primal thrust, holiness is finding release from a divided heart and learning to love God wholly. In my church tradition we have sometimes used the phrase *full salvation*. I like that concept too because I think many of us experience a very shallow version of our faith rather than the fullness intended in the gospel. Occasionally I speak of full salvation in this text, but not often. It can be an ambiguous concept. *Full salvation* has been used to mean different things over the centuries. Saint Augustine,[1] Charles Finney, Charles Spurgeon, Dwight Moody and the growing Pentecostal movement[2] have all used the terminology to mean different things. For this study, however, we are pursuing John Wesley's understanding of holiness and full salvation. In his usage, full salvation is freedom from both the *guilt* and the *power* of sin while still in this world. "It is thus we wait for entire sanctification; for a full salvation from all our sins, —from pride, self-will, anger, unbelief; or, as the apostle expressed it, 'go on unto perfection'."[3] John Fletcher, one of Wesley's protégés, countered Augustine's understanding of full salvation as glorification after death, writing, "Some of thy people look at death for full salvation from sin; but at thy command, Lord, I look unto thee... Thou can save from sin to the uttermost all that come to God through thee."[4]

Freedom from the power of sin was a fundamental tenet of Wesley's Methodism, and the teaching was the cause of abiding conflict with the Anglicans and those Evangelicals who held a Calvinist theology. An understanding of that conflict is helpful in grasping just how radical Wesley and his followers were. Therefore, a brief historic overview is provided in Chapter 1, and after that a systematic treatment of repentance, salvation, assurance, holiness and perseverance is undertaken. I pray that you are provoked and challenged as much as I have been in the research and writing.

Lindsay Cameron

---

[1] Augustine, *Complete Works*, Book 1, "Moral Treatises: On Continence , Point 21, loc. 139, 783; and Book 15, "Reproving the Manichaeans , Point 8, loc. 179, 827.
[2] For example, see Carter, *The Atonement for Sin and Sickness or, Full Salvation for Soul and Body* (Philadelphia: Willard Tract Repository, 1884), 213–222.
[3] Wesley, "Sermon 43, The Scripture Way of Salvation , in *Works*, vol. 6: 46
[4] Fletcher, *Fletcher on Christian Perfection*, Section 2, Point 12, loc. 740.

Chapter 1: **THE HISTORICAL CONTEXT**

*Since we have so great a cloud of witnesses surrounding us, let us
also lay aside every encumbrance and the sin which so easily
entangles us, and let us run with endurance the race that is set before
us, fixing our eyes on Jesus, the author and perfecter of faith.*
Hebrews 12:1–2

In the 1730s nation-wide revivals burst upon the mainstream church
in Britain and the colonies in North America. The revivals, dubbed
evangelical,[1] occurred almost simultaneously in the New England
colonies of America, in Wales and in England from 1735, and spread
from there around the globe. These Evangelical Revivals, including the
Great Awakenings of North America, were understood by the
Evangelicals to be rooted in the founding principles of continental
Protestantism, with threads extending centuries earlier to Catholic
reformers and patriarchs. Evangelicalism was not a new thing, and
yet, clearly something new occurred in the English-speaking world in
the 1730s that exceeded what had been building for generations in
continental Europe.

From the 1600s the reform movements within Lutheranism (that is,
Pietism) and Anglicanism (that is, Puritanism) had extensive contact
with each other, sharing and encouraging concepts of the new birth,
bible-study, small-group meetings, lay-preaching and organized
societies for community action. Furthermore, since much of the
immigration to America was from Germany, Poland and other
European nations, the continental pursuit of salvation by faith and
personal piety was sown directly in the New World.

Localized revivals with clear evangelical tones began breaking out in
central Europe from 1701–08.[2] Lutheran-Pietists and the more-recent

---

[1] The term *evangelical* has been dated as early as the 1530s, as used by William
Tyndale and Sir Thomas More.
[2] The border country between Poland and Czechia, known then as Silesia.
Ward, *Protestant Evangelical Awakening*, 72–79.

Moravian preachers actively worked with local preachers and printed literature to encourage isolated revivals in Sweden, the Baltic States and Russia. Continental dispersion of this pre-evangelical teaching was still expanding vigorously even while the famed Oxford Club was beginning to meet in England. The Moravian sect, which incorporated Count Zinzendorf's Pietism and the Brethren faith of Moravian and Bohemian refugees, began to promote an instantaneous experiential salvation,[3] and the components of full-blown Evangelicalism were in place. In the relative religious tolerance of Britain and the separation of church and state in the New World, localized evangelical revivals became nation-wide, culture-changing phenomena.

The Methodists

John and Charles Wesley played a significant part in the evangelical revivals, although their own conversions were some three years after most of the initial evangelical leaders.[4] After several years of wrestling with the simple teaching of salvation by faith, the Wesley brothers both found assurance of salvation within days of each other in May 1738.[5] Their conversions (and perhaps, sanctifications) marked the introduction of a fiercely contested theological rift between them and the other evangelical leaders. This rift was a major schism, but it can sometimes overshadow the fact that all Evangelicals shared many theological essentials, including the full inspiration of the Bible, the absolute necessity of a miraculous conversion, the promise of Spirit-given assurance of salvation and the clear teaching that born-again believers cannot continue in willful sin.

Nonetheless, the theological differences between the Wesleyan Methodists and the other Evangelicals was a prominent historical event, and it was brutal. The global history of Evangelicalism does not make sense without an understanding of this conflict. The Wesley brothers taught from a modified Arminian theological basis, while the other evangelical leaders were either of Moravian or Calvinist theologies. The Moravian missionaries (Lutheran-Pietist-Brethren heritage) together with Jonathan Edwards, George Whitefield, Howell Harris, Benjamin Ingham and the Countess of Huntingdon (Calvinist-Puritan heritage) all followed the teaching of predestination. The

---

[3] Ward, *Protestant Evangelical Awakening*, 136–39.
[4] That is Jonathan Edwards of Connecticut, George Whitefield, Benjamin Ingham and Lady Huntingdon of England, and Howell Harris of Wales.
[5] Charles Wesley on May 21, 1738, John Wesley on May 24, 1738.

Wesleys followed a teaching that emphasized free-will, which violently clashed with the concept of predestination.

Like Jacobus Arminius (1560–1609) before them,6 the Wesley brothers taught that the atoning merit of Christ's death is freely available to every member of the human race, but it is only effective for those who respond to Christ in saving faith. All people can be saved by faith, but not all people will respond to Christ in faith. However, like Martin Luther (1483–1546) and John Calvin (1509–64) before them, the Lutheran and Calvinist leaders taught that every person was assigned to either salvation or damnation before their birth, even before the foundations of the world.7 For those who promoted this doctrine of predestination, an individual response was not possible for anyone who had not been preselected by God. There were subtle differences between the Moravians and the Calvinists, which ultimately alienated the Moravians as well but the major schisms of 1740–41 and 1770–71, that brought an end to Oxford Club unity, were the result of the division over predestination and free-will.

The Wesleys taught that all converts must strive for their own salvation and sanctification, while the Moravian/Calvinist teaching opposed the concept of *striving* as an affront to God's sovereign choice and an outrageous heresy. Both camps taught the doctrine of salvation by faith, which was the cornerstone doctrine of the Protestant Reformation, but they interpreted the doctrine differently to each other. The Moravians and Calvinists understood that saving faith was granted to some people, rather than exercised by them. For them, there was nothing an individual could do to influence their eternal destiny, and any striving would be to seek salvation through works. The predestinarian teaching of reprobation[8] —the necessary corollary to predestination—and its potential to promote antinomianism[9] were focal points for the Wesleyan objection to Moravian/Calvinist

---

[6] The General Baptists were another group in London   of the Dissenting stream   which pursued free will teaching prior to the Wesleys.

[7] The Supralapsarian / Infralapsarian debate (arguing whether predestination was assigned before or after Adam and Eve s original sin) was the debate into which Jacobus Arminius entered in the Netherlands as a staunch Calvinist and emerged believing neither viewpoint, thereby establishing the Remonstrants and what would become known as Arminian theology.

[8] That is, that some people are created for the express purpose of suffering eternally in hell. See Wesley, "Sermon 78, Free Grace , in *Works*, vol. 7: 383.

[9] That is the concept that, since salvation is by grace alone, then believers are free to continue to sin without risk to their salvation. See Fletcher, *Five Checks to Antinomianism.*

doctrine, while the Wesleyan teaching of Christian Perfection (holiness) became the focal point of the Moravian/Calvinist opposition to the Wesleys.[10]

After John and Charles Wesley's conversions, this theological rift quickly widened and divided the former evangelical comrades. In July 1740, John and Charles Wesley separated from the Moravian leadership at the Fetter Lane Society in London over the doctrines of predestination and holiness. The recently arrived Moravian leader, Philip Molther, began teaching a radical form of predestination that required *stillness*,[11] and the Wesleys separated from the society, forming the United Society in Moorfields. The Foundry at Moorfields became the first uniquely Wesleyan Methodist society in London. The Wesleys and the Moravians were never reconciled, so that in 1770, John Wesley was still describing the extreme theological error of the Moravian "Zinzendorf 'heresy'."[12]

At the same time, in 1740, John Wesley and George Whitefield published against each other's doctrinal views despite their close friendship.[13] In June, Wesley's sermon, *Free Grace*, was printed and widely distributed,[14] and in December Whitefield wrote his rebuttal. The heat of the disagreement can be glimpsed in Whitefield's response to Wesley:

> Down with your carnal reasoning. Be a little child; and then, instead of pawning your salvation, as you have done in a late hymn book, if the doctrine of universal redemption be not true; instead of talking of sinless perfection as you have done in the preface to that hymn book, and making man's salvation to depend on his own free-will as you have in this sermon; you will compose an hymn in praise of sovereign distinguishing love. You will caution believers against striving to work a perfection

---

[10] The Wesleyan understanding of holiness required personal discipline and diligence.

[11] The Moravians taught that, because of predestination, all true believers were fully sanctified holy. Furthermore, Molther applied the doctrine of predestination (and election) to mean that reading the Bible, praying, church going, or doing good works was an evil expression of salvation by works, when undertaken before being fully saved. See Wesley, "Journal, November 1, 1739 – July 20, 1740 , in *Works*, vol. 1: 248–82.

[12] That is that all true believers are sanctified holy. See Wood, *Meaning of Pentecost in Early Methodism*, chapt. 3: 48, loc. 402.

[13] Keeping in mind that it was only in April 1740 that Whitefield handed over his field preaching enterprise in Bristol to John Wesley.

[14] Wesley, "Sermon 78, Free Grace , in *Works*, vol. 7: 373–386.

out of their own hearts, and print another sermon the reverse of this, and entitle it free-grace indeed.[15]

The relationship between the Wesleys and the Moravians was never properly restored, but the rift between the Wesleyan Methodists and the Calvinist Evangelicals was gradually healed, to the extent that two of Wesley's prominent young men were recruited to lead Lady Huntingdon's *Trevecca College* in Wales in 1768.[16] In 1770, George Whitefield died while on preaching tour in America and, at his specific request, John Wesley preached his London memorial sermon at the Tottenham-Court Road Chapel on Sunday, November 18, 1770.

The timing of these events is rather extraordinary, because in the shadow of Whitefield's death, the Evangelicals were about to be torn apart again. In August 1770, John Wesley led his annual Methodist Conference to adopt a minute,[17] reflecting upon the Wesleyan Methodist tendency to embrace Calvinist assumptions:

"We have leaned too much toward Calvinism." Wherein?

1. With regard to man's faithfulness. Our Lord Himself taught to use the expression. And we ought never to be ashamed of it. We ought steadily to assert, on His authority, that if a man is not "faithful in the unrighteous mammon money]," God will not give him the true riches.

2. With regard to working for life. This also our Lord has expressly commanded us. "Labor for the meat that endures to everlasting life." And, in fact, every believer, till he comes to glory, works for as well as from life.

3. We have received it as a maxim, that "a man is to do nothing in order to justification." Nothing can be more false. Whoever desires to find favor with God should "cease from evil, and learn to do well." Whoever repents should do "works meet for repentance." And if this is not in order to find favor, what does he do them for? italics are from the Minutes][18]

---

[15] Whitefield, "A Letter to the Reverend Mr. John Wesley in Answer to His Sermon Entitled] Free Grace , in *Works*, vol. 4: 72.

[16] They were John Fletcher as founding President and Joseph Benson as Principal. Wood, *The Meaning of Pentecost in Early Methodism*, 17–18.

[17] That is, an official written record.

[18] Wesleyan Methodist Conference, *Minutes of the Methodist Conferences*, 95–96. See Appendix B for the full minute.

Lady Huntingdon's faithful supporter, Rev. Walter Shirley,19 called upon Calvinists from across the British Isles to disrupt the August 1771 Methodist Conference and force John Wesley to recant the heresies contained in that 1770 Minute. Therefore, in July 1771, one of John Wesley's most articulate supporters and his "designated successor,"20 John Fletcher, published his first of five Checks to Antinomianism. Fletcher's systematic use of the Bible and of Shirley's own publications to defend Wesleyan-Arminianism became one of Methodism's greatest theological statements, and Fletcher is given the unusual acknowledgement of having influenced the theology of John Wesley himself in his later years.21

The concept that John Wesley's Methodism has repeatedly shown a tendency to drift from its early understanding of salvation and holiness is central to our search to rediscover the power of an undivided heart. Over the following centuries Wesleyan-Arminianism became increasingly influenced by Calvinism, affluence and complacency. Altar-call theology and presumptuous assurance of salvation22 replaced early Methodism's call to "flee the wrath to come." At the same time, Calvinism found sufficient common ground with the holiness revivals, so that a uniquely-Calvinistic version of holiness teaching was promoted through the Oberlin College in America and the Keswick Conventions in Britain.

A more conciliatory theology

The purpose of this historic overview is to frame the discussion before us. The early holiness teaching was so controversial, so aggressive in its pursuit of a balance between faith and good works, that it can still shock us today. If Wesley's preachers were warned to resist the temptation to dilute their doctrines while Wesley was still alive, then it seems extremely likely that the teaching we have inherited in the twenty-first century has indeed been substantially softened (or even reinvented) since early Methodism. If simple Methodist doctrines stirred a nation-wide call for Calvinists to picket the Methodist Conference in 1771, then no greater evidence of theological compromise can be offered than the readjustments required to

---

[19] Shirley was second cousin to Lady Huntingdon.
[20] Wood, *The Meaning of Pentecost in Early Methodism*, 75–100.
[21] Wood, *The Meaning of Pentecost in Early Methodism*, 7.
[22] See Chapter 4.

facilitate mergers of Methodist, Presbyterian and Congregational groups around the globe in the twentieth century.

In the 1770 Minutes, the question was asked, "What have we then been disputing about for these thirty years?" The answer supplied was, "I am afraid, about words."[23] Some of the words that separated the Wesleyans and the Calvinists were worth disputing and some were distorted to create a disagreement where little truly existed. There were ardent Arminians and Calvinists on both sides who believed in the inerrancy of the Bible, the miraculous born-again conversion and the impossibility for a true Christian willfully sinning.[24] However, the Calvinistic doctrines of predestination and reprobation were fundamentally offensive to the Wesleyans,[25] while the Wesleyan teaching of free-will was unbiblical to Calvinists and working out salvation was "Popery."[26] A wall between them was built and at times it was sustained by belligerently overstated rhetoric. John Wesley's teaching of Christian perfection encountered resistance from Anglican Church leaders for many years, most notably from the Bishop of London, Revd Dr Edmund Gibson. Gibson publicly criticized the enthusiasm of Methodist meetings and denied that anything exceptional had ever come from these revivals.[27] However, when Wesley explained his teachings in person to Gibson, the Bishop replied, "If this be all you mean, publish it to all the world. If anyone can confute what you say, he may have free leave."[28] Three decades later, John Fletcher took great advantage of the writings of several prominent Calvinists to show that Calvinists often taught the same things that the Wesleyans taught, albeit in different words. Fletcher quoted Rev. Shirley's own sermons back at him in support of Methodist teachings, with the result that Shirley took the extraordinary action of removing twelve of his own sermons from

---

[23] Appendix B.

[24] See Chapter 2.

[25] Although, the term *predestination* can be interpreted differently to the traditional Reformed definition. It can, with solid biblical reason, be interpreted to mean that God planned beforehand the pathway of salvation and sanctification, rather than the individuals who would be saved or damned.

[26] Wesley, "Journal, August 27, 1739, February 28 and August 14, 1741, March 28, 1743 , in *Works*, vol. 1: 218, 301, 322, 418.

[27] See Gibson, *Observations Upon the Conduct and Behavior of ... Methodists.* Also, Wesley, "Sermon 66, The Signs of the Times , vol. 6: 307 and "Sermon 132, Foundation of the City Road Chapel , in *Works*, vol. 7: 420.

[28] Wesley, *A Plain Account of Christian Perfection*, Section 12, p.21.

publication. Fletcher chastised Shirley for destroying his own sermons out of humiliation:

> O! Sir, what have you done! Do you not know that your sermons contain not only the legally evangelical doctrine of the Methodist] Minutes, but likewise all the doctrine which moderate Calvinists esteem as the marrow of the Gospels?... Now sir, spare a valuable book for the sake of a "thousand" excellent things it contains. But if you are inflexible, and still wish it "burned," imitate, at least, the kind angels who sent Lot out of the fiery overthrow of Sodom and Gomorrah], and except all the evangelical pages of the unfortunate volume.[29]

The Methodists were not without fault in stoking the flames of a difficult theological division though. Indeed, it seems to have been an era that reveled in theological thrust and parry. Wesley doggedly retained his *Christian perfection* terminology, despite the misconceptions that the word *perfection* invariably generated,[30] while in following centuries, many Methodists adopted the less confronting term, *holiness*. Fletcher, likewise, seemed to gravitate to provocative language. In the second of his *Five Checks to Antinomianism*, Fletcher developed his argument for the "second justification by works," which he then carried over into his subsequent *Checks*:

> Or will you insinuate that our Lord "recanted" the legal sermons written Matthew 5, and 12? If you do, his particular account of the day of judgment, chapter 25, which strongly confirms and clearly explains the doctrine of our second justification by works, will prove you greatly mistaken, as will also his declaration to St. John, above forty years after, "Behold, I am coming quickly, and my reward is with me, to give to every man as his work (not faith) shall be." emphasis Fletcher's][31]

Fletcher was arguing that many biblical statements point to the final judgment when our good-works will be examined to confirm or repudiate our claims to a living faith. However, by dubbing this truth a *second justification*, Fletcher allowed a perception that salvation by faith will ultimately be superseded by salvation by works—a theology that all Wesleyans rejected. Fletcher's argument was that our actions illustrate whether we have truly lived in abiding love and

---

[29] Fletcher, *Five Checks to Antinomianism*, Second Check, Letter 2, loc. 1768.
[30] More on this topic in Chapter 5.
[31] Fletcher, *Five Checks to Antinomianism*, Second Check, Letter 1, loc. 1418.

repentance,[32] but his choice of terminology appears to have been chosen for maximum shock-value.

By the end of George Whitefield's and John Wesley's lives, some of the personal attack had dissipated between the British Evangelicals.[33] In the nineteenth century, developments in America resulted in some grudging agreement in the previously-divisive topic of holiness. The American Methodists, after neglecting the holiness teaching during the slavery divisions, experienced a profound resurgence of holiness teaching with the development of camp meetings from 1800. Camp meetings initially appeared as an extension of the traditional Methodist quarterly meetings[34] and by 1802, the aging Francis Asbury acknowledged that camp meetings were a central and effective means of revival.[35] The Methodists and the Baptists both grew exponentially in the early decades of the nineteenth century, with the result that the old Calvinist anti-holiness sentiment was reignited and gained wide publicity. However, this divide was thrown into turmoil in 1836, when the leaders of the Calvinist Oberlin College, evangelist Charles Finney and principal Asa Mahan, both claimed to have experienced sanctification. There followed a rush of non-Methodist publications on holiness as the Calvinists embraced their own form of the doctrine.[36] Finney's *Views on Sanctification* (1840), Mahan's *Scripture Doctrine of Christian Perfection* (1844) and W.E. Boardman's *The Higher Christian Life* (1858) flowed back into Methodism, breaking down old barriers and drawing the Methodists and Calvinists closer to a common view of holiness. This reformation of the holiness doctrine was accelerated by the formation of the National Camp Meeting Association for the Promotion of Christian Holiness in Georgia in 1867.[37] By the end of the century, interdenominationalism had become a feature of the holiness camp meetings, where Baptists, Methodists, Quakers and Campbellites (American Restoration Theology) sought the Spirit's filling together.[38]

---

[32] More on this topic in Chapter 9.
[33] However, it might be argued that the Baptists and Methodists in America continued to pursue the debate.
[34] Wigger, *American Saint*, 59, 318. As the Second Great Awakening changed the religious face of the American nation, 600 camp meetings were planned in the Methodist Church in 1810 alone. Wigger, 365.
[35] Wigger, *American Saint*, 317.
[36] Bebbington, *Evangelicalism in Modern Britain*, 164–65.
[37] Synan, *The Holiness Pentecostal Tradition*, chapt. 2, loc. 294.
[38] Thomas and Thomas, *Days of Our Pilgrimage*, 14–17, 30.

Through the neglect and rediscovery of the holiness teaching, and with a more conciliatory approach to the old evangelical divide, a new understanding of holiness doctrine evolved, with a greater focus on God's work in holiness and a lesser emphasis on human striving. This new holiness theology can be illustrated in the dynamic ministry of Phoebe Palmer. Palmer was a Methodist who's personal search for holiness mirrored John Wesley's search for assurance of salvation. "From a sense of responsibility before God], she began to be more abundant in labors" as she sought to be the person she should be. Yet, despite her constant good-works and prayer, Palmer remained, "conscious that she had not the witness of entire consecration to God."[39] Eventually, Palmer concluded that she had been leaning too heavily upon her need for an experience when she simply needed to take the truths of the Bible as her promise regardless of feelings. She concluded that feelings will develop once faith is in place. Therefore, Palmer offered herself to God at the altar and claimed God's sanctifying grace in that same moment:

> O, Lord, I call heaven and earth to witness that I now lay my body, soul, and spirit, with all these redeeming powers, upon thine altar, to be forever THINE! 'TIS DONE! Thou hast promised to receive me! Thou canst not be unfaithful! Thou dost receive me now! From this time henceforth I am thine wholly thine![40]

This new immediate-holiness-through-an-altar-call was dubbed the *shorter way*,[41] and became Palmer's mantra as she preached and published in America and Britain until her death in 1874. Phoebe Palmer's search and discovery of holiness through trusting consecration at the altar became the abiding standard of the holiness movement in the later decades of the nineteenth century. Without doubting Palmer's commitment or experience, it is instructive to note how far the *shorter way* had taken Methodism from its roots and how much it favored the Calvinistic viewpoint. This can be illustrated in three ways:

1. Note that Palmer had to "reckon herself dead unto sin" in her quest for holiness. This was the terminology that Wesley, Whitefield and Fletcher used to describe salvation, not

---

[39] Palmer, *The Way of Holiness*, Section 2, loc. 137; Section 3, loc. 188.

[40] Palmer, *The Way of Holiness*, Section 6, loc. 394. There is a clear connection between Palmer s thinking/teachings and the growth of healing ministries in the late 1800s.

[41] Palmer, *The Way of Holiness*, Section 7, loc. 436.

sanctification. For the early evangelicals, all born-again believers must cease willful sin—it was not delayed until holiness![42] Nudging repentance further along in the Christian experience opened the way for several tragic consequences, including condoning lukewarm Christianity, turning holiness into an often-legalistic, culture-driven freedom from social mores, and drawing attention away from the historic and biblical purpose of holiness as perfect love.

2. One obvious difference between Wesley's "heart-warming" conversion experience and Palmer's holiness teaching is that Wesley did not set aside his regimen of good-works once he had assurance of salvation. To the end of his life, he maintained that good-works and other means of grace were central pillars of abiding holiness. Wesley wrote:

> We do not allow, but earnestly contend, that there is no perfection in this life, which implies any excusing of the believer] from attending all the ordinances of God, or from doing good unto all men while we have time, though "especially unto the household of faith." We believe, that not only the babes in Christ, who have newly found redemption in his blood, but those who are "grown up into perfect men," are indispensably obliged, as often as they have opportunity, "to eat bread and drink wine in remembrance to him," and to "search the Scriptures"; by fasting, as well as temperance, "to keep their bodies under, and bring them into subjection"; and, above all, to pour out their souls in prayer, both secretly, and in the great congregation.[43]

3. Palmer's new altar-call holiness was considerably influenced by Calvinism, in that she now encouraged a perception that the work of holiness was God's work to do and the believer's to receive by faith. Holiness became something that God did, to the detriment of the believer's responsibility. John and Charles Wesley broke from the Moravian-led Fetter Lane Society over the latter's teaching of stillness in 1740, and hints of stillness can be seen in the new shorter-way. Class meetings had been the pillar of accountability in John Wesley's system, so it should be no surprise that, within decades of Palmer's ministry

---

[42] Inbred sin was dealt with at holiness, not acts of willful sin. See Chapter 7.
[43] Wesley, *A Plain Account of Christian Perfection*, Section 15: 34–35.

much of Methodism no longer considered class meetings an essential for church membership.

The evidence suggests that Phoebe Palmer was a faithful worker for the gospel and for holiness. She neither invented the altar call nor manufactured a new understanding of holiness—she is merely a useful pointer to the shifting teaching of holiness, first within Methodism and then in the wider denominational context. Altar calls were the fruit of camp meetings from the early 1800s[44] and of Charles Finney's "anxious seat."[45] The contention here is that altar-call theology refocused holiness onto the *miraculous moment* rather than the *lifetime of discipline*. Both the miraculous and the self-discipline were vitally important to John Wesley, but the altar call moved the holiness experience closer to a Calvinistic understanding of an all-controlling sovereign God and away from the responsibility of believers.

These developments in American Methodism flowed back into British Methodism. Early signs of this can be seen in the formation of the Primitive Methodist denomination in Britain, centered around camp-meetings from 1811.[46] This development in England's midland counties occurred within a decade of the widespread use of camp meetings in America. Another is seen in the formation of the Keswick Conventions in England from 1875. Charles Finney had toured England in 1849 and Phoebe Palmer from 1859–63. Their visits illustrate the growing desire of non-Methodists for a modified message of holiness. William Pennefather, an Anglican priest, initiated annual revival meetings in Barnet from 1856 and in Mildmay from 1864, where "personal holiness" was a central theme.[47] From 1873, American evangelists, Robert and Hannah Pearsall Smith, began ministry in Britain. With a mix of Quaker heritage and American Methodist experience, the Keswick Conventions were born. Their "new spirituality" was presented at the first Keswick Convention in 1875, where, in keeping with a predominately Calvinist heritage, the Keswick leadership rejected "effort, conflict and] endeavor" as they sought "the rest of faith."[48] Hints of the Moravian *stillness* and Phoebe

---

[44] Peter Cartwright described altar ministry in 1806 at the New Lancaster OH Methodist Camp meeting. Cartwright, *Autobiography*, 77.

[45] Or "anxious bench , became especially well known during Finney s Rochester campaign from 1831. See Finney, *Autobiography*, chapt. 20, p. 158.

[46] Petty, *The History of the Primitive Methodist Connexion*, 25.

[47] Bebbington, *Evangelicalism in Modern Britain*, 159–61.

[48] Bebbington, *Evangelicalism in Modern Britain*, 155.

Palmer's *shorter way* can be heard to echo through the new Calvinist holiness emphasis of waiting upon God for his anointing.

Other culture changing influences in the nineteenth and twentieth centuries included the rise of higher biblical-criticism, liberal theology and social gospel, and the emergence of the Pentecostal movement. Both profoundly impacted the Methodist message, further obscuring the original message of the Evangelicals and dragging the Methodist message away from its role in nation-wide revivals. Liberal theology broke with evangelical fundamentals by denying the complete inspiration of the Bible and redefining conversion as a social phenomenon rather than a miraculous personal indwelling of the Spirit of God.[49] Mainline Methodist denominations around the globe have since fought internal battles between their liberal intellectual elite and their conservative congregations, resulting in massive numerical decline in Western nations. In circles where a miraculous conversion is disavowed, the message of holiness has largely disappeared.

The Pentecostal movement's influence upon Methodism, however, was not an attack upon the Methodist message, but a development out of it. It has been widely acknowledged that Pentecostalism rose to fill the void left by Methodism's declining message,[50] and it reinforced conservative, Bible-believing Evangelicalism.[51] Nonetheless, the outcome of Pentecostalism's rise is that Palmer's altar-call theology was cemented in church tradition and the holiness message was superseded by the focus upon power-in-witness. Pentecostal theology's capacity to infiltrate mainline denominations has done much to promote a doctrine of the Holy Spirit and to defend the inerrancy of the Bible, but it has not upheld the early Methodist emphasis on good-works. And, how could it, if indeed Pentecostalism was born out of waning Methodism that had itself drifted from its early priorities?

This historic overview draws attention to the changes that have reshaped holiness teaching from the vitality of early evangelical expansion to the powerlessness of modern-day, culture-pleasing irrelevance. It is written to prepare the reader for some of the chapters to come. The remainder of this book is primarily presented as a Bible

---

[49] Cameron, *Methodism Reborn*, 85–94.
[50] Hempton, *Empire of the Spirit*, chapt. 1, loc. 436; Synan, *The Holiness Pentecostal Tradition*, preface, loc. 37 and chapt. 1, loc. 50; and Dayton, *Theological Roots of Pentecostalism*, 175.
[51] Bebbington, *Evangelicalism in Modern Britain*, 198.

study, with illustrations from the seminal writings of John Wesley, John Fletcher and George Whitefield. In these chapters we glimpse the gripping, even shocking, demands of an unwavering gospel. The goal is not simply to understand Methodist heritage, but to rediscover the joy of loving God with an undivided heart.

Calvinism's underlying premise is that God's purpose on the earth is to rescue his elect from this world of sin. Wesleyanism's underlying assumption is that God's purpose is to use this broken world as a training ground, a place of refinement, for those who will carry God's name in eternity. That difference is immense. If the biblical term *predestination* is properly understood to be a pathway of refinement that some will pass while others fail, rather than pre-selection of specific individuals, then it is essential that individuals must be allowed to strive and grow so the process of changed character is achieved. If pre-selection is the only purpose, then the elect can arrive in heaven no better for their time on earth. This is a profound discussion and the launching point for the rest of our study.

STUDY QUESTIONS

These following "Questions for Reflection and Discussion" are intended for review of the corresponding chapters of *An Undivided Heart: God's gift to his children*. It is expected that the related chapter will be read prior to considering the study questions.

These questions are provided for a wide range of applications, from local church small-group discussion to college coursework. The questions provide for review and an opportunity to consider specific concepts more deeply. The group-leader/teacher might assign all the questions or only selected questions, as best suits the need.

Consider these questions and take some notes, or if you are with a group, discuss your answers. Do not judge another person's answers! Every one of us comes to study the Christian faith from a different background. It is good to have some different perspectives. It makes the discussion richer.

QUESTIONS FOR REFLECTION AND DISCUSSION

1. Have you encountered the distinction between Calvinism and Arminianism before? Explain the differences in your own words. Do you think these distinctions are important today? Explain your reasons.

2. We are told here that the Wesleys taught "free will" and the Calvinists taught "predestination". Explain the difference.

3. Calvinism and Arminianism are not the only theological options. Calvinism is part of a larger grouping called Reformed theology, which in many ways is aligned with Lutheranism. The third option in the early Evangelical arena was Sacramentalism, which would be typified by the High-Anglicans and the Catholics. Do you know much about any of these? Do you identify with one of them? Do an internet search and find out more.

4. What four things are we told were the theological essentials of all Evangelicals? Discuss whether a modern group could still be Evangelical if they did not hold one or more of those "essentials".

5. Research and define the terms *reprobation* and *antinomianism.* Include your own responses to these doctrines.

6. What is your understanding of being born-again? How does that happen? When does it happen? What happens to the person who is born-again? Where did you hear about this teaching?

7. What do you understand about the Bible? Is it accurate and true? From where did your thoughts about the Bible originate? How much of the Bible have you read?

8. Explain John Fletcher's teaching on the "Second Justification by Works"? Have you heard this taught in church? How would this teaching be received if it was taught in your congregation?

9. Explain Phoebe Palmer's "Shorter Way". Compare that to John Wesley's understanding of "Christian Perfection" and to modern Pentecostal teachings.

10. In this chapter it is stated, "Where miraculous conversion is disavowed, the message of holiness has largely disappeared." Why is that conclusion warranted? Do you agree?

11. The final paragraph of Chapter 1 suggests that, for Arminians, the struggles of this world are a training ground for building eternal character. How do you respond to that concept?

12. Consider the following chart of Evangelical connections in eighteenth-century London. Describe what each group agreed on and what they disagreed on.

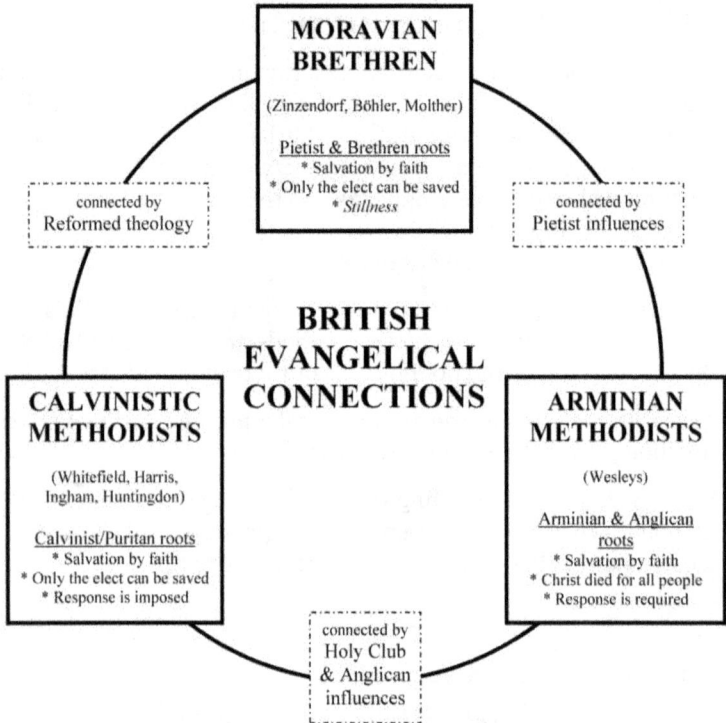

MORAVIAN BRETHREN

(Zinzendorf, Böhler, Molther)

Pietist & Brethren roots
* Salvation by faith
* Only the elect can be saved
* *Stillness*

connected by
Reformed theology

connected by
Pietist influences

BRITISH EVANGELICAL CONNECTIONS

CALVINISTIC METHODISTS

(Whitefield, Harris, Ingham, Huntingdon)

Calvinist/Puritan roots
* Salvation by faith
* Only the elect can be saved
* Response is imposed

ARMINIAN METHODISTS

(Wesleys)

Arminian & Anglican roots
* Salvation by faith
* Christ died for all people
* Response is required

connected by
Holy Club
& Anglican
influences

Chapter 2: **THE GOAL OF OUR FAITH**

He chose us in Him before the foundation of the world,
that we would be holy and blameless before Him.
Ephesians 1:4

The Apostle Paul explained the goal of Christianity as "love from a pure heart and a good conscience and a sincere faith."[1] These words complement the central teachings of Jesus, "'You shall love the LORD your God with all your heart, and with all your soul, and with all your mind.' This is the great and foremost commandment. The second is like it, 'You shall love your neighbor as yourself'."[2] Neither Jesus nor Paul offered any alternative to single-minded love for God. That is holiness, and unconditional love is always the intended outcome of Christianity.

In his first letter to the Corinthian Church, Paul again asserted that, on this earth, the three most desirable characteristics are "faith, hope, love... but the greatest of these is love."[3] The Apostle Peter similarly explained the process of Christian growth, outlining the process from saving faith to moral excellence (or goodness), knowledge, self-control, perseverance and godliness, and from brotherly love to unconditional love.[4] Unwavering, unconditional, undivided love is, therefore, the primary goal of the Christian faith. This goal should not be obscured by a misunderstanding of sinless perfection or a misdirection toward Christian service.

Interestingly, the love described by Paul in 1 Timothy 1 rises not only out of pure intentions and sincere motives, but it also draws upon "a good conscience." The inclusion of a good conscience affirms that the mature Christian should be unaware of any personal willful sin, since a guilty conscience would make a mockery of purity and sincerity and

---

[1] 1 Timothy 1:5.
[2] Matthew 22:37–39.
[3] 1 Corinthians 13:13.
[4] 2 Peter 1:5 7. This text will be examined in greater detail in Chapter 3.

it would undermine confident faith. Furthermore, a guilty conscience is often associated with a legalistic, critical spirit because finding fault in others is one way of minimizing one's own sense of guilt. A pure heart and a sincere faith both build upon a conscience that is free from guilt. It is not possible to experience the love that Paul describes while sin is knowingly tolerated in the life of the believer.

Of course, only God can truly know the conscious and subconscious machinations of the heart. Our understanding of other people, and even of ourselves, is at best partial. As King Solomon said, "All the ways of a man are clean in his own sight, but the LORD weighs the motives."[5] God has testified himself, "Man looks at the outward appearance, but the LORD looks at the heart,"[6] and King David affirmed, "For the LORD searches all hearts, and understands every intent of the thoughts."[7] Because of our limitations, we are prone to look upon people's actions to judge their motives, often through the lens of our own experiences, and since we see the external rather than the internal, the biblical call to a pure heart is too often translated into a list of outward regulations. This leads to the ugliness of legalism. The test of a pure heart should be one of purity of intention, not of actions.

Our inability to know each other's motives is somewhat countered by the recurring teaching of the New Testament that people's hidden motives will be evidenced by the "fruit" of their lives;[8] meaning that the visible results of a person's life provide a reliable window into the invisible motivations. It should be noted though, that fruit is not produced in a single day, but over a period of time. In due time the condition of a person's heart will be revealed through the results of their life and ministry. Have they left health or hurt where they have been? How do the members of their family relate to each other? Have they remained faithful? A person's heart is not revealed in one day, but the out-workings are inescapable over time.

Even the self-assessment of the believer is unreliable. We may know ourselves better than we know others, but we can still hide our true motivations from ourselves. The human capacity for rationalization and self-deceit is enormous. The prophet Jeremiah confirmed that, "The heart is more deceitful than all else and is desperately sick; who can understand it?"[9] Any person may be deluded by their own self-

---

[5] Proverbs 16:2.
[6] 1 Samuel 16:7.
[7] 1 Chronicles 28:9. See also Revelation 2:23 and Jeremiah 17:10.
[8] Matthew 7:15–20; 12:33–35; James 5:12.
[9] Jeremiah 17:9.

interest, and only God can truly see into the heart. King David pleaded, "Search me, O God, and know my heart; try me and know my anxious thoughts; and see if there be any hurtful way in me, and lead me in the everlasting way."[10]

Every person is born with a deceitful heart

From the first sin of Adam and Eve, the unregenerate human heart has always been inclined toward selfish rebellion. In our natural state, we are not capable of consistently loving God, even when we sincerely desire him and desperately need him. Jews and Greeks alike are under sin, as it is written, "There is none righteous, not even one; there is none who understands, there is none who seeks for God; all have turned aside, together they have become useless; there is none who does good, there is not even one."[11]

Moses' understudy, Joshua, spoke of humanity's inability to love God. When the Israelites declared, "We also will serve the LORD, for he is our God," Joshua replied:

> You will not be able to serve the LORD, for He is a holy God. He is a jealous God; He will not forgive your transgression or your sins. If you forsake the LORD and serve foreign gods, then He will turn and do you harm and consume you after He has done good to you.[12]

The natural human condition gives us no hope of living up to the demands of love. Even our best intentions are defeated by our inner agenda of selfishness. Fortunately, while we in our natural selves are hopelessly corrupted, God announced new hope associated with the coming of the Christ and the outpouring of his Spirit. In God's eternal plan, sins and sinfulness are forgiven through the atonement of the Cross, and hearts are renewed through the indwelling Spirit of God. The conclusion is that Paul's goal of "a pure heart and a good conscience and a sincere faith" is an impossibility for a person who does not have the supernatural indwelling of the Spirit, but it is absolutely required of all who claim to be born-again of God.

---

[10] Psalm 139:23–24.
[11] Romans 3:9–12.
[12] Joshua 24:19–20.

The promise of a new heart

Through the prophet Ezekiel, God had promised the Israelites new hearts; that is, undivided hearts, no longer crippled by sin, hearts made capable of perfect love:

> I will give them one heart an undivided heart, NIV], and put a new spirit within them. And I will take the heart of stone out of their flesh and give them a heart of flesh, that they may walk in My statutes and keep My ordinances and do them. Then they will be My people, and I shall be their God.[13]

Again, Ezekiel affirmed:

> I will give you a new heart and put a new spirit within you; and I will remove the heart of stone from your flesh and give you a heart of flesh. I will put My Spirit within you and cause you to walk in My statutes, and you will be careful to observe My ordinances. You will live in the land that I gave to your forefathers; so you will be My people, and I will be your God.[14]

Ezekiel's prophecy was not a new promise. It first appeared in the books of Moses, where it is written, "The LORD your God will circumcise your heart and the heart of your descendants, to love the LORD your God with all your heart and with all your soul, so that you may live."[15] Ezekiel spoke of the fulfilment of Moses' promise, and his prophecy coincided with other prophets. In the same era, Jeremiah said, "I will put My law within them and on their heart I will write it; and I will be their God, and they shall be My people."[16] It was not unreasonable then that when the Jewish teacher, Nicodemus, came to Jesus he was scolded for not understanding the fundamental promise of new birth.[17]

In the New Testament, John the Baptist announced, "As for me, I baptize you with water for repentance, but He who is coming after me is mightier than I, and I am not fit to remove His sandals; He will baptize you with the Holy Spirit and fire."[18] John called those seeking God to demonstrate their commitment in the waters of baptism, but John knew very well that his followers did not have the moral capacity

---

[13] Ezekiel 11:19–20.
[14] Ezekiel 36:26–28. See also Jeremiah 31:31–33 and Hebrews 8:10.
[15] Deuteronomy 30:6.
[16] Jeremiah 31:31–33.
[17] John 3:1–10.
[18] Matthew 3:11.

to repent, despite their best intentions. Their hearts were still corrupted by sin, so John eagerly announced that the promise of the Holy Spirit was about to be fulfilled. The Christ was coming with life-changing power! After Jesus Christ's death on the Cross, sin was atoned for and the temple curtain was torn apart: God and his people were no longer separated by sin. Before Pentecost, Jesus confirmed, "John baptized with water, but you will be baptized with the Holy Spirit not many days from now."[19] At the Day of Pentecost, Christ poured out the heart-changing power of the Holy Spirit. The apostles began preaching the good news with increasing boldness and soon discovered, to their wonderment, that the new heart was available to all Gentiles as well as Jews. From the Jewish mindset, Peter's report of the conversion of Cornelius's household was world-changing: now they understood that even the non-Jews could be saved, and Ezekiel's Israel-specific promise was shown to be a global provision through the coming of Jesus:

> God gave to them the same gift as He gave to us also after believing in the Lord Jesus Christ... and] When they heard this, they quieted down and glorified God, saying, "Well then, God has granted to the Gentiles also the repentance that leads to life."[20]

New terminology was added to Ezekiel's prophecy. Jesus taught, "You must be born-again,"[21] that is, you must have a new type of birth through the indwelling Spirit. Paul proclaimed, "Therefore if anyone is in Christ, he is a new creature; the old things passed away; behold, new things have come."[22] Again, in his letter to the Galatians, Paul wrote, "For neither is circumcision anything, nor uncircumcision, but a new creation is what matters]."[23] James challenged his readers, "Cleanse your hands, you sinners; and purify your hearts, you double-minded."[24]

In his later years, Peter wrote under the inspiration of the Holy Spirit:

> His divine power has granted to us everything pertaining to life and godliness, through the true knowledge of Him who called us by His own glory and excellence. For by these He has granted

---

[19] Acts 1:5.
[20] Acts 11:17–18.
[21] John 3:7.
[22] 2 Corinthians 5:17.
[23] Galatians 6:15.
[24] James 4:8.

> to us His precious and magnificent promises, so that by them you may become partakers of the divine nature, having escaped the corruption that is in the world by lust.[25]

Peter had experienced the power of a changed heart, an undivided heart, with the removal of his old hard-heartedness. Through the indwelling Holy Spirit, he spoke with confidence that believers may share in the divine nature, escaping the corruption of evil desires and living a godly life. He knew the fulfilment of Ezekiel's prophetic announcement and he affirmed it to his readers with unshakable confidence. Paul confirmed that the coming of the Holy Spirit was the fulfilment of Moses' prophecy of a circumcised heart: "In Christ] you were also circumcised with a circumcision made without hands, in the removal of the body of the flesh by the circumcision of Christ."[26]

The New Testament apostles and the Old Testament prophets are in agreement: under the New Covenant,[27] if a born-again believer is not free from corruption and evil desires, then something is not right.

The eternal plan

From the beginning of Creation, our world was planned and purposeful. Out of nothingness, God fashioned the physical universe, plant life and animal life, all leading to his master-plan on the sixth day. The divine purpose was fulfilled when God breathed life and spirit into the first human being—a creature imbued with physical and spiritual capacity, made to reflect the character of God himself.

You and I are part of that great plan—we are the living remnant of God's masterpiece. We are direct descendants of the first man and we carry the same creative purpose. Although we are morally disfigured and wretchedly weakened by subsequent willful rebellion, the promise of a pure heart remains. Before the Creation was initiated, God had each of us in mind. His purpose was that we might be holy and blameless, the pinnacle of his creation, reflecting his glory in this world and in the world to come. "For those whom He foreknew, He also predestined to become conformed to the image of His Son, so that He would be the firstborn among many brethren."[28] This, then, is the Arminian understanding of the biblical doctrine of predestination.

---

[25] 2 Peter 1:3–4.
[26] Colossians 2:11.
[27] This terminology of Old and New Covenants is used in applying the promise of an undivided heart in Hebrews 8:7–13.
[28] Romans 8:29.

God, in his omniscience, knew in advance that some would respond to Christ and some would not, and therefore he laid out a pathway to spiritual maturity. The substance of that pathway is Christ-likeness through repentance, forgiveness, new birth, holiness and perseverance. Again in Paul's writings, we read:

> In him also we have obtained an inheritance, having been predestined according to His purpose who works all things after the counsel of His will, to the end that we who were the first to hope in Christ would be to the praise of His glory.[29]

Despite declaring that his Creation was "good" and pleasing on the sixth day, God's creative purposes were not yet finished. He had another creation still planned, a "new creation." Adam's corruption and Christ's regeneration were already on the horizon. The first creation was "good", but the new creation was to be "perfect":

> By this we know that we have come to know Him, if we keep His commandments. The one who says, "I have come to know Him," and does not keep His commandments, is a liar, and the truth is not in him; but whoever keeps His word, in him the love of God has truly been perfected. By this we know that we are in Him: the one who says he abides in Him ought himself to walk in the same manner as He walked.[30]

If God could create the universe with just a word, how glorious would this new creation be that required the blood of his only begotten son! In the incarnation of Jesus, deity took on human flesh, making Jesus the first-fruits of the new creation.[31] Christ was the first of the New Creation. He was God-clothed-in-humanity. In his wake, previously-wretched humans were born-again and made holy through the invisible work of God. In a reversal of Christ's incarnation, the born-again believer's humanity is now clothed in the Spirit's divinity. Divided hearts are healed, and hard hearts are softened. This is the eternal plan, now revealed in all who would surrender themselves to Christ.

In the born-again believer, human flesh is indwelt by divinity, making us joint heirs with Jesus. As children of God, we have become "partakers of the divine nature" and now have "everything we need for a godly life." Sadly though, for too many of us, a godly life seems an unreachable ideal. The beginning of new life is seizing the promise by

---

[29] Ephesians 1:11–12.
[30] 1 John 2:3–6. See also 2 Corinthians 7:1; Colossians 4:12, Matthew 5:48.
[31] 1 Corinthians 15:20–23.

faith. In his letter to the Ephesians, Paul strongly contends that we must know and understand the hope, inheritance and power of being a Christian.[32] Further in his letter, he repeated himself:

> For this reason I bow my knees before the Father... that He would grant you, according to the riches of His glory, to be strengthened with power through His Spirit in the inner man, so that Christ may dwell in your hearts through faith; and that you, being rooted and grounded in love, may be able to comprehend with all the m]saints what is the breadth and length and height and depth, and to know the love of Christ which surpasses knowledge, that you may be filled up to all the fullness of God.[33]

Take hold of the promise! God meant us for greater things!

The Two Trees gospel plan

An outline of the *Two Trees* gospel presentation that follows illustrates God's two-fold plan of justification and regeneration.[34] These themes will then be developed more fully in subsequent chapters.

There are several places in the Bible where people are pictured to be trees. If a person has a good heart, like a good tree they will produce good fruit. If they have a sinful heart, like a bad tree they will produce bad fruit.[35] A tree must produce fruit in keeping with its nature.[36] Sadly, we are all born as bad trees—we have sinful hearts and we are not able to consistently bear good fruit. This is our heritage as descendants of Adam, "Through one man sin entered into the world, and death through sin, and so death spread to all men, because all sinned."[37] We are all born as sinful humans, or as "bad trees." The Bible describes this as our "natural", "worldly" or "fleshly" state.[38] "A natural man does not accept the things of the Spirit of God, for they are foolishness to him; and he cannot understand them, because they are spiritually appraised."[39] This natural person produces the fruit of a sinful nature, as Jesus explained:

---

[32] Ephesians 1:18–23.
[33] Ephesians 3:14–19.
[34] Cameron, *Two Trees*.
[35] Matthew 7:17–18.
[36] Luke 6:43–45.
[37] Romans 5:12. This topic is pursued in Chapter 4.
[38] 1 Corinthians 3:3.
[39] 1 Corinthians 2:14.

For from within, out of the heart of men, proceed the evil thoughts, fornications, thefts, murders, adulteries, deeds of coveting and wickedness, as well as deceit, sensuality, envy, slander, pride and foolishness. All these evil things proceed from within and defile the man.[40]

We can picture the natural person as a tree bearing bad fruit, with a sinful root system (heart). This tree cannot bear good fruit because its roots dictate what sort of tree it is.

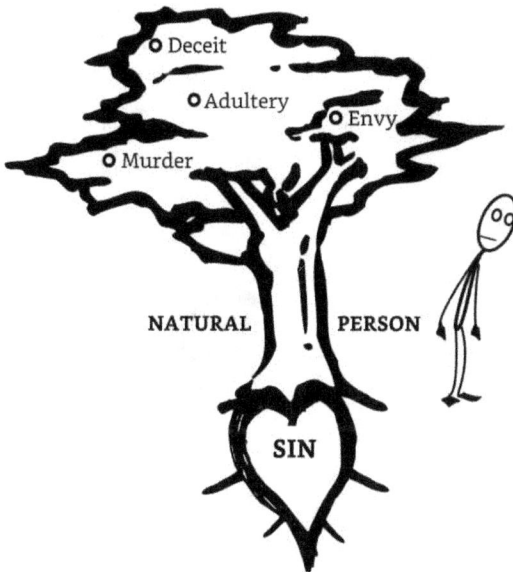

Apart from the pain that sin causes in this world, it also separates us from God. God is perfect, and anyone who wants to live in his presence in heaven or have a relationship with him on earth is restricted because of sin. We cannot dwell in the presence of a holy God and he cannot dwell in the presence of sinful people. Separation from God, the source of all life, is the sentence on those who sin, which means that death hangs over every human being. As Paul said, "For the wages of sin is death."[41] People attempt to change their behavior by making resolutions and adjusting their environment, but with limited results. They still fail to live up to their own expectations or to God's standards,

---

[40] Mark 7:21–23.
[41] Romans 6:23.

and furthermore, picking the fruit does nothing to change the sinful heart. Because of our corrupted heart we cannot live as we ought. The tree (every natural person) is sentenced to death. "Every tree that does not bear good fruit is cut down and thrown into the fire."[42]

It seems hopeless! As Paul wrote, "Wretched man that I am! Who will set me free from the body of this death?"[43] Fortunately, God has seen our desperate situation, and he has come to save us himself.

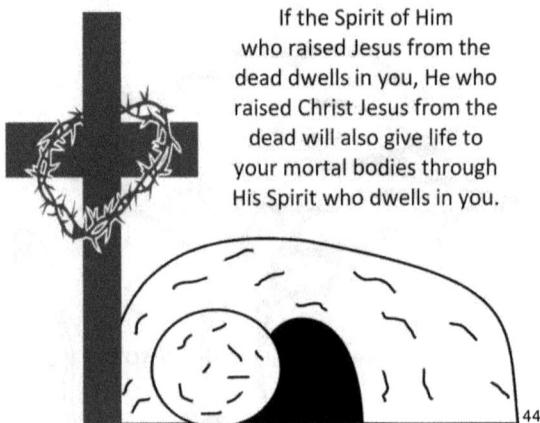

If the Spirit of Him who raised Jesus from the dead dwells in you, He who raised Christ Jesus from the dead will also give life to your mortal bodies through His Spirit who dwells in you.[44]

God came to earth as the man, Jesus Christ, and lived amongst us.[45] He lived a perfect life, without any sin.[46] He was the only person who ever lived who did not deserve to die, but the people crucified him anyway. However, God, in his wisdom, turned this wicked act into the undoing of sin. The death of Jesus Christ is now offered in exchange for our sins—his death is credited to you and me. Jesus takes on our sinfulness and we take on his righteousness. We can be forgiven for every sin we have ever committed, as the Bible declares, "We beg you on behalf of Christ, be reconciled to God. God] made Him who knew no sin to be sin on our behalf, so that we might become the righteousness of God in Him."[47]

---

[42] Luke 3:9.
[43] Romans 7:24.
[44] Romans 8:11.
[45] John 1:14.
[46] Hebrews 4:15.
[47] 2 Corinthians 5:20–21.

When we choose to turn away from our sinful ways and call upon Jesus Christ for forgiveness,[48] God comes to us through his Holy Spirit, changing our hearts from sinful to righteous.[49] The Spirit is able to live within us because the guilt of our sins has been removed at the Cross, and once indwelling us, the Spirit begins to change us from the inside out.

The Natural Person is forgiven of sins through the Cross of Jesus and the sinful heart is renewed through the indwelling Spirit of God. The believer is now a new person, with a new heart. "Therefore if anyone is in Christ, he is a new creature; the old things passed away; behold, new things have come."[50]

> Repent, and each of you be baptized in the name of Jesus Christ for the forgiveness of your sins; and you will receive the gift of the Holy Spirit. For the promise is for you and your children and for all who are far off, as many as the Lord our God will call to Himself.[51]

We are a new type of tree, with a new root system that can now produce good fruit. This new person is a spiritual person,[52] producing a crop that is pleasing to God: "The fruit of the Spirit is love, joy, peace, patience, kindness, goodness, faithfulness, gentleness, self-control; against such things there is no law."[53]

---

[48] Repentance is discussed in Chapter 3.
[49] Regeneration is discussed in Chapters 4 and 6.
[50] 2 Corinthians 5:17.
[51] Acts 2:38–39.
[52] 1 Corinthians 2:14–15.
[53] Galatians 5:22–23.

The extent of the new life we now share is often understated in our pulpits. Freedom from the penalty of sin, a clear conscience, peace that passes understanding, freedom from a divided heart, power to live faithfully before God, and wisdom to know God's values; these are available to every Christian. Those who have sought to end old sinful habits and to adopt new ways of relating to people will have discovered that it is not possible to consistently be a different person while the heart remains under the power of sin. The gospel of forgiveness and new birth is the only hope of a genuinely victorious life.

God's eternal plan, predestined before the creation of the world, was that those who would humble themselves in repentance[54] would follow the pathway to Christ-likeness through justification and new birth,[55] holiness[56] and perseverance.[57]

---

[54] Chapter 3.
[55] Chapter 4.
[56] Chapter 6.
[57] Chapter 9.

QUESTIONS FOR REFLECTION AND DISCUSSION

1. In this chapter we read, "The test of a pure heart should be one of purity of intention, not of actions." State this in your own words. Give an example of when a person might mean well but perform badly. Give an example of when a person might have malicious intentions but appear to be doing a good thing.

2. Read Proverbs 20:9. This is a rhetorical question that assumes the answer is understood. What is the answer?

3. Do you agree that the human heart is not capable of consistent (perfect) love?

4. Read Mark 7:20–23. How do these words of Jesus relate to the Two Trees? Have you seen this truth in life? Have you ever done something or said something that is embarrassing, and then wondered where that came from?

5. Read Galatians 4:5–6. How does this verse support the concept that we must be forgiven (justified) before we can be born-again? Has this been your experience?

6. Read 1 Peter 1:23. Peter is the only other biblical author who uses Jesus' term *born-again*. What would be the perishable seed? What would be the imperishable seed? Compare this concept to 1 Corinthians 15:47–49. From where did these two types of seed originate?

7. Peter wrote of believers becoming "partakers of the divine nature" in 2 Peter 1:3–4. Do you agree with this? Do you think some might find this unbelievable? Has this been your experience?

8. In this chapter it is suggested that the Creation was not complete on the sixth day, but that a "new creation" was yet to come. Of course, this is something of a play on words, because the new creation is really the perfecting or fulfillment of the original creation. How do you respond to these concepts? Was the creation incomplete after the sixth day? Are we merely returning to Adam's original created state? Or is the perfected believer improved from Adam's original state?

9. Do you agree with the concept that the human's regeneration is the reversal of Christ's incarnation? Read Hebrews 2:10–12. What implications does this have on our earthly existence and on our heavenly existence?

10. Read John 3:1–15. What question do you think is implied in Nicodemus's opening statement? Read John 2:11, 18, 23. Does this context help explain Nicodemus's question? How do Paul's words in 1 Corinthians 1:22 support what was happening in this discussion?

11. What is recorded as Jesus first response to Nicodemus in John chapt. 3? Does this seem a strange response to Nicodemus's opening statement? What does it tell you about Jesus' priorities? Before Jesus begins to speak about his impending death from John 3:14, Jesus pushes Nicodemus to understand which concept?

12. In your experience, has the miraculous power of the gospel been understated from the pulpit?

13. Review the Two Trees gospel plan below. Explain why a person cannot simply cross from "bad fruit" to "good fruit". Explain why the two elements of salvation—justification and new birth—are both essential.

Chapter 3: **REPENTANCE**

I did not shrink from declaring to you anything that was profitable,
and teaching you publicly and from house to house,
solemnly testifying to both Jews and Greeks of repentance
toward God and faith in our Lord Jesus Christ.
Acts 20:20–21

Repentance is a prerequisite for salvation, which includes turning away from sin and facing toward God in surrender and trust. This change of life necessarily implies some limited awareness of one's previous sinfulness and avoidance of God, perhaps even outright animosity toward God. Repentance is a far-reaching decision which, if pursued faithfully, will impact all of life's future decisions.

A decision of lasting impact

For some people, repentance centers on ceasing a specific behavior or a cluster of guilt-laden practices at the time of conversion.[1] This is right and proper, but it should not obscure the truth that repentance is primarily a change of attitude, a new direction, a change of allegiance, a commitment with life-long repercussions. For believers, repentance is worked out daily throughout their earthly existence. At the point of first surrender to Christ we do not know ourselves fully, and neither do we fully understand God's ways. There is more to learn about oneself and about God. Repentance is a decision to follow God's ways, wherever that might lead. It is fundamentally a reorientation of one's whole life to follow God's leading, and as such, it is a profound expression of trust in God. Repentance, therefore, is never fully complete in this world. It must be sincere, and should be joyful and eager, but the need for personal correction remains a lifelong discipline.

---

[1] For others, repentance might be focused upon the desire for assurance of salvation or God s help in a time of trouble.

It is useful to understand that both repentance and saving faith are acts of trust. Expressing faith in eternal rewards through the blood of Jesus is grasping something that cannot be seen in this world.[2] Similarly, walking away from learned behaviors and selfish ambitions in submission to God's will is an act of trust that cannot be entirely explained by human logic. The Spirit of God has been stirring the seeker's heart toward conviction of sin and faith in Christ. Both saving faith and repentance reflect the convert's budding trust in Christ, and since both draw upon the same trust, it is not possible to have saving faith and not also have repenting faith. For this reason, preachers should beware that it is inappropriate to preach a gospel of salvation that does not include repentance.

Nonetheless, there are some differences between saving faith and repenting faith: unlike saving faith, repentance is necessarily revisited many times throughout the life. The *decision* to repent of an ungodly lifestyle can be located at a moment in time but *acts* of repentance are progressive because they are worked out only as the believer becomes aware of improper attitudes or behaviors. We are learning as we go, although in a rare few cases the attitude of repentance barely has time to be worked out before death, such as in the death of the thief on the cross.[3] At the point of surrender, the new believer may be deeply convicted of the need to forgive someone or the need to break an addiction. Weeks or months later, the believer begins to recognize that God desires greater kindness in the home, or regular attendance in public worship, or honesty in financial transactions, or purity of thought, or an end to vulgar language, or greater sacrifice in service and giving. The Christian life is often a long walk home. It is intended to be a long, joyful, victorious walk home, but too often we cheapen our own faith by failing to pursue a lifetime of repentance.

Sometimes believers start out with a strong commitment to Christ, but as they become re-immersed in their worldly concerns, they grow numb to the need for repentance. The resulting loss of repentance, humility and passion in the Christian's life is addressed in Jesus' words, "You are the salt of the earth; but if the salt has become tasteless, how can it be made salty again? It is no longer good for anything, except to be thrown out and trampled under foot by men."[4] Peter, likewise, employs picturesque language to affirm that repentance is essential throughout the Christian journey:

---

[2] Hebrews 11:1.
[3] Luke 23:38–43.
[4] Matthew 5:13. See also the parable of the sower Matthew 13:1–23.

For if, after they have escaped the defilements of the world by the knowledge of the Lord and Savior Jesus Christ, they are again entangled in them and are overcome, the last state has become worse for them than the first. For it would be better for them not to have known the way of righteousness, than having known it, to turn away from the holy commandment handed on to them. It has happened to them according to the true proverb, "A dog returns to its own vomit," and, "A sow, after washing, returns to wallowing in the mire."[5]

Stages of life

Various sinful temptations are more prominent at different stages of life. There are some temptations that prevail in youthful years and some that gain a foothold in later years. Sadly, after decades of sacrificial service, the temptation toward self-importance, pride, self-righteousness and entitlement can overcome mature spiritual leaders in a way that was not possible when they were younger and less accomplished. Many of Israel's greatest kings and prophets succumbed after outstanding ministry, and the same can be said of too many modern-day church leaders. It seems unlikely that King David, in his younger years, could have imagined his later acts of adultery and murder in the saga of Uriah and Bathsheba. Certainly, David could not have repented before the temptation arrived. The stern warning of Ezekiel reminds us that repentance is a lifelong essential:

> But when a righteous man turns away from his righteousness, commits iniquity and does according to all the abominations that a wicked man does, will he live? All his righteous deeds which he has done will not be remembered for his treachery which he has committed and his sin which he has committed; for them he will die.[6]

This must not be confused with salvation by works. Remember that repentance is an act of faith—as much an act of faith as trusting Jesus is an act of faith. If a person has faith, that faith will evidence itself through consistent repentance and other acts of godliness. If a believer ceases to live in repentance, the deep-seated problem is not their wayward actions as much as it is their loss of sincere faith. Faith, working through the indwelling Spirit, must goad us forward in our

---

[5] 2 Peter 2:20–22.
[6] Ezekiel 18:24.

Christian journey. It does not condone falling back into a former way of life.

Repentance is required for salvation

The holiness emphasis within evangelicalism is traced from the preaching of John Wesley (1703–91). Wesley considered the doctrine of Christian Perfection (perfect love) to be the "grand depositum" of the Methodists.[7] In Wesley's estimation, holiness teaching was the reason the Methodists were raised up by God. However, perfect love was not to be confused with freedom from willful sin. Freedom from willful sin was to be expected of every born-again believer, even prior to a holiness experience. Repentance is not something that can wait until the deeper work of holiness is experienced. In fact the opposite is true: a lack of sincere repentance will hinder any deeper experience of the Spirit.

Wesley taught that the miraculous work of salvation contained repentance and saving faith, with holiness stretching ahead to the undivided heart. In his own words:

> Our main doctrines, which include all the rest, are three—that of repentance, of faith, and of holiness. The first of these we account, as it were, the porch of religion; the next, the door; the third, religion itself. Repentance, or conviction of sin, ... is always previous to faith, (either in a higher or lower degree, as it pleases God) ... The gate of religion, —of the true, Christian, saving faith... is, not only to believe that the Holy Scriptures and articles of faith are true, but also to have a sure trust and confidence to be saved from everlasting damnation, through Christ... Religion itself... we define, "The loving God with all our heart, and our neighbor as ourselves; and in that love abstaining from all evil, and doing all possible good to all men."[8]

The Bible speaks on repentance

John Wesley was a preacher who considered the Bible to be fully inspired by God, inerrant in every part. He wrote, "Nay, if there be any mistakes in the Bible, there may as well be a thousand. If there be one

---

[7] Wesley, "Letters to Various Persons , in *Works*, vol. 13: 9.
[8] Wesley, "Principles of a Methodist Farther Explained , in *Works*, vol. 8: 472–74.

falsehood in that book, it did not come from the God of truth."[9] In retrospect, he wrote of his regret that he had not stated this more clearly from the beginning:

> I might have said peremptorily and expressly, "Here I am: I and my Bible. I will not, I dare not, vary from this book, either in great things or small. I have no power to dispense with one jot or tittle of what is contained therein. I am determined to be a Bible Christian, not almost, but altogether. Who will meet me on this ground? Join me on this, or not at all."[10]

Wesley considered confidence in the Bible necessary to enable seekers to take hold of, otherwise unknowable, eternal truths.[11] When Wesley was twenty-six years of age and returning to Oxford to join what would become the Holy Club, he made a conscious decision in his own life to set the Bible above all other sources of wisdom, "In the year 1729, I began not only to read, but to study, the Bible, as the one, the only standard of truth, and the only model of pure religion."[12] In the preface to his sermons, Wesley later described himself as *a man of one book*, "Let me be *homo unius libri*."[13] The final authority in Wesley's teaching on repentance, salvation and holiness was, therefore, the Bible. Fortunately, the same truths are still evident in the Bible today and we can test Wesley's teachings against biblical truths.

In two seemingly contradictory statements, the Apostle John challenges us to think more deeply about sin and repentance. Initially, John says:

> If we say that we have no sin, we are deceiving ourselves and the truth is not in us. If we confess our sins, He is faithful and righteous to forgive us our sins and to cleanse us from all unrighteousness. If we say that we have not sinned, we make Him a liar and His word is not in us.[14]

---

[9] Wesley, "Journal, Jul. 24, 1776 , in *Works*, vol. 4: 82. See also "no defect, no excess in the Bible, "Preface to Notes on the New Testament , in *Works*, vol. 14: 238.

[10] Wesley, "Sermon 116, Causes of the Inefficacy of Christianity , in *Works*, vol. 7: 287.

[11] Wesley s co worker, John Fletcher promoted this same view. Fletcher, *Fletcher on Christian Perfection*, Section 2, X.1, location 518.

[12] Wesley, *A Plain Account of Christian Perfection*, Section 5: 7.

[13] Wesley, "Preface to Sermons , in *Works*, vol. 5: 1. This Latin phrase is similar to a phrase that Thomas Aquinas (1225–74) is reputed to have employed.

[14] 1 John 1:8–10.

A few paragraphs further the apostle seems to take a different view, emphatically stressing that living without sin is essential for born-again believers:

> You know that He appeared in order to take away sins; and in Him there is no sin. No one who abides in Him sins; no one who sins has seen Him or knows Him. Little children, make sure no one deceives you; the one who practices righteousness is righteous, just as He is righteous; the one who practices sin is of the devil; for the devil has sinned from the beginning. The Son of God appeared for this purpose, to destroy the works of the devil. No one who is born of God practices sin, because His seed abides in him; and he cannot sin, because he is born of God. By this the children of God and the children of the devil are obvious: anyone who does not practice righteousness is not of God, nor the one who does not love his brother.[15]

The sense of conflict in these passages, written by one man in a single sitting under the inspiration of the Holy Spirit, is dispelled when we follow Wesley's logic. Humans are desperately damaged by sin. Like a sheet of glass shattered by a large rock, we are fractured in every direction. Our moral incapacity and our propensity to wickedness touches every part of our beings. To claim that we are not severely impacted by this indwelling sin would either be foolishness or deceit. Furthermore, to claim that we have never committed acts of sin would be to call God a liar. However, God offers us an escape from our hopelessness—he can forgive us of our sins and he is able to restore us to moral integrity. The clear outcome is that anyone who continues in acts of sin does not belong to Jesus Christ and has not been revived by his Spirit.

Again, toward the end of this letter, John confirms, "We know that no one who is born of God sins; but He who was born of God keeps him, and the evil one does not touch him."[16] John Wesley and the apostle are in clear alignment in these matters.

In the book of Romans, Paul wrote:

> What shall we say then? Are we to continue in sin so that grace may increase? May it never be! How shall we who died to sin still live in it? Or do you not know that all of us who have been baptized into Christ Jesus have been baptized into His

---

[15] 1 John 3:5–10.
[16] 1 John 5:18.

death? Therefore we have been buried with Him through baptism into death, so that as Christ was raised from the dead through the glory of the Father, so we too might walk in newness of life.[17]

As highlighted in Chapter 2, Peter affirmed that all believers have received the divine nature and "escaped the corruption that is in the world by lust."[18] The author of the book of Hebrews describes willful sin plainly when he addresses those who have been forgiven through the blood of Jesus and sanctified through the indwelling Spirit:

> For if we go on sinning willfully after receiving the knowledge of the truth, there no longer remains a sacrifice for sins, but a terrifying expectation of judgment and the fury of a fire which will consume the adversaries. Anyone who has set aside the Law of Moses dies without mercy on the testimony of two or three witnesses. How much severer punishment do you think he will deserve who has trampled under foot the Son of God, and has regarded as unclean the blood of the covenant by which he was sanctified, and has insulted the Spirit of grace?[19]

Those who seek to defend ongoing willful sin by assuring believers that they are washed clean by the blood of Christ, even while they are sinning daily, can be corrected with the words of Jesus in Matthew 5, in which he said:

> Do not think that I came to abolish the Law or the Prophets; I did not come to abolish but to fulfill. For truly I say to you, until heaven and earth pass away, not the smallest letter or stroke shall pass from the Law until all is accomplished. Whoever then annuls one of the least of these commandments, and teaches others to do the same, shall be called least in the kingdom of heaven; but whoever keeps and teaches them, he shall be called great in the kingdom of heaven. For I say to you that unless your righteousness surpasses that of the scribes and Pharisees, you will not enter the kingdom of heaven.[20]

The last sentence here might be construed to mean that the blood of Christ covers our sins, so that we stand before God dressed in Christ's perfection, despite our ongoing, willful sin. However, in the context, Jesus is not speaking about such *imputed righteousness*. He is saying

[17] Romans 6:1–4.
[18] 2 Peter 1:4.
[19] Hebrews 10:26–29.
[20] Matthew 5:17–20.

that whoever fulfills the Old Testament laws is great in the Kingdom, and in fact, one cannot even enter into salvation unless one's acts of righteousness are better than the scribes and Pharisees. The context, which affirms that Christ is speaking about our deeds, stretches further back in the Sermon on the Mount. In verse 16, Jesus told us, "Let your light shine before men in such a way that they **may see your good works**, and glorify your Father who is in heaven." emphasis mine][21] Throughout the Sermon on the Mount, Jesus Christ was promoting, and insisting upon, good works.

In another place Jesus spoke of the actions that we are required to take up as Christians, not just the sins that we are to turn away from. Jesus said, "Why do you call Me, 'Lord, Lord,' and do not do what I say?"[22] This passage is similar to his "new commandment" of love for each other,[23] and includes giving food to the hungry and drink to the thirsty, hosting strangers, clothing the naked, and visiting the sick and the prisoners.[24] Repentance includes adopting good works as much as ceasing wicked practices.

The possibility of failure

While the Bible speaks with forceful clarity of the Christian's obligation to ongoing repentance, it also provides for mercy in times of failure. John explained:

> My little children, I am writing these things to you so that you may not sin. And if anyone sins, we have an Advocate with the Father, Jesus Christ the righteous; and He Himself is the propitiation for our sins; and not for ours only, but also for those of the whole world.[25]

When these words of John are contrasted to the warnings of Hebrews 10:26–29, the discussion is seen to focus not only on *willfulness*, but upon *ongoing willfulness*. If a Christian willfully *continues* to defy the command of the Father or of the Son, then that person shows contempt for the sacrifice of Jesus and for the indwelling Spirit. However, if a believer fails from time to time, shocking themselves by their willful disregard for God's ways, there is mercy. God looks upon the heart. John specifically notes that Christ's blood atones for "our"

---

[21] Matthew 5:16.
[22] Luke 6:46; Matthew 7:21–23.
[23] John 13:34.
[24] Matthew 25:34–46.
[25] 1 John 2:1–2.

sins, even sins of believers, as well as the sins of the unsaved population. Therefore, where there is repentance, mercy remains; where there is ongoing contempt, eternal judgment remains.

This concept of intentional and unintentional sin is reflected in both the New and Old Testaments. For example, in Exodus 21:12–14 different penalties are provided for intentional killings and accidental killings, and in Numbers chapt. 35, cities of refuge are provided for perpetrators of accidental killings while death is the uncompromising penalty for intentional murder. Leviticus chapts. 4–5 addresses unintentional sins, while chapts. 5–6, intentional sins are addressed. This concept of two broad categories of sin is repeated in the New Testament. John wrote:

> If anyone sees his brother committing a sin not leading to death, he shall ask and God will for him give life to those who commit sin not leading to death. There is a sin leading to death; I do not say that he should make request for this. All unrighteousness is sin, and there is a sin not leading to death.[26]

Exodus, Leviticus and Numbers plainly state which sins lead to death; that is, intentional sins. In Old Testament terms, when a person sins willfully, they must repent and offer a blood-sacrifice to receive forgiveness, which is to say that something must die for their sin. The blood of Jesus Christ became the permanent blood-sacrifice for our sinfulness, and that sacrifice is only available through repentance. This is the same principle that John applied in New Testament terms. The prayers of a third party cannot circumvent the need for personal repentance; one person cannot repent for known sin on behalf of another person. Rather, pray that the willful sinner would come to repentance, because repentance is essential to salvation. However, when someone is falling short of loving, respectful behavior, but not willfully defying God, pray for God's mercy for them so that they might live and come to understand a better way.

King David illustrated the difference between willful and unintentional sins through, what he called, "great transgressions" and "hidden faults." He said:

> Who can discern his errors? Acquit me of hidden faults. Also keep back Your servant from presumptuous willful] sins; let

---

[26] 1 John 5:16–17.

them not rule over me; Then I will be blameless, and I shall be acquitted of great transgression.[27]

The careful use of the term *blameless* in the Scriptures highlights the truth that all believers unintentionally fail God's perfect laws, but they are not blamed for that of which they are unaware. To be sure, a believer may unknowingly violate God's laws in the most heinous ways, living for years in brutality, greed, hatefulness or deceit. Do you doubt that this could be so? Then do not consider your neighbor but look into your own heart. How many years did it take to recognize your unloving behavior? Did it take some decades? Were you close to the grave before you awoke one night, tormented by a memory of a harsh response to your child, your spouse, or some wretched lost soul? We are all fortunate that the blood of Jesus atones for unintentional sins.

Sin is deceitful. It creeps into your life, and often you are the last to recognize that you are flirting with sin. It is like an acquaintance coming toward you up an escalator. First you see only the empty, endless stairs, and then a few hairs, and then a forehead. Something in your mind stirs with recognition, but your mind is elsewhere. You weren't expecting to see someone you knew here, so you continue in your daydream. Then, when almost in front you, they wave or call your name, and you are caught out by your lack of attention. In the same way, at some point an unintentional sin becomes known. When does a sin become willful? When you recognize it for what it is, and the Spirit says, "Enough of that!"

> And yet, for all this, they are not condemned. Although they feel the flesh, the evil nature in them; although they are more sensible, day by day, that their "heart is deceitful and desperately wicked;" yet, so long as they do not yield thereto; so long as they give no place to the devil; so long as they maintain a continual war with all sin, with pride, anger, desire, so that the flesh hath not dominion over them, but they still "walk after the Spirit;" "there is no condemnation to them which are in Christ Jesus." God is well-pleased with their sincere, though imperfect, obedience.[28]

When you recognize your sin, it is time for immediate action: go and apologize, burn those books, break those relationships, forgive, humble yourself, give your wealth away, confess your sins to God, confide in a friend who will hold you accountable, and pray for

---

[27] Psalm 19:12–13.

[28] Wesley, "Sermon 8, The First Fruits of the Spirit , in *Works*, vol. 5: 91.

cleansing. Some sins can be jettisoned in a moment of decision, but other habitual sins are considerably harder to break. Some "cannot come out by anything but prayer."[29] Besetting sins are those that have deep roots in our habits or memories. They can be very difficult to break. It may be that the Spirit is guiding the believer to break some other habit; some preceding practice that repeatedly places the believer in temptation's way. It may be that the believer needs to fill their life up with sacrificial service, bible study and prayer. Remember that God's purpose is character development—he will guide you through the process of unlearning sinful behaviors and he will fill your heart with his own love. Nonetheless, though the struggle takes months or even years, the believer does not joyfully, willingly return to their sin. Jesus confirmed, "If anyone wishes to come after Me, he must deny himself, and take up his cross daily and follow Me."[30]

We are counted blameless for unintentional sin and for our failures. However, a blameless person does not, cannot, continue in willful sin. Some believers have been trained to recite a concept that all people sin daily "in thought, word and deed."[31] This is both correct and incorrect, depending upon which definition for sin is intended. It is correct that we fail unintentionally daily, and that prayer for the blood of Christ is appropriate, but it is unbiblical to say that Christians sin willfully every day. A willfully-sinning Christian is an oxymoron. If a "Christian" is sinning recklessly, willfully every day, then that person is simply not a Christian.

John Wesley differentiated between unintentional sins and intentional sins when he wrote:

> By sin, I here understand outward sin, according to the plain, common acceptance of the word; an actual, voluntary transgression of the law; of the revealed, written law of God; of any commandment of God, acknowledged to be such at the time that it is transgressed.[32]

> Nothing is sin, strictly speaking, but a voluntary transgression of a known law of God... However] there may be ten thousand wandering thoughts, and forgetful intervals, without any

---

[29] Mark 9:29. Some manuscripts say, "prayer and fasting .

[30] Luke 9:23.

[31] Drawn from Matthew 5:21–37 and the *Westminster Confession*.

[32] Wesley, "Sermon 19, The Great Privilege of Those that are Born of God , in *Works*, vol. 5: 227.

breach of love, though not without transgressing the Adamic law.[33]

Wesley acknowledged that failures are a form of sin (that is, not living in Adam's original righteousness) but sin, engaged in knowingly and willfully, destroys faith. Paul alluded to the same principle when he wrote, "Whatever is not from faith is sin."[34]

We have spoken earlier of the theological differences that separated the Arminian and the Calvinist Evangelicals, but this insistence that a born-again believer shall not continue in willful sin is not one such difference. George Whitefield, arguably the greatest of the early Calvinistic Evangelicals, preached as strongly as Wesley against continued sin. In his sermon, *Marks of Having Received the Holy Ghost*, Whitefield assured his hearers that one mark of receiving the Spirit is to cease willfully committing sin:

> *Neither can he sin.* This expression does not imply the impossibility of a Christian's sinning: for we are told, that "in many things we offend all:" It only means thus much; that a man who is really born-again of God, doth not willfully commit sin, much less live in the habitual practice of it. For how shall he that is dead to sin, as every converted person is, live any longer therein? It is true, a man that is born-again of God, may, through surprise, or the violence of a temptation, fall into an act of sin: witness the adultery of *David*, and *Peter's* denial of his Master. But then, like them, he quickly rises again, goes out from the world, and weeps bitterly; washes the guilt of sin away by the tears of a sincere repentance, joined with faith in the blood of Jesus Christ; takes double heed to his ways for the future, and perfects holiness in the fear of God. Italics Whitefield's][35]

Moving ahead

In this chapter we have affirmed the truth that all born-again believers have the power and the obligation to repent of known, willful sin. Satan has sought to contradict this truth from the beginning. Satan lied to Eve in the Garden of Eden when he flatly contradicted God,

---

[33] Wesley, "Letters to Mrs. Elizabeth Bennis , in *Works*, vol. 12: 394.

[34] Romans 14:23.

[35] Whitefield, "Sermon 42, Marks of Having Received the Holy Ghost , in *Works*, vol. 6: 166.

claiming that willful sin would not lead to death, "You surely will not die!"[36] The devil still whispers the same lie today, even in the Church, saying, "You are a Christian, saved by grace. You will not die if you indulge yourself a little more." God's Word remains: willful sin always leads toward death, whether for a believer or an unbeliever.

Further to this, we have explored three sin-concepts. There is the moral corruption, inherited by each one of us, that is traditionally named "original sin", "the sinful nature", "the flesh"[37] or "inbred sin;" there are acts of sin which are willful and defiant, and of which we must personally repent; and, there are acts of unintentional sin which, for clarity, we shall refer to as "failures." However, even unintentional failures are a form of sin, as John stated in 1 John 5:17, and failures require the blood of Jesus for remission. In as much as failures are unknown, mercy is applied, and repentance is not required until they are recognized, at which time, confession and restitution are appropriate. To be sure, there is no stage of maturity in the life of a Christian when the blood of the Lamb is no longer required.

---

[36] Genesis 3:4.
[37] Romans 7:25. In NASB "my flesh" is in NIV "the sinful nature".

QUESTIONS FOR REFLECTION AND DISCUSSION

1. This chapter speaks of repentance and receiving salvation as acts of faith. Explain why repentance requires faith.

2. Read 1 Corinthians 10:12–13. Restate these verses in your own words, without using Paul's descriptive words— such as "standing firm", "don't fall", "common to man", etc. How does God fulfil this promise? Have you had any experiences that fit this promise?

3. Read 1 Peter 4:1–6. Can you think of some ways you lived for evil human desires? Can you see your own life in this passage? Do you feel confident to say, "I am done with sin"? Have you lost any friendships (verse 4) because you became a Christian?

4. Read Psalm 51:1–12. What were the circumstances in which David wrote this Psalm? How are those circumstances reflected in his words in this Psalm, for example in verse 3? Where is inbred sin referenced in this Psalm? Consider David's reference to the Holy Spirit—how do you think David understood about the work of the Holy Spirit so many centuries before the New Testament Pentecost?

5. Our text book speaks of different temptations at stages of life. What temptations might teenagers and single young adults be especially vulnerable to? What temptations might parents with families be susceptible to? What temptations might older people be drawn to?

6. Read 1 John 5:16–17. Did you agree with the interpretation given in this chapter? What has been your previous understanding of "a sin leading to death"?

7. Explain why repentance is not "salvation by works".

8. If repentance is a life-long pursuit, how can repentance be required before salvation? Would that mean that you cannot be saved until you have dealt with every temptation in your life?

9. Read Luke 6:46–49. To whom is this teaching directed? Who says, "Lord, Lord"? Does Jesus mean that some "believers" are building on sand? What is the ultimate destiny of those who build, a) on the rock, and b) on the sand?

10. This chapter claims that John Wesley believed in the inerrancy of the Bible. However, the term *inerrancy* is a more recent term; *inspired* and *infallible* are traditional terms. Write out Wesley's

quote from this chapter where he links inspiration and inerrancy. "If there be one...

11. This chapter claims, "Repentance includes adopting good works as much as ceasing wicked practices." What good works should Christians in your culture/society be doing? How often are you engaged in good works?

12. Can you think of an instance when you were close to sin without realizing it—like the man watching the escalator?

13. Do you agree that there is no time in our Christian life when we do not need the Blood of the Lamb? Explain how that could be true, if we are already justified and going to heaven.

Chapter 4: **SALVATION**

Repent, and each of you be baptized in the name of Jesus Christ
for the forgiveness of your sins;
and you will receive the gift of the Holy Spirit.
Acts 2:38

The good news of salvation includes two major elements: Jesus Christ's death on the cross to pay for sins and the Holy Spirit's indwelling of the believer, resulting in new birth. There are numerous theological terms that are aligned with these two elements. The death of Jesus was substitutionary (Jesus took our place); he provided atonement for us (Jesus made amends or reparation for our sins); Jesus provided justification (Jesus' death made us righteous before God); he was our propitiation (Jesus appeased the wrath of God); Jesus redeemed us (he brought us back from slavery); and we received imputed righteousness (Jesus' righteousness was assigned to each of us—as if we were the perfect ones). New birth through the Holy Spirit provides regeneration (our corrupt nature is renewed); we are sanctified (set apart and empowered for service); and we receive imparted righteousness (through the renewal of the Holy Spirit we are enabled to consistently live according to God's commands). This teaching of two elements of salvation was part of the rediscovered truths of the first Evangelicals. They understood afresh that salvation includes assurance that sins are forgiven and a miraculous infilling of the Holy Spirit. Wesley wrote:

> Is there any conversion that is not miraculous? Is conversion a natural or supernatural work? I suppose all who allow there is any such thing as conversion] believe it to be supernatural. And what is the difference between a supernatural and a miraculous work, I am yet to learn.[1]

---

[1] Wesley, "Letter to The Reverend Mr. Potter ", in *Works*, vol. 9: 92.

Thus, Wesley confirmed the commonly held two-part teaching of all early Evangelicals; that salvation, "consists of two general parts, justification and sanctification."[2] In John 15, Jesus described a similar principle when he told the disciples that they were "already clean" because of his teaching, but that the production of new fruit was now an urgent second phase of the gospel.[3] This two-part salvation was necessary because we suffer a two-part problem: we are estranged from God and incapable of living a life pleasing to him.

A world lost in sin

God loves all his creation and does not desire anyone to be lost eternally. "The Lord is not slow about His promise, as some count slowness, but is patient toward you, not wishing for any to perish but for all to come to repentance."[4] However, when God decided to create a new being with free will—similar to the angels—he knew that many would therefore choose to defy him and follow a pathway to destruction. Tragedy and suffering would necessarily follow, the beautiful creation would be spoiled, and God would pay a high price to rescue his faithful remnant. The creation of humanity with free-will introduced the inevitability of rebellion.

Why would God initiate a plan that included so much hurt? We know that God is not the creator of sin and temptation,[5] but we also know that, when God the Trinity created human-beings with free-will, God opened the doorway for the suffering that would surely follow as rebellion spread.[6] The answer to the persistent question of why sin and suffering was allowed into the perfect creation lies in the future glory of the Redeemed. The unimaginable magnificence for which the Children of God are destined has not yet been revealed,[7] but when the time comes, those who have walked with God on the earth will be elevated above all creatures of the universe, even above the angels. This future glory explains why the earthly testing must be intense, for, "After you have suffered for a little while, the God of all grace, who

---

[2] Wesley, "Sermon 43, The Scripture Way of Salvation , in *Works*, vol. 6: 44. Note that, in this context, sanctification is speaking of the born again renewal rather that the entire sanctification ot Wesley s controversial Christian Perfection.

[3] John 15:1–8.

[4] 2 Peter 3:9.

[5] James 1:13.

[6] See Genesis 1:26–27.

[7] 1 Corinthians 2:9. See also 1 John 3:1.

called you to His eternal glory in Christ, will Himself perfect, confirm, strengthen and establish you."[8]

> Therefore we do not lose heart, but though our outer man is decaying, yet our inner man is being renewed day by day. For momentary, light affliction is producing for us an eternal weight of glory far beyond all comparison, while we look not at the things which are seen, but at the things which are not seen; for the things which are seen are temporal, but the things which are not seen are eternal.[9]

The glory of God's purified and perfected children is what places the trial of this earth in perspective. The Children of God were created to be vessels that carry the presence of God—his Spirit and his character—throughout the universe. Those who have been found faithful in this broken world will be highly regarded in the next world because they will have a special relationship, a special familial union, with God. We do not know the details of the next world, but we know that our place will be close beside the Master himself. The intensity of earthly suffering refines the Children of God for their eternal work.

Just as we do not know all the details of the future, we are not given all the details of the past. We are not told how long it took the first humans, Adam and Eve, to break trust with God, but they did so, and we understand that it happened before their first offspring were conceived because our original parents lost their moral and spiritual strength before Eve bore children to Adam. Adam and Eve's spiritual "death" therefore flowed on to every one of their descendants. The truth that no descendants were conceived before the Fall is borne out by the fact that the natural state of all humanity was corrupted through Adam and Eve's actions. When Adam and Eve choose to distrust God's warning about the tree of the knowledge of good and evil,[10] they lost their spiritual union with God. Something died within them, with the result that they no longer had spiritual life to pass on to their children.

In human terms, we can describe spiritual death by comparing it to physical death. If Adam had died physically before any children were conceived, then all of humanity would have died with him because he did not have physical life to pass on. Adam did not immediately die physically, but he did die spiritually, and consequently, he did not

---

[8] 1 Peter 5:10. See also 1 Corinthians 6:2–4 and Hebrews 1:4; 2:8–11.
[9] 2 Corinthians 4:16–18.
[10] Genesis chapt. 3.

have spiritual life to pass on to his descendants. All humans were then born lacking Adam's original spiritual life because of his sin.

All humans are created with a spiritual capacity, awareness and desire, but in their fallen state their desires remain unsatisfied. The Spirit of God has withdrawn from them, leaving them to need what they do not have. They live like people who are thirsty for water in a desert, and in the absence of water their thirst drives them to harmful alternatives. This spiritual thirst, or spiritual vacuum, has several theological and biblical names, but in this publication, we shall speak of it as *inbred sin*.[11] It is not an *act* of sin, but rather the *condition* of moral weakness.

Describing inbred sin as a vacuum and a thirst are not perfect analogies, but these do provide some significant answers. Importantly, these illustrate how sin entered the world without ever actually being created. God did not *create* sin. Inbred sin is the absence of God's goodness within a human; inbred sin is not an entity in itself, but rather, the *absence* of a spiritual entity. Inbred sin, like all vacuums, will by nature draw foreign objects into itself. Vacuums are a void that must be filled, and thus it is for the human soul: we must have a purpose in the world, and in the absence of God's spiritual presence, we find other things for which to live. These worldly desires and hopes become our idols and our gods, and in these illegitimate gods, we are sentenced to abiding dissatisfaction and increasing hatred for God.[12]

We ask, why did God not intervene to stop the rebellion? Why didn't he wipe out the sin, or at least, destroy the worst of the sinners? The reasons are two-fold. First, God was committed to free-will. If he removed all opportunity for sin, then he had not created true free-will. No form of genetic or spiritual interference could be undertaken without the loss of free-will.[13] Furthermore, if God wiped out all who had inbred sin, he would have to kill all of humanity because no one was spiritually whole. This truth was shown through the Great Flood,[14] when, even though humanity was reduced back to just one

---

[11] Traditionally often called "original sin . Inbred sin is discussed further in Chapter 7.

[12] Romans 8:7; James 4:4; 1 John 2:15–17.

[13] The Calvinist understanding of predestination and perseverance does just that it denies select humans the possibility of rebellion.

[14] Genesis chaps. 7–9.

God-fearing family, sin quickly reasserted itself in the lives of Noah and his descendants in the renewed world.[15]

Death was the penalty ascribed to Adam and Eve for their sin, and similarly for every human since then. God had forewarned Adam of the penalty for violation of the first regulation given to him, "But from the tree of the knowledge of good and evil you shall not eat, for in the day that you eat from it you will surely die."[16] In the New Testament, Paul reaffirms this regulation: "For the wages of sin is death."[17] This death-sentence included both immediate and long-term components.

Adam and Eve died spiritually at the moment of their disobedience. In that instant, they lost their innocence and their spiritual lives, and that loss cannot be overstated. Adam and Eve's journey to the eternal suffering of hell began when they decided to pick the forbidden fruit, because by doing so they forfeited their relationship with God and their capacity to live according to God's values. When they made that decision, they turned away from God and began to follow the devil. God brought a temporary remedy to them through the death of innocent animals,[18] which was a symbol of the future atoning and redemptive death of Christ for all humanity. Nonetheless, for the remainder of their years, Adam and Eve battled their own broken natures and the constant knowledge of their failure.

Adam and Eve were also given over to *physical* death after their rebellion. *Spiritual* separation was the central punishment for sin, but separation from God necessarily introduced physical aging and death as well. In Adam and Eve's original homeland a second tree was planted beside the tree of the knowledge of good and evil. It was the tree of life. The presence of the tree of life explains much of the first days and years of the creation. The provision of this tree suggests that, in the beginning, all creatures were created to grow and mature and age and die, while special provision was made for mankind. By eating the fruit of the tree of life, humans matured but never aged. While the animals were reproducing and living a normal life-span, Adam and Eve matured but were spared the negative processes of aging. After their sin, however, God decreed that they must no longer have access to the tree of life, where they could "eat, and live forever."[19] This was

---

[15] Genesis 9:18–27. Clearly both Noah and Ham behaved in ungodliness in this story.

[16] Genesis 2:17.

[17] Romans 6:23.

[18] Genesis 3:21.

[19] Genesis 3:22.

an act of mercy by God, because it would have been no kindness to assign Adam and Eve to endless suffering as their family fractured, as murder entered creation, and humanity's proclivity toward evil spiraled to ever-greater depths of depravity.[20]

Inbred sin (spiritual death) was bequeathed to you and me as a birthright by the first parents, and because we do not have the capacity to live sinless lives, we also earn the penalty of death when we inevitably sin. Paul wrote, "Through one man sin entered into the world, and death through sin, and so death spread to all men, because all sinned."[21]

Adam was the forebear of all humans, with the unique potential to determine our spiritual makeup. Adam brought death to us all. No other human was the father of all humans, and therefore no other human could reverse Adam's curse. How could anyone else interrupt this hopeless cycle of sin and death (that is, we sin because we are spiritually dead, and we are spiritually dead and physically dying because we sin)? Paul asked the same question and gave us the answer: "Wretched man that I am! Who will set me free from the body of this death? Thanks be to God through Jesus Christ our Lord!"[22] Jesus, the Son of God, was uniquely qualified to redeem us. He was the Maker (effectively, the owner of the human race) and he was without sin. Christ preceded Adam, and he alone could enter the human race as our Savior and Representative. Adam brought a curse upon us as the father of our race, but Jesus brought hope back again because he was the Creator of all humans, even of Adam himself.

> So also it is written, "The first man, Adam, became a living soul." The last Adam became a life-giving spirit. However, the spiritual is not first, but the natural; then the spiritual. The first man is from the earth, earthy; the second man is from heaven. As is the earthy, so also are those who are earthy; and as is the heavenly, so also are those who are heavenly. Just as we have borne the image of the earthy, we will also bear the image of the heavenly. The use of the unusual word "earthy" is an accurate translation of the Greek][23]

Christ's intervention was God's eternal plan, but we are told that no one knew the timing nor the details of God's radical solution. The

---

[20] See Genesis 6:5.
[21] Romans 5:12.
[22] Romans 7:24–25.
[23] 1 Corinthians 15:45–49.

angels saw the worsening corruption of the created world, the prophets spoke of a future time of holiness, and the demons relished the worldly decay. All awaited God's eternal plan to be revealed:

> As to this salvation, the prophets who prophesied of the grace that would come to you made careful searches and inquiries, seeking to know what person or time the Spirit of Christ within them was indicating as He predicted the sufferings of Christ and the glories to follow. It was revealed to them that they were not serving themselves, but you, in these things which now have been announced to you through those who preached the gospel to you by the Holy Spirit sent from heaven—things into which angels long to look.[24]

The sacrifice of Christ

The greatest mystery of the ages was revealed when the eternal Christ, the Son of God, accepted his role as the ultimate representative of humanity. In his incarnation, the life of God fused with human flesh to create a new version of humanity—one who was not hindered by inbred sin but driven by an undivided love for God the Father. Jesus Christ was born and lived amongst his own creation, without sin, the first of a new type of human. The writer of the book of Hebrews explained:

> Therefore, since we have a great high priest who has passed through the heavens, Jesus the Son of God, let us hold fast our confession. For we do not have a high priest who cannot sympathize with our weaknesses, but One who has been tempted in all things as we are, yet without sin.[25]

Sadly, many did not welcome the Christ. The synagogue leaders were amongst those most threatened by his appearance because his priorities competed too sharply with their own worldly ambitions. Jesus was falsely accused by the religious leaders and put to death by crucifixion. As he died on the cross, Jesus said, "It is finished."[26] The payment for our sins was paid in full through the death of the innocent Creator.

However, while the work of death was completed, the work of new life was just beginning. Payment for sins was paid in full, but the remedy

---

[24] 1 Peter 1:10–12.
[25] Hebrews 4:14–15.
[26] John 19:30.

for inbred sin was only now to be revealed. As Jesus lay in the tomb, the power of the Holy Spirit came upon him and raised him back to life. We are told that this same power of the Spirit is now made available to every believer. Paul wrote, "If the Spirit of Him who raised Jesus from the dead dwells in you, He who raised Christ Jesus from the dead will also give life to your mortal bodies through His Spirit who dwells in you."[27] Elsewhere Paul wrote, "If anyone is in Christ, he is a new creature; the old things passed away; behold, new things have come."[28]

The indwelling Spirit

There is an essential logic to the stages of repentance, forgiveness and new birth. After the sin of Adam and Eve, God's own nature would not allow him to dwell amongst willful wickedness or to draw near to us. The Old Testament prophet, Isaiah, said:

> Behold, the LORD s hand is not so short that it cannot save; nor is His ear so dull that it cannot hear. But your iniquities have made a separation between you and your God, and your sins have hidden His face from you so that He does not hear.[29]

Our sins create a barrier that keeps God from entering into dialogue and relationship with us. God made his goodness and his desire for relationship known through the Creation, his prophets, the Scriptures and the visitation of his own Son, but despite these gracious offerings, humanity continued to reject the knowledge of God and to shun relationship with him.[30] Nonetheless, in the face of willful rebellion, God continued to announce his presence and goodness,[31] and those few who sought him in repentance and humility, found him.[32] In the New Testament era, the goodness of God took on human flesh,[33] so that believing in Christ became the most poignant symbol of faith in God's goodness.[34] Jesus said, "Truly, truly, I say to you, he who hears My word, and believes Him who sent Me, has eternal life, and does not come into judgment, but has passed out of death into life."[35] In the

[27] Romans 8:11.
[28] 2 Corinthians 5:17.
[29] Isaiah 59:1–2.
[30] For example, see John 1:11 and Romans 1:21, 28.
[31] See Hebrews 11:6.
[32] Jeremiah 29:13.
[33] John 1:14.
[34] John 1:10–13.
[35] John 5:24.

crucifixion of the Christ, the love of God was demonstrated and the penalty for our sins was paid in full, for "God demonstrates His own love toward us, in that while we were yet sinners, Christ died for us."[36]

The sacrifice was offered, but sinners must first reject willful rebellion through humility and repentance. Repentance, while it does not settle the matter of *guilt*, does remove the obstruction of *willfulness*, and therefore, repentance always precedes God's return to his people.[37] Repentance unlocks our relationship with God, and the Blood of Christ can be brought to bear, washing away guilt and shame. When the guilt is cleansed, the Spirit of God enters the cleansed believer to bring new life.

The connection between the death of Christ and the outpouring of the Spirit is evident in numerous places in the Bible. The Spirit of God had empowered various individuals prior to the New Testament Pentecost, but it wasn't until the debt of sin was settled in full on the cross of Calvary that the Spirit of God was poured out upon all who would repent and believe. In the Gospel of John we are told, "He spoke of the Spirit, whom those who believed in Him were to receive; for the Spirit was not yet given, because Jesus was not yet glorified."[38] Jesus was even more explicit, stating that the Spirit would not come until Christ had returned to heaven and sent him, "For if I do not go away, the Helper will not come to you; but if I go, I will send Him to you."[39] One author has suggested that the link between Christ's ascension and the Spirit's coming was connected to the Baptism of the Spirit and fire (Matthew 3:11). If the Spirit came before Christ's blood was offered, the Spirit would have brought only consuming fire of judgement upon people, whereas after the ascension, the Spirit brought holiness and power.[40] This conclusion seems unwarranted though, since the baptism of fire might just as easily be understood to be a prediction of the second crisis of holiness (that is, "Spirit and fire" correlates to being "born-again and sanctified"). Regardless of the reason, it is clear that the giving of the Holy Spirit awaited the completion of Christ's redemptive work.[41]

Repentance necessarily precedes forgiveness, just as surely as forgiveness precedes the indwelling of the Holy Spirit. Nonetheless,

---

[36] Romans 5:8.
[37] See 2 Chronicles 7:14–15.
[38] John 7:39.
[39] John 16:7.
[40] Dunn, *Baptism in the Holy Spirit*, chapt. 4, loc. 1166.
[41] More on this later in this chapter.

there is some blurring between repentance, justification and new birth. God is the active force that enables all three, so it should be no surprise that God is fulfilling a second purpose even as the first is still being accomplished. In describing justification and new birth, John Wesley wrote:

> In order of *time*, neither of these is before the other; in the moment we are justified by the grace of God, through the redemption that is in Jesus, we are also "born of the Spirit;" but in order of *thinking*, as it is termed, justification precedes the new birth. We first conceive his wrath to be turned away, and then his Spirit to work in our hearts. Italics Wesley's][42]

After Pentecost, Peter proclaimed:

> Repent, and each of you be baptized in the name of Jesus Christ for the forgiveness of your sins; and you will receive the gift of the Holy Spirit. For the promise is for you and your children and for all who are far off, as many as the Lord our God will call to Himself.[43]

In repentance we reject sinful ways, in justification we are forgiven of sins, and in new birth we are given inner capacity to live according to our new resolution. However, the indwelling Spirit has other purposes in the life of the believer. The Spirit grants wisdom and insight into spiritual truths,[44] he ministers assurance of salvation,[45] he holds believers steady during times of weakness and difficulty,[46] he empowers for the increasingly godly life,[47] he helps in prayer,[48] he endows with new abilities in the service of the Christian community[49] and he reveals our inner-most secrets and failures.[50] The importance of being indwelt by the Spirit of God is revealed in Christ's teaching that it was to our benefit that the Spirit come, even more than it would have been if Jesus had remained in person.[51]

---

[42] Wesley, "Sermon 45, The New Birth , in *Works*, vol. 6: 65–66.
[43] Acts 2:38–39; John 14:26.
[44] 1 Corinthians 2:10–16.
[45] Romans 8:16.
[46] John 14:16. The Spirit is the *Paracletos*, one who stands beside us to help, a comforter, an advocate, a counselor.
[47] Galatians 5:22–23.
[48] Romans 8:26–27.
[49] Romans 12:6–8; 1 Corinthians 12:8–10.
[50] John 16:8; Ephesians 6:17; Hebrews 4:12.
[51] John 16:7.

The urgency

In the next chapter we shall consider the urgency given to being born-again, as seen in Peter and John's ministry in Samaria[52] and in Paul's ministry in Ephesus.[53] This urgency originates in the two-fold gospel, as discussed here—the gospel was not complete until believers were both justified and born-again, because the New Covenant was to be deeper and more effective than the old temple-system of forgiveness ever was.[54] The coming of the Messiah was not just to provide forgiveness of sins, since forgiveness had long been available, but he provided a better high priest and an inner moral capacity. He brought back the spiritual life lost millennia earlier by Adam. The death and resurrection of Jesus encapsulate the dual truths of forgiveness from sins and a new life of faithfulness.

God had long awaited the time when his followers would worship in spirit and in truth, and through Christ's ministry that time had finally arrived.[55] The urgency lay in the truth that the new beginning was not complete until the Spirit was poured out, just as our salvation is not complete until we have been redeemed and born-again.

In the book to the Romans, Paul systematically described the hopeless situation of all humans—Jews and Gentiles, those who have the Bible and those who do not— "for all have sinned and fall short of the glory of God."[56] He explained that the perfect laws of God do not help us in our hopelessness, since God's laws merely reveal to us the depth of our depravity. We have no moral capacity in ourselves to consistently be faithful to God's laws, or even to our own values. The only hope has ever been to throw ourselves upon the mercy of God, as Abraham did.[57] As Paul progressed in the book of Romans, he showed that, in due time, "while we were still helpless," God's merciful plan was revealed in the sacrificial death of Jesus Christ.[58] Furthermore, with that mercy, God granted us the power of the Holy Spirit, "so that we serve in newness of the Spirit and not in oldness of the letter."[59] That is to say, serving under law was impossible for us, but serving through the Spirit is eminently achievable. In the later paragraphs of Romans

---

[52] Acts chapt. 8.
[53] Acts chapts. 18–19.
[54] Hebrews chapts. 8–10, especially 9:9, 14.
[55] John 4:23.
[56] Romans 3:23.
[57] Romans 4:1–3, 13–15.
[58] Romans 5:6.
[59] Romans 7:6.

7, Paul described the impossibility of trying to be faithful to God while internally weakened by sin,[60] even when justified by the blood of Christ. Consider the turmoil and confusion of the last verses of Chapter 7:

> Wretched man that I am! Who will set me free from the body of this death? Thanks be to God through Jesus Christ our Lord! So then, on the one hand I myself with my mind am serving the law of God, but on the other, with my flesh the law of sin.[61]

Through the cross of Jesus Christ, we are set free from the penalty of death, and yet, the battle between my desire to please God (repentance) and my weakened human state (inbred sin) continues to be an unwinnable struggle, as described in the Romans 7 summary.

It is only in Chapter 8 that the narrative changes. Verse 1 begins with *imputed righteousness*, when we are forgiven for our sins— "there is now no condemnation"[62] —and then moves on to *imparted righteousness*, when the shackles of the sinful nature are finally broken and we can live "according to the Spirit."[63] When Christ died for humanity, he not only paid the price for sins (*justification*), but he reclaimed ownership of us (*redemption*).[64] Now Christ has the legal right to place his own Spirit within those who repent and are justified because they are now his possession.[65] Now he can regenerate us in his own image. Earlier in this chapter we asked why the outpouring of the Holy Spirit could only occur after the crucifixion. The answer lies in this concept that, since the sin of Adam and Eve, we were sold as slaves to sin and the devil. We were children of the devil, because in the Garden, Adam had swung his allegiance from God to Satan by trusting the devil's word rather than God's word. Only after the crucifixion could Christ place his own seal upon us, when we were redeemed (purchased back from the devil).[66]

Romans 8:10–11 summarize these concepts:

> If Christ is in you, though the body is dead because of sin, yet the spirit is alive because of righteousness. But if the Spirit of Him who raised Jesus from the dead dwells in you, He who

---

[60] Romans 7:7 25.
[61] Romans 7:24–25.
[62] Romans 8:1.
[63] Romans 8:4.
[64] Review the first paragraph of this chapter.
[65] Ephesians 1:14; Titus 2:14.
[66] 2 Corinthians 1:22.

raised Christ Jesus from the dead will also give life to your mortal bodies through His Spirit who dwells in you.[67]

If a believer is justified (has received Christ's mercy), but has not been born-again, the human spirit is alive to God, but the sinful nature still dominates the spirit. But, when the power of the Holy Spirit comes upon the believer, the Spirit overcomes the power of the sinful nature. It is only in the Spirit, that repentance can be lived out. In the understanding of Paul, salvation is not complete until the believer is both justified and born-again. Hence the urgency of being born-again. Repentance, which is required prior to salvation, cannot be fully activated until the believer is born-again and has the moral power to live according to their new convictions. Hence, an attitude of repentance is necessary prior to forgiveness, but complete acts of repentance are not possible until after new birth.

---

[67] Romans 8:10–11; see also Ephesians 1:18–20.

QUESTIONS FOR REFLECTION AND DISCUSSION

1. Explain how Christ's death and resurrection are the remedies for our two-part problem of guilt and moral incapacity.

2. What Bible verses can you find that speak of "the unimaginable magnificence for which the Children of God are destined."

3. Read 1 Corinthians 2:6–10. Rephrase this in your own words.

4. Read 1 Corinthians 15:45–49. Discuss the concept that Adam was of the earth and Jesus was of heaven. Explain the difference between them.

5. Adam became a living soul, but Jesus became a life-giving spirit. What do you understand is the difference between a soul and a spirit?

6. Read Ephesians 1:19–20. In what way does this passage agree with Romans 8:11?

7. Explain the statement, "Repentance, while it does not settle the matter of *guilt*, does remove the obstruction of *willfulness*…"

8. Read and contrast John 1:19–34 and Matthew 11:1–6. What was happening with John the Baptist between these two passages? He had such a strong confidence in Jesus' identity in the beginning, but in prison he seemed to lose that confidence. He asked, "Jesus, did I get it wrong? Is there still someone else to come?" What caused John to hesitate? Was it imprisonment that affected John? Was it some form of depression or other human frailty? Perhaps John was not wavering, but simply wanted his disciples to hear Jesus say it themselves. What do you think?

   What part might *urgency* have played in John's question? John seems to have understood the great urgency of being born of the Spirit. (After all, he was filled with the Spirit in the womb![68]) Perhaps he wondered why Jesus was not immediately pouring out the Spirit.[69] Perhaps the delay in the baptism of the Spirit until after the crucifixion caused John to ask whether he had misunderstood. See John 3:31–36.

9. Read John 15:1–8. Note especially verses 3–4. What did Jesus mean that the disciples were "clean," and how did that happen? What

---

[68] Luke 1:15.
[69] Dunn, *Baptism in the Holy Spirit*, chapt. 4, loc. 1124.

was the condition of fruitfulness? Explain the difference between these two phases of Christian life.

10. What "other purposes" does this chapter describe for the Spirit's presence in our lives? Can you suggest other ways that the Spirit helps us?

11. Consider the concept of *redemption*. Can you find some Bible verses that describe us as belonging to the devil or to sin? In what way were we redeemed when Jesus was crucified?

12. While a missionary in the colony of Georgia, North America, John Wesley met the Moravian missionary, August Spangenberg. As they talked, Spangenberg said to Wesley, "My brother, I must first ask you one or two questions. Have you the witness within yourself? Does the Spirit of God bear witness with your spirit, that you are a child of God? Do you know Jesus Christ?" ... Wesley] answered, "I hope he has died to save me..."[70] How would you characterize Wesley's response?

How would you answer those questions? Do you know that Jesus has saved you? Have you been forgiven of your sins? Have you been born-again? How do you know what you know?

---

[70] Wesley, "Journal, February 7, 1736 , in *Works*, vol. 1: 20.

Chapter 5: **ASSURANCE OF SALVATION**

God has sent forth the Spirit of His Son into our hearts,
crying, "Abba! Father!"
Galatians 4:6

Assurance of salvation was one of the key emphases of the Evangelical Revival in the eighteenth century. In the early 1700s, Anglicans, Puritans and other Non-Conformists in Britain and North America rediscovered the biblical teaching that believers could experience a miraculous conversion and an abiding inner assurance that their sins were forgiven by Christ. This was a radical break from the somber Calvinistic teaching of the time that held seekers in "a persistent phase of gloom" as they sought salvation, with little or no assurance in their lifetime. Assurance of salvation was, therefore, the very engine of Evangelicalism. "The dynamism of the Evangelical movement was possible only because its adherents were assured in their faith."[1]

In the teachings of the Bible, assurance of salvation is directly connected to the miraculous indwelling of the Holy Spirit. In his letter to the Galatian Church, Paul wrote, "Because you are sons, God has sent forth the Spirit of His Son into our hearts, crying, 'Abba! Father!' Therefore you are no longer a slave, but a son; and if a son, then an heir through God."[2] In the book of Romans, Paul explained more fully the connection between repentance, salvation, new birth and assurance of salvation:

> So then, brethren, we are under obligation, not to the flesh, to live according to the flesh—for if you are living according to the flesh, you must die; but if by the Spirit you are putting to death the deeds of the body, you will live. For all who are being led by the Spirit of God, these are sons of God. For you have not received a spirit of slavery leading to fear again, but you have

---

[1] Bebbington, *Evangelicalism in Modern Britain*, 42–45.
[2] Galatians 4:6–7.

received a spirit of adoption as sons by which we cry out, "Abba! Father!" The Spirit Himself testifies with our spirit that we are children of God, and if children, heirs also, heirs of God and fellow heirs with Christ, if indeed we suffer with Him so that we may also be glorified with Him.[3]

This concept of assurance of salvation was prone to readjustment over the centuries following the Evangelical Revivals, and today Evangelicals are tempted to teach a personal confidence rather than a miraculous witness of assurance. The difference is subtle, but real. For the early evangelical leaders, notwithstanding their differences over predestination, assurance of salvation resulted from the miraculous action of God. God sent his Spirit into the soul of the believer, and the Spirit himself ministered assurance. Assurance was neither presumed nor experienced prior to an experience of the Spirit. Waiting for assurance was intense, often exhausting, and sometimes took weeks or months. Wesley's preaching was accompanied by penitent seekers, moaning and weeping as they awaited God's miraculous visitation. When the Spirit came, assurance of salvation was generally realized. Wesley wrote:

Indeed it is the same Spirit who works in them that clear and cheerful confidence that their heart is upright toward God; that good assurance, that they now do, through his grace, the things which are acceptable in his sight, that they are now in the path which leadeth to life, and shall, by the mercy of God, endure therein to the end.[4]

George Whitefield boldly preached of the assurance which only the born-again can have:

For Christ came not only to save us from the guilt, but from the power of our sins: till he has done this, however he may be a Savior to others, we can have no assurance or well-grounded hope, that he has saved us: for it is by receiving his blessed Spirit into our hearts, and feeling him witnessing with our spirits, that we are the sons of God, that we can be certified of our being sealed to the day of redemption.[5]

---

[3] Romans 8:12–16. Note the concept in this paragraph that suffering through this world is one thing that qualifies the Children of God to reign with him in eternity.

[4] Wesley, "Sermon 17, The Circumcision of the Heart", in *Works*, vol. 5: 206.

[5] Whitefield, "Sermon 24, What Think Ye of Christ?", in *Works*, vol. 5: 368

Across the Atlantic Ocean, Jonathan Edwards described the same fresh assurance of salvation, although using different terminology to his London-based evangelical counterparts. Edwards wrote:

> Those amongst us who had formerly been converted, were greatly enlivened, and renewed with fresh and extraordinary incomes of the Spirit of God; though some much more than others, according to the measure of the gift of Christ: many that before had labored under difficulties about their own state, had now their doubts removed by more satisfying experience, and more clear discoveries of God's love.[6]

Nonetheless, both Wesley and Whitefield allowed that there were exceptional situations in which the internal sense of assurance was elusive. Whitefield wrote:

> Not that I dare affirm, that there is no real Christian, but what has this full assurance of faith, and clearly knows, that his Maker is his husband. In speaking thus, I should undoubtedly condemn some of the generation of God's dear children, who through the prevalence of unbelief, indwelling sin, spiritual sloth, or it may be, for want of being informed of the privileges of believers, may walk in darkness, and see no light: therefore, though I dare not affirm, that a full assurance of faith is absolutely necessary for the very being, yet I dare assert, that it is absolutely necessary, for the well-being of a Christian. And for my own part, I cannot conceive, how any persons, that pretend to Christianity, can rest satisfied or contented without it...[7]

Wesley tried to avoid using the term *assurance of salvation*, preferring to speak of "divine evidence or conviction."[8] This allowed Wesley to shift the conversation away from a future hope of heaven, and refocus it to a present experience of the work of Christ in the believer's life. He spoke of "a divine conviction that Christ loved me, and gave himself for me; and still more clearly in the Spirit's bearing witness with my spirit, that I am a child of God." Assurance of salvation was of this present salvation, rather than an inheritance in glory. When asked whether Christians must have this conviction, he tempered his words slightly, "My belief, in general, is this, — that every Christian believer has a divine conviction of his reconciliation with God. The sum of my]

---

[6] Edwards, *A Faithful Narrative of the Surprising Work of God*, chapt. 1, loc. 138.
[7] Whitefield, *Works*, vol. 5: 178–79.
[8] Wesley, "Letters to Rev. Mr. Walker , in *Works*, vol. 13: 201.

concessions is, 'I am inclined to think, there may be some exceptions.'"[9] Wesley's focus on the current experience was consistent with his theology, since he had a high expectation of the direct intervention of the Holy Spirit in the life of the believer. For him, an evangelical conversion was miraculous and life-changing, and it was hard to imagine such an event occurring without the believer's awareness. Therefore, Wesley's "internal witness" of the Spirit might be considered to be similar to "the peace of God, which surpasses all comprehension,"[10] as described by Paul. Although Paul is speaking in a broader sense of peace that comforts through worldly troubles, both are the Spirit's ministry in present experience, and the work is always that of the Holy Spirit, whispering peace and confidence to the spirit of the believer.

Today we are often instructed that assurance of salvation is a matter of trusting the biblical promises, as a logical extension of God's love. The rationale is that God wants us to repent and to be saved; we want to repent and be saved; so, our act of consecration is the catalyst for our new birth and assurance. Pastors and evangelists are trained to lead seekers in a prayer of repentance and faith, after which penitents are assured that they are now members of the family of God and born-again of the Spirit. Sometimes they might be instructed that a lack of any real internal assurance of a miraculous transformation should be set aside, and rather they should fix their faith on the promises of the Bible. This modern "external assurance" is, thus, clearly a shift from the expectation of the early Evangelicals.

Are justification and new birth simultaneous?

One possible reason for an absence of Spirit-whispered internal assurance is that justification and new birth do not necessarily occur at the same time. Perhaps the absence of a miraculous inner assurance is because the convert has been justified by faith (forgiven of their sins) but not yet born-again. If that is so, then it greatly impacts the next steps for the evangelist.

However, before further consideration of this separation of justification and new birth, it should be noted that John Wesley consistently taught that the two events always occur simultaneously. Wesley's viewpoint can be shown to have developed over some years. Two months after his own conversion, Wesley visited Germany and

---

[9] Wesley, "Letters to Mr. Richard Tompson , in *Works*, vol. 12: 471, 473.
[10] Philippians 4:7.

met with the Moravian leadership. On Sunday July 9, 1738, Count Zinzendorf preached a message on his eight points of justification and new birth.[11] Wesley carefully recorded these points in his journal, and he took the time to note his own disagreement with point 7. "To be justified is the same thing as to be born of God. (Not so.)"[12] For the remainder of his ministry, Wesley's maintained this view that justification and new birth are separate but simultaneous events. He taught that, with salvation by faith, the new believer, "instantly received the Spirit of adoption, whereby he now cried, 'Abba Father'."[13] The new birth is, "the immediate fruit of justification, but, nevertheless, is a distinct gift of God, and of a totally different nature."[14] Toward the end of his ministry, Wesley detailed this teaching:

> Justification implies only a relative, the new birth a real, change. God in justifying us does something *for* us; in begetting us again, he does the work *in* us... The one restores us to the favor, the other to the image, of God. The one is the taking away the guilt, the other the taking away the power, of sin: So that, although they are joined together in point of time, yet are they of wholly distinct natures. emphasis Wesley's][15]

This understanding that new birth is given immediately upon justification does not require that the convert have any knowledge of the Holy Spirit or of his work, because the act of believing in Christ is what brings about new birth in the Spirit. Paul's writings have traditionally been cited to support this concept that justification and new birth occur simultaneously, or to put it in the negative, a person is not properly justified if they are not born-again:

> Those who are in the flesh cannot please God. However, you are not in the flesh but in the Spirit, if indeed the Spirit of God dwells in you. **But if anyone does not have the Spirit of Christ, he does not belong to Him**... So then, brethren, we are under obligation, not to the flesh, to live according to the flesh— for if you are living according to the flesh, you must die; but if by the Spirit you are putting to death the deeds of the body, you

---

[11] See Appendix A.

[12] Wesley, "Journal, July 9, 1738 , in *Works*, vol. 1: 111.

[13] Wesley, "Sermon 4, Scriptural Christianity , in *Works*, vol. 5: 39.

[14] Wesley, "Sermon 5, Justification by Faith , in *Works*, vol. 5: 56.

[15] Wesley, "Sermon 19, The Great Privilege of Those That are Born of God , in *Works*, vol. 5: 224.

will live. For all who are being led by the Spirit of God, these are sons of God. emphasis mine][16]

There are, nonetheless, a good number of biblical passages that appear to contradict the interpretation that justification and new birth are necessarily concurrent. Three obvious cases follow after Pentecost in the scattered Church of Samaria,[17] the conversion of Cornelius's household,[18] and the new congregation of Ephesus.[19] If the Cornelius episode is set aside, because it is not clear that these Gentiles were justified before the Spirit came upon them, then two confronting narratives remain. In Samaria, Christ was "proclaimed" and "believed in," so that the Jerusalem Church heard that "Samaria had received the word of God."[20] However, the Holy Spirit "had not yet fallen upon any of them; they had simply been baptized in the name of the Lord Jesus," and the Spirit only came when Peter and John went to them from Jerusalem.[21] (Verse 16 also removes the argument that the Samaritans actually received the second experience of the Spirit through the ministry of Peter and John.) The Samaritans believed in Christ but had not yet received the Spirit. Similarly, in Ephesus a group had been taught about John's baptism of repentance and about Jesus Christ, so that they are identified as "disciples."[22] When Paul arrived and found that these disciples knew nothing of the Holy Spirit, he rebaptized them into the name of Jesus and laid hands upon them to receive the Holy Spirit.[23] In both instances people are taught about Jesus Christ and presented in the Bible as justified believers who are not yet born-again. It was only after they were taught about the Holy Spirit that they received the Spirit. These examples support the view that receiving the Spirit is an act of faith after hearing about the Spirit, as much as justification through Christ is an act of faith after hearing about Jesus. "How then will they call on Him in whom they have not believed? How will they believe in Him whom they have not heard? And how will they hear without a preacher?"[24]

---

[16] Romans 8:8–9, 12–14. Some translations go so far as to render the bold section as "… he does not belong to Christ. This is an unwarranted translation though, which rules out the option that "him refers to the Spirit.
[17] Acts 8:4–25.
[18] Acts 10:23–48.
[19] Acts 18:24–19:7.
[20] Acts 8:5, 12, 14.
[21] Acts 8:16–17.
[22] Acts 19:1.
[23] Acts 19:1–7.
[24] Romans 10:14.

One interpretation is that these followers had some elementary form of belief but were not yet "Christians."[25] To maintain this view it becomes necessary to redefine the terms *disciple* and *believe in* as found in Acts chapt. 8 and chapts. 18–19. Furthermore, the examples would press us to adopt a theology that a person must have knowledge of the Holy Spirit before being justified/born-again. It would therefore be necessary to redefine the numerous verses that make no mention of the Holy Spirit, but rather, "He who believes in the Son has eternal life."[26] If knowledge of the Spirit is necessary, and if justification and new birth are always concurrent, those verses need to be understood to mean, "He who believes in the Son (and the Spirit) has eternal life." Surely, this is not an acceptable reshaping of God's Word.

The logical inconsistencies to a doctrinal statement that justification and new birth are always concurrent are numerous:

1. If all new believers in Christ are automatically born-again of the Spirit, then new believers do not need to have any knowledge of the Spirit's ministry at all. The work of new birth is entirely God's initiative, with no faith in the Spirit required.[27] It follows that all people around the globe who have trusted in Christ since Pentecost have been born-again. This goes against the events in the book of Acts which have been cited above; that is, Paul was wrong in his dealings with the Ephesians, as were Peter and John in their dealings with the Samaritans and Luke in his recording of Acts 8:16.

2. Alternatively, believers cannot be born-again until they are taught about the Holy Spirit and responded to him, and therefore, they cannot be properly justified either until they are taught about the Spirit and born-again. That defies the multitude of biblical passages that insist that faith in Jesus Christ is the condition of salvation,[28] and some New testament

---

[25] This is an argument that James Dunn develops in his book, *Baptism in The Holy Spirit* (2011), as part of his thesis that the New Testament does not provide for a doctrine of two fillings with the Holy Spirit (at salvation and at holiness). Specifically see Dunn, *Baptism in The Holy Spirit*, chapt. 8, loc. 2018.

[26] John 3:36.

[27] This might fit a Calvinist theology, but not an Arminian theology.

[28] There are, of course, too many references to give. As examples, read John 6:47; 12:31. Note that if they have believed in the name of Jesus, they are already justified not that they *will be* saved, but they *already have* eternal life.

passages that simply state that faith in God is all that is required.[29] If justification is not possible until a believer is taught about the Spirit and born-again, then it could promote an ugly denominational division, concluding that almost no one who was not trained in a born-again tradition will go to heaven.

3. Furthermore, if it is maintained that the Holy Spirit is immediately received with justification by the unilateral action of God, then it would not be necessary to submit to a second filling of the Holy Spirit at a later time. Why would God not complete the work, first time, every time? The call to a deeper work is centered on the increasing faith and submission of the believer, which suggests that it was the believer's relatively shallow commitment that limited the saturation of the Spirit in the born-again experience.

The option is, therefore, that there is indeed a possibility of being justified while not yet born-again—an experience we might normally associate with the Old Covenant. To hold this view, one must reconsider Paul's statement in Romans 8:9, "If anyone does not have the Spirit of Christ, he does not belong to Him." To do so, we must first set aside those paraphrases that impose their own view on the passage by substituting "Christ" in place of "him", when "Spirit" might be a more correct interpretation. In the Greek, the same tone of rejection is not implied when reading that the person who does not have the Spirit "is not of him" (οὐκ ἔστιν αὐτοῦ), or perhaps "is not sharing the Spirit's nature." In this, Paul may simply be stating that the believer who does not yet have the Spirit is not yet sharing in the spiritual nature of Christ, and this deficiency must be addressed as a priority. This would find agreement with the urgency of Jesus in John 3 and Paul in Acts 19. It may not mean that such a person is not forgiven of their sins, but that they are without the essential experience of the Spirit for which Paul was so strongly arguing. This translation fits better with Paul's whole Chapter 7 argument, that to desire consistent repentance without the indwelling Spirit is a hopeless pursuit. You cannot hope to overcome sin without the indwelling Spirit.

The Spirit's outpouring upon the household of Cornelius might, at first glance be used to show that sometimes the Spirit might come prior to the explicit teaching of the new birth, but upon closer examination, it can also be seen to support the separation of justification and new

---

[29] Hebrews 11:6; John 5:24; 12:44.

birth.[30] Unlike the Samaritans or the Ephesians, Cornelius's household had a prior knowledge of events in Jerusalem. It is quite possible, even likely, that these God-fearers had heard of the Pentecostal episode and perhaps even of John the Baptist's message. An angel appeared to Cornelius, instructing him to send for Peter in response to his prayers.[31] Perhaps Cornelius had been praying for guidance about this new work of God, and if so, then this illustrates the concept that new birth is granted when believers have sufficient understanding to ask of God.

One consistent theme of Jesus' teaching was that believers receive according to their faith. "All things you ask in prayer, believing, you will receive."[32] He healed the sick, the blind and the deaf with the words, "It shall be done to you according to your faith,"[33] while miracles were withheld where faith was lacking.[34] Peter walked on water until his faith wavered.[35] Most importantly, salvation depends on faith, and faith depends on hearing the good news.[36] It is only consistent then, that a believer who expects forgiveness but knows nothing of the indwelling Spirit, receives justification but not new birth. Peter's message in Acts 2:38[37] is in harmony with this abiding biblical principal.

To maintain that new birth necessarily accompanies justification flounders in the face of too many biblical teachings. John Wesley's experience may have been, because of his strong evangelical teaching, that he only encountered believers who were both justified and born-again. Alternatively, Wesley may not have counted believers to be Christians[38] until they had the Spirit-given assurance of salvation. In either case, experience must be submitted to the spectrum of biblical

---

[30] Acts 10:1–48, 11:15.
[31] Acts 10:30.
[32] Matthew 21:22.
[33] Matthew 9:29, and also in Mark 5:34, Luke 7:50.
[34] Matthew 17:20; Mark 6:1–6.
[35] Matthew 14:22–27; see also Luke 8:22–25.
[36] Romans 10:12–15.
[37] "Repent, and each of you be baptized in the name of Jesus Christ for the forgiveness of your sins; and you will receive the gift of the Holy Spirit.
[38] This leads to an interesting discussion: Can a person be justified by faith but not a true Christian if one assumes that a Christian, by definition, has a clean heart like Jesus? We might say, are there still Old Testament believers as well as Spirit led New Testament believers? Or, as in our discussion above, if the definition of a Christian is one who "merely believes in Jesus, then can a person be a Christian but not born again?

examples. Justification by faith has been available to believers throughout history, with Abraham as the prime example.[39] However, under the New Covenant, the power of the Spirit revolutionizes salvation by making an undivided heart possible. The New Covenant fulfilled that which the Old Covenant failed to deliver "because of its weakness and uselessness."[40] Salvation by faith is not novel to the New Testament but being born-again is.

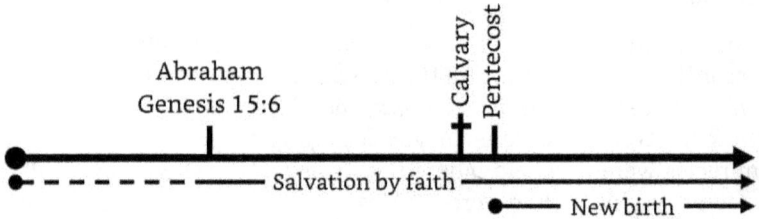

Salvation by faith has not been superseded—that is why Abraham remains our example and the father of our faith under the New Covenant.[41] Christians look to Abraham just as Jews did and still do—he is the father of salvation by faith. The pathway to salvation has not changed, for "he who comes to God must still] believe that He is and that He is a rewarder of those who seek Him."[42] The New Covenant, however, provides us with the addition of the power of the indwelling Holy Spirit to live faithfully before God. Thus, Jesus said, "Among those born of women there is no one greater than John the Baptist]; yet he who is least in the kingdom of God is greater than he."[43] To live in Old Testament faith is sufficient for forgiveness of sins, but to live in victory over sin requires the regeneration of the New Covenant.

Many are trained in churches today that do not preach the indwelling of the Spirit of God, and therefore, it is probable that their listeners may have turned to Christ in faith but never been born-again. Surely the luke-warm end-times church of Revelation points to such a conclusion.[44] Despite the Bible teachings and centuries of faithful

---

[39] Romans 4:18–25.
[40] Hebrews 7:18.
[41] John 8:39; Romans 9:6–8.
[42] Hebrews 11:6.
[43] Luke 7:28.
[44] Revelation 3:15–16.

witnesses, there are potentially millions of genuine believers today who are no better trained in the full gospel than the Ephesians or the Samaritans and have not experienced the indwelling Spirit. If so, that has an enormous bearing upon how we preach the gospel, and it sheds light on the prevalence of new converts who have no Spirit-whispered assurance. It cannot be assumed that a person who has offered a prayer of repentance has been born-again. Justification may be realized, but New Covenant full-salvation should be recognized as yet-incomplete if the believer has not been born-again.

The external witness

John is the author most often referenced in ministering external assurance. "These things I have written to you who believe in the name of the Son of God, so that you may know that you have eternal life."[45] This can be taken to imply that assurance of salvation comes through reading the Scriptures, but in his gospel, John had written:

> But as many as received Him, to them He gave the right to become children of God, even to those who believe in His name, who were born, not of blood nor of the will of the flesh nor of the will of man, but of God.[46]

As in the verse above (1 John 5:13), the "things that John wrote" were always centered on receiving Christ's Spirit or being born of God. He wrote emphatically, "The one who keeps His commandments abides in Him, and He in him. We know by this that He abides in us, by the Spirit whom He has given us."[47]

Receiving the Spirit of God and having the capacity to keep Jesus commandment of love are essentially connected. It is not possible to live a life of love through repentance and will-power alone. We must be born-again. Thus, John wrote:

> By this we know that we have come to know Him, if we keep His commandments. The one who says, "I have come to know Him," and does not keep His commandments, is a liar, and the truth is not in him; but whoever keeps His word, in him the love of God has truly been perfected. By this we know that we are in

---

[45] 1 John 5:13.
[46] John 1:12–13.
[47] 1 John 3:24.

Him: the one who says he abides in Him ought himself to walk in the same manner as He walked.[48]

Biblically, it is therefore argued that the witness of the Holy Spirit to the believer's human spirit is the immediate assurance available to the new convert. Believing the promises of the Bible is an important part of faith, but since one of the promises of the Bible is Spirit-whispered assurance, it is not consistent to believe the Bible and dispense with this promise. Nonetheless, over time, a lifestyle of obedience becomes an objective (external) source of assurance as well, bearing a similarity to the "fruit by which we are known."[49] Paul urged his readers:

> Test yourselves to see if you are in the faith; examine yourselves! Or do you not recognize this about yourselves, that Jesus Christ is in you—unless indeed you fail the test? But I trust that you will realize that we ourselves do not fail the test.[50]

If an evangelist promises assurance of salvation to seekers simply because they knelt at an altar, then that ministry has become one of presumption. The emphasis has been shifted from what God does when sending the Spirit, to what the seeker does when submitting to God. A more biblical teaching is based upon these truths:

1. God "is patient toward you, not wishing for any to perish but for all to come to repentance."[51] Until there is true repentance, there is no saving faith, no new birth, and no assurance of salvation. Although the Spirit of God is pursuing lost humanity, it is a mistake to conclude that he is in a hurry, but rather "he is patient toward you." He wants us to be truly free from our sinful habits and hidden thoughts. He will persist with seekers until they are ready to be set free.

2. Our capacity for self-deceit is beyond understanding: "The heart is more deceitful than all else and is desperately sick; who can understand it?"[52] Even when we believe we are truly surrendered, we may still be jealously withholding some part of our lives or we may still harbor disbelief. Esau, Jacob's brother, was an outstanding example of someone who

---

[48] 1 John 2:3–6.
[49] Matthew 7:15–20.
[50] 2 Corinthians 13:5–6.
[51] 2 Peter 3:9.
[52] Jeremiah 17:9.

believed in and coveted the blessing of God, and yet his "faith" was very shallow indeed.[53]

3. Only God can see into the heart.[54] He alone knows when real repentance is offered, and doubt is abandoned. He alone sends his Spirit to whisper to the seeker's heart that they are a child of God.

4. Even true repentance and faith does not guarantee that believers have the inner capacity to consistently repent. In fact, until believers are born-again, they simply do not have the power to overcome inbred sin. Therefore, the believer must be taught about the new birth and encouraged to receive the indwelling Spirit as a matter of urgency.

The role of God the Father

With these truths as a foundation, the role of God the Father in saving faith, new birth and assurance is given context. Jesus insisted that no one can find saving faith unless the Father enables them:

"No one can come to Me unless the Father who sent Me draws him... It is the Spirit who gives life; the flesh profits nothing; the words that I have spoken to you are spirit and are life. But there are some of you who do not believe." For Jesus knew from the beginning who they were who did not believe, and who it was that would betray Him. And He was saying, "For this reason I have said to you, that no one can come to Me unless it has been granted him from the Father." As a result of this many of His disciples withdrew and were not walking with Him anymore.[55]

When the Father, the Son and the Spirit manage the work of supernatural conversion, regeneration and assurance, seekers are coached toward a truly life-changing start to their Christian journey and the Church is spared untransformed members. God is committed to the salvation of all those who present themselves in repentance and faith, but only God knows when the heart is truly surrendered. Evangelicals today must learn to expect more of God's miraculous intervention in the preaching of the gospel—the gospel is not simply a logical premise to be argued and accepted. Seekers should be coached

---

[53] See Genesis 25:29–34 and Hebrews 12:16.
[54] 1 Samuel 16:7. See also Jeremiah 17:10.
[55] John 6:44, 63–66; see also Matthew 16:17.

to wait before the Lord, to search their hearts and look for a miraculous salvation.

Waiting upon the Lord

Sometimes a seeker finds immediate faith and assurance, but at other times there is a period of knocking, seeking and soul-searching. One convert from the 1920s described his extended journey toward saving faith and assurance, despite the best efforts of church leaders. As a twenty-year-old Methodist local preacher, while preaching to others, he was still unsure of his own salvation. He went to hear a visiting evangelist[56] in September 1922:

> At the close of her address, which was on the subject of the second coming of Christ, she invited seekers to come forward to the penitent form. True to my resolve, I was the first to kneel there, but as I began to pray, an usher tapped me on the shoulder and asked for my name and address, enquiring also what church I wished to join! We seekers were then marched onto the platform to shake hands with the evangelist, first having a little ribbon pinned on us to show the Lord whether we had been saved or just restored. "And this is the first time you have been saved!" gushed the evangelist, eyeing the red-and-white ribbon on my lapel. "Oh, no," I said in disappointment, "I've had this before." "Well," she said, "they have given you the wrong ribbon. It should have been a red ribbon to show that you have been restored." I felt it should have been a black one; and walked from the platform feeling disillusioned. When next evening came, the hunger was still there, so I again came to receive, if it were only a crumb of comfort for my soul.[57]

Meanwhile, the young man continued his own preaching ministry, but with no rest in his own soul:

> With deepening convictions and uncertainty of soul condition, preaching had become drudgery. I despaired of finding something to say. Beside me in the pulpit would stand another, accusing self, whispering, "You are not fit to preach to these people. You are not right yourself!" ... I had discovered I was not even converted, and unfitted to preach, and never expected to preach again unless and until I received the experience I needed.

---

[56] Aimee Semple MacPherson on preaching tour in Melbourne, Australia.
[57] Ridgway, *In Search of God*, 178.

My mentor] was very sympathetic. "You will be all right," he said. "I have other students who felt as you do, but they got over it after a while."[58]

The following weekend, despite a nasty fall from his horse, he attended a small prayer meeting:

Aching and weary, sin-sick and heart-sore, I dropped on my knees and began to seek God in good earnest. As I talked with God, He reasoned with unworthy me. I need not now go into His dealings. Suffice it to say, that finally all "my ambitions, plans and wishes; At His feet in ashes lay." And then it happened! I received the key to understanding those people who could get a hilarious joy out of religion. I found what made David dance in ecstasy before the Lord, and what was the glory of the Lord which so filled the temple of old that the priests could not minister. One moment, weeping unashamed in misery, half-fainting, almost despairing, crying like Peter, "Save, Lord! I perish." The next moment, conscious of a warm glow within and the shining of a great light into the blackness of my heart's deep night—the lead was gone, I was borne away out on the vast sea of God's eternal love, where there was no ripple, no bottom, no shore; and such a sense of calm, sweet, uncaring peace throbbed in my soul that neither] death, nor life, nor angels, nor principalities nor powers nor height nor depth nor any other creature disturbed those blissful moments of ecstatic communion with my Maker.[59]

---

[58] Ridgway, *In Search of God*, 180–81.
[59] Ridgway, *In Search of God*, 182.

QUESTIONS FOR REFLECTION AND DISCUSSION

1. What do you think of Wesley's preference for "a divine conviction" of reconciliation to God rather than "assurance of salvation"? Describe the difference between the two terms. Suggest your own phrase that does not use either "conviction" or "assurance".

2. Count von Zinzendorf was the founder of the Moravians (or the United Brethren). Zinzendorf was trained as a Lutheran-Pietist but built his lasting work upon Brethren refugees from Moravia and Bohemia. His was a mixture of theologies, but it was hugely important in opening the Evangelicals' understanding of instantaneous salvation and assurance. Find Moravia and Bohemia on a map. What modern cities are the centers of these regions today? How far are they from the community of Herrnhut, the town they established on Zinzendorf's estate?

   How did Zinzendorf's theology differ from Wesley's in Chapter 1? How did Wesley differ from Zinzendorf in Chapter 5? —see Appendix A, point 7. What are the implications of this difference?

3. Read Romans 4:1–8. When was Abraham's belief "credited as righteous"? Find the passage in Genesis. What family did he have at that time? What was God's promise that Abram believed? Did Abraham see the promise fulfilled during his years on the earth? How is that similar to our confidence in Christ? Read Galatians 3:6–9.

4. Read Acts 2:38–39. According to this passage, what was baptism a sign of? Was it of justification (forgiveness for sins through the blood of Jesus) or sanctification (freedom from the power of sin through the Holy Spirit)? Which baptism was Peter referencing—baptism of water or baptism of the Spirit? Note how even the language of "baptism" separates the concepts of justification and sanctification. Then again, note how quickly Peter links new birth to forgiveness.

   Is it possible that Peter's words were chosen because of his Jewish audience, in that Judaism believed in the Father and (somewhat) in the Spirit, but they did not accept Jesus? Hence, the reference to being baptized in the name of Jesus. In whose name/s were you baptized?

5. Read Acts 8:1–17. Do you think the Samaritans were converted before Peter and John came from Jerusalem? Why so?

6. Read Acts 19:1–7. How would you explain this event? Were the Ephesians "Christians" before Paul arrived? Why? Do you think it is possible to be saved but not born-again? Is it possible for someone to be saved and (unknowingly) born-again? Explain your reasoning.

7. When did you first learn about the Holy Spirit? Can you name a time when you were born-again? Can you name a time when you repented and believed in Jesus?

8. Read Hebrews 11:1–7. Were these pre-Abraham heroes saved by faith? Do you agree that "Salvation has only ever been by faith"? (as stated in the Chapter 12 conclusion) What are some alternative theories?[60]

9. Read Genesis 25:27–34. What was the root of Esau's sin? Esau is described as "godless" person in Hebrews 12:16. How does that fit with your understanding of Genesis 25?

10. Read Genesis 6:9. Noah is given credit for three attributes in this passage. What are they in your bible version? Describe Noah in your own words.

   Now, read Genesis 9:20–27. In this passage Noah became drunk and lay naked where his family could find him. The next day (it would seem) Noah remembered what had happened and cursed his youngest son's descendants for Ham's disrespect. Does that sound like the same man that you read about in Genesis 6? Do you think Noah bears some of the fault for Ham's behavior? How then, can Noah be reported as a righteous and blameless man? In the New testament Noah is credited as "an heir of the righteousness which is according to faith."[61]

11. Read 1 Corinthians 1:8; Ephesians 1:4; Philippians 1:10, 2:15; 2 Peter 3:14; and Jude v. 24. Does God expect us to be blameless? Explain the difference between blamelessness and sinless perfection. Do you agree that Noah, King David, Peter, Paul, John Wesley, Mother Teresa, you and me—we all need the blood of the Lamb, but we can live without willful rebellion against God. How

---

[60] Advanced students might be asked within which theory does *An Undivided Heart* most readily fall: Dispensationalism, Covenant Theology, New Covenant Theology, or another?

[61] Hebrews 11:7.

does living blamelessly impact our divine conviction or assurance of relationship with God?

Chapter 6: **HOLINESS**

Therefore leaving the elementary teaching about the Christ,
let us press on to maturity, not laying again a foundation of
repentance from dead works and of faith toward God,
of instruction about washings and laying on of hands,
and the resurrection of the dead and eternal judgment.
And this we will do, if God permits.
Hebrews 6:1–3

When discussing the holiness doctrine, teachers will usually describe a second event in the lives of Christians, a filling with the Holy Spirit subsequent to conversion. We will do likewise here, and then later in the chapter, discuss why there are some exceptions to this process.

The day of Pentecost, in Acts 2:1–41, is considered to be the time when the apostles received the second blessing and were greatly empowered in witness and boldness.[1] This concept of a second event is supported in the experience of the apostles, because they had previously received the Spirit. The first time the disciples received the Spirit was immediately after the resurrection. John recorded:

> When it was evening on that day the day of Christ's resurrection], the first day of the week, and when the doors were shut where the disciples were, for fear of the Jews, Jesus came and stood in their midst and said to them, "Peace be with you." And when He had said this, He showed them both His hands and His side. The disciples then rejoiced when they saw the Lord. So, Jesus said to them again, "Peace be with you; as the Father has sent Me, I also send you." And when He had said this, He breathed on them and said to them, "Receive the Holy Spirit. If you forgive the sins of any, their sins have been forgiven them; if you retain the sins of any, they have been retained."[2]

---

[1] There were other times of filling, such as Acts 4:31.
[2] John 20:19–23.

The Gospel of Luke also recounts the events of the same evening, but with different details, including Jesus' instructions, "But you are to stay in the city until you are clothed with power from on high."[3] This instruction is referenced again by Luke in the opening verses of the book of Acts. This emphasis of Luke's, taken together with John's assurance they the apostles received the Spirit on the first day of Christ's resurrection, might indicate that a second filling is to be a common expectation.[4] In the seven weeks between receiving the Holy Spirit (John 20) and the Pentecostal filling with the Holy Spirit (Acts 2), the disciples were consistently meeting in secret, timidly avoiding recognition as followers of Christ. However, after the Pentecostal filling, they began boldly preaching in the temple and the marketplaces that the Messiah had been crucified by the Jewish leaders and that salvation could only be found through the name of Jesus. By the apostles' example and their written words, we are confident that willful sin was finished at conversion, but power and boldness came with the second blessing.

The second event has been described variously as holiness, Christian perfection, perfect love, baptism of the Spirit, fullness of the Spirit, entire sanctification, the baptism of fire, and other terms. These terms all describe the fulfilment of Ezekiel's promise of an undivided heart, although some denominations tend to focus more on power-in-witness than on purity of heart. Truth be told, purity of heart *is* the power of witnessing: perfect love drives out all fear,[5] and the effect of a godly life upon unbelievers is powerful.[6]

The period of growth between conversion and holiness has been compared to the period when the Israelites wandered in the Sinai wilderness, free from Egypt but not yet courageous enough to enter the promised land.[7] Indeed, it can be a time of failure and frustration, but it need not be so. For some new believers, this is a time of new-found peace, new experiences and growing confidence. For a new convert, coming out of the harshness of worldly relationships into the loving care of a Christian congregation can be an overwhelming experience. Whether it is a difficult or a wonderful time, rather depends upon how ready the convert is to accept the Spirit's leading.

---

[3] Luke 24:49.
[4] Acts 1:5.
[5] 1 John 4:18.
[6] Matthew 5:16.
[7] The books from Exodus to Deuteronomy.

Some of the terms named above have been, and still are, disputed. In Wesley's ministry, the term *Christian perfection* was the source of much contention. Although perfection is a biblical teaching, its use was often misconstrued to mean sinless perfection; that is, that a Christian can live without any failings at all. Wesley maintained that Christians (from conversion) must live without willful sin and can be filled with perfect love, but he pressed the point that all people continue in unintentional failure, writing, "I believe there is no such perfection in this life as excludes these involuntary transgressions which I apprehend to be naturally consequent on the ignorance and mistakes inseparable from mortality."[8]

For this reason, Wesley wrote, "Therefore sinless perfection is a phrase I never use, lest I should seem to contradict myself."[9] John Fletcher,[10] however, was less concerned with being misunderstood, employing the term "an evangelically sinless perfection."[11] The use of the word *perfection* has fallen out of favor since Wesley's era because of the ease with which it is misunderstood. There is a time and a place for the term *perfection*, but it is not when the term can be easily misunderstood.

Another of the terms used to describe the second experience of the Holy Spirit is "baptism of the Spirit." Again, while Wesley opted not to employ the phrase to describe the holiness experience, John Fletcher used it freely:

> Should you ask how many baptisms, or effusions of the sanctifying Spirit, are necessary to cleanse the believer from all sin, and to kindle his soul into perfect love; I reply... If one baptism of the Spirit seals you unto the day of redemption, and cleanses you from all moral filthiness, so much the better. If two or more are necessary, the Lord can repeat them.[12]

A simple review of the biblical use of *baptism of* or *baptized with* the Holy Spirit shows that Wesley was more consistent with biblical

---

[8] Wesley, *A Plain Account of Christian Perfection*, sect. 19: 55.

[9] Wesley, *A Plain Account of Christian Perfection*, sect. 19: 56.

[10] Fletcher remained an Anglican priest at Madeley, Shropshire while ardently supporting John Wesley and the Methodists. Fletcher s untimely death in 1785 curtailed the suggestion that he might succeed Wesley as the Methodist leader.

[11] John Fletcher, on the other hand, did not shy from the phrase of *sinless perfection* although he modified it, calling it "an evangelically sinless perfection . Fletcher, *On Christian Perfection*, sect. 2, loc. 52.

[12] Fletcher, *On Christian Perfection*, sect. 2, loc. 188.

usage, although there is some flexibility. In the New testament, baptism of the Holy Spirit is almost always associated with being born-again. Apart from those times that are clearly referring to baptism with water, there are eleven times that the concept of baptism is connected to the initial receipt of the Holy Spirit. Four times it speaks specifically of regeneration,[13] three times baptism is more generally used as a descriptor of being born-again,[14] four times John the Baptist describes Jesus as the One who would baptize with the Holy Spirit,[15] and two times it is a reference to the Day of Pentecost.[16] These last two occurrences, both in the book of Acts, are the two which are best understood to reference the Pentecostal filling, however, for the majority of situations where the Pentecostal gift, holiness or second-blessing power is referenced, it is described as being "filled" with the Holy Spirit.[17] This leaves the impression that "baptism with the Holy Spirit" was used to describe the regenerating work of new birth and retained briefly in the transition period as the Pentecostal experience was understood. In time, though, "filled with the Holy Spirit" came to be the best descriptor for the experience of holiness and power. "Baptism of the Spirit" referenced being born-again, while "filled with the Spirit" referenced holiness and power.

Why would it matter whether *baptism* or *filled* is used for the second experience of the Holy Spirit? Biblical usage indicates that this is not an essential issue, but rather, there was simply some preference for using baptism consistently as a descriptor of new birth. Baptism with water has symbolized repentance, death and new birth (for immersion), or cleansing and receiving the Holy Spirit (for sprinkling or pouring). Therefore, it is less confusing to use the baptism imagery when speaking of being born-again of the Spirit. Water baptism was a conversion symbol, not a holiness image. More importantly, however, there is a substantial misunderstanding of the difference between conversion and holiness—and the word *filling* better explains what happens in the holiness experience. Holiness is not an external application of the Spirit (a baptism), it is in internal surrender of every motive and passion to the Spirit (a filling).

---

[13] Romans 6:3–4; Colossians 2:12 and 1 Peter 3:21.

[14] 1 Corinthians 12:13; Galatians 3:27 and Mark 16:16 (if you allow that this must speak of baptism of the Spirit since water baptism never saved anyone).

[15] Matthew 3:11; Mark 1:8; Luke 3:16 and John 1:33. Note also that Matthew and Luke include baptism "with fire in John s words.

[16] Acts 1:5 and 11:16.

[17] Luke 1:15; Acts 2:2, 4; 4:8; 15:9 and Ephesians 5:18.

John the Baptist said, when testifying about the Christ:

> He who comes from heaven is above all. What He has seen and
> heard, of that He testifies; and no one receives His testimony.
> He who has received His testimony has set his seal to this, that
> God is true. For He whom God has sent speaks the words of God;
> **for He gives the Spirit without measure**. emphasis mine][18]

There is only one salvation, which includes repentance, belief in Jesus
Christ and being born of, and filled with, the Holy Spirit. John
celebrated the coming of the dispensation of the Holy Spirit in the
confidence that the Spirit would be given without limit. There is no
partial filling! Salvation is not a preliminary taste of the Spirit of God,
followed by a complete filling at a later time. God gives the Spirit
without measure, and if there is any blockage it is because of the
receptivity of the believer, not the gift of God. Most importantly, any
teaching that implies a partial filling at conversion works against the
clear teaching that *all* believers must cease willful sin and have the
power to do so from conversion; it subtly introduces a possibility that
repentance is only truly possible at the point of holiness. This teaching
encourages the new believer to defy the Word of God by postponing
repentance and it misdirects the teaching of holiness away from its
real purpose. Victory over acts of willful sin is not the focus of holiness;
holiness is the fullness of love. Repentance is necessary for salvation.

So, we ask, how is being "filled with the Spirit" any more useful than
being "baptized with the Spirit"? The use of the term *filled* is very
helpful indeed because it encourages us to think of holiness as an
internal event when we are filled with perfect love. However, fullness
of the Spirit should not be understood as receiving more of the Spirit,
but rather, when the Spirit claims more of us as our love and our
willingness to open up to the Spirit increases. Imagine a car drives off
the road and is fully immersed in a river, sinking to the very river-bed.
The car is "baptized" and appears to be completely invaded by the
water, and yet we understand that pockets of air remain in sealed
sections of the panel-work. The water cannot press into those pockets
because the air pressure pushes back against it. And so it is for most
people when they are born-again. They do not yet know all that will be
asked of them by God, and they do not fully understand their own
weakness and their own points of stubborn rebellion. A deeper
surrender is yet to come, often a very emotional time of release and
cleansing, as the Spirit is given free access to the most sensitive,

---

[18] John 3:31–34.

hidden parts of our hearts and wills. Being filled with the Spirit can be both exhausting and thrilling at the same time.

For John Wesley, pressing on to holiness was to do with achieving perfect love, not gaining victory over willful sin. Even though, from conversion, victory over willful acts of sin was possible, the presence of a divided heart remained in the experience of believers. Through the Spirit's indwelling, the sinful nature, "has not now dominion over them," but they are increasingly convicted of their need for inner cleansing.

> It is a conviction, wrought by the Holy Ghost, of the *sin* which still *remains* in our heart... our proneness to evil, of an heart bent to backsliding, of the still continuing tendency of the flesh to lust against the spirit. Sometimes, unless we continually watch and pray, it lusts to pride, sometimes to anger, sometimes to love of the world, love of ease, love of honor, or love of pleasure more than of God. It is a conviction of the tendency of our heart to self-will, to Atheism, or idolatry; and above all, to unbelief; whereby, in a thousand ways, and under a thousand pretenses, we are ever departing, more or less, from the living God. Italics are Wesley's][19]

When the Israelites came out of Egypt, they were free from the bondage of slavery. They were saved by the presence of God in their midst, "a pillar of cloud by day... and a pillar of fire by night", which did not depart from them.[20] God was fully present with the Israelites, but they were not fully committed to him. They accepted him, and they followed him, but they grumbled, they yearned for their old food, and they did not fully trust that God could protect them from the giants in their world. That is why the period between salvation and sanctification is sometimes likened to "wandering in the wilderness," as the Israelites did because of their lack of trust. Ezekiel described it as a time when we still have a divided heart or a hard heart. We have only to look around us in the Church and ask, "How many here are truly enjoying their faith? How many grumble their way through their new life in Christ? And, how can this be so?" The answer is two-fold: there are some who have been deceived into thinking that repentance is not necessary for salvation, and there are others who still have "pockets of air" in their lives where they do not allow their faith to penetrate.

---

[19] Wesley, "Sermon 43, The Scripture Way of Salvation , in *Works*, vol. 6: 50.
[20] Exodus 13:21.

Most converts go through a time of growth in their spiritual experience and biblical knowledge after conversion, if for no other reason than that they cannot properly understand God's truth until they have the indwelling Spirit of God.[21] At the same time, they become increasingly aware of how inconsistent their own discipline is and how desperately they find themselves longing for some old pleasures. This process may take weeks or years. The growing awareness of one's own divided heart leads to a second crisis of faith as the believer seeks a deeper work of the Spirit.

This experience can be very different for each person because we have all come from different struggles and we have engaged in different sins. The human part of holiness is trust and consecration, the miraculous part is the Spirit's cleansing (freedom). "For just as you presented your members as slaves to impurity and to lawlessness, resulting in further lawlessness, so now present your members as slaves to righteousness, resulting in sanctification."[22] Where there is real trust, consecration is not difficult:

- Do you believe that God's plans for your life are better than your own plans? Can you eagerly, joyfully pray, "God, whatever you want me to do, please show me and I will gladly comply. Wherever you want me to go, just tell me and I will go. I know that your plans are good and perfect."

- Do you believe that God's ways are perfect? Can you pray, "God, I don't care what others are doing around me, I only want to know your ways and to be like Jesus in this world."

- Do you believe that God forgave your sins at great cost? Then pray, "God I freely forgive (_name_) for what they did, and I ask you to be merciful to them as well. Please God, release them from their sin and set them free."

- Do you believe that Jesus is preparing a better home for you in heaven? Then pray, "Jesus, I know my future with you is better than anything here on earth. I gladly give it all up, just so that I can walk closely with you. Use my resources, my health, my career, my relationships—use me up, but just stay close beside me."

- Do you love the very presence of God? He is perfect, he is faithful, he is good in all his ways. How amazing that the all-

---

[21] 1 Corinthians 2:14–15.
[22] Romans 6:19.

powerful God is so gracious and so unwavering. "God, I want to walk with you, to know you, and to know that you are pleased with me."

You see, the real issue in the Garden of Eden was that Adam and Eve did not trust God. God told them quite simply what would happen if they ate the forbidden fruit, but the devil contradicted God, and Eve made her own decision based upon what looked good in her own eyes. Eve was deceived while Adam watched on.[23] Adam never offered any objection, but simply allowed his wife to make the first move and then joined her. Both Adam and Eve were guilty of that first sin, and they passed the curse of distrust on to us all. The human tendency to distrust God, or to trust our own opinions more than God's instructions, is at the heart of sin. Therefore, salvation is by faith, because faith is the reversal of distrust and addresses the sentiment underlying every sin.

Similarly, if the things that Jesus and the prophets taught are true, then we have no reason to cling to this world. It should be an easy thing to say, "Here I am Lord. I want to walk with you. Use me and my life as you see fit." But we hesitate; we are held back by fear, greed, lust and self-will. The Spirit of God can deal with those things, but the first step is human consecration. Just as repentance precedes justification, so consecration precedes sanctification. Like the submerged car, consecration invites the Spirit of God to enter our most sensitive places, our most jealously guarded secrets. It can take some time. Sometimes, we know what we must do, but we are fighting against ourselves. We don't want to forgive, or to quit, or to give away. In those cases, the starting point is to ask God to help you to *want* to do what must be done, "for it is God who is at work in you, both to will and to work for His good pleasure."[24] In Wesley's words, "God breathes into us every good desire, and brings every good desire to good effect."[25]

When this second miraculous experience comes, the Christian enters a new era of faith, usually accompanied by greater growth. Growth in knowledge and grace never ceases, but once the believer's will be fully surrendered to God, growth accelerates because the believer is not resisting God. This second event is not the end of spiritual growth, it is the beginning of unhindered growth. John Wesley taught:

---

[23] Genesis 3:6.

[24] Philippians 2:13.

[25] Wesley, "Sermon 85, Working Out Our Own Salvation , in *Works*, vol. 6: 508.

At conversion] we are born-again, born from above, born of the Spirit: there is a real as well as a relative change. We are inwardly renewed by the power of God...

But soon] Temptations return, and sin revives; showing it was but stunned before, not dead. They now feel two principles in themselves, plainly contrary to each other; "the flesh lusting against the Spirit"; nature opposing the grace of God. They cannot deny, that although they still feel power to believe in Christ, and to love God; and although His "Spirit" still "witnesses with their spirits, that they are children of God"; yet they feel in themselves sometimes pride or self-will, sometimes anger or unbelief. They find one or more of these frequently stirring in their heart, though not conquering; yea, perhaps, "thrusting sore at them that they may fall"; but the Lord is their help...

It is thus that we wait for entire sanctification; for a full salvation from all our sins... perfect love. It is love excluding sin; love filling the heart, taking up the whole capacity of the soul.[26]

Progressive sanctification

So much attention is necessarily placed upon repentance and faith in the process toward conversion, that it can leave the new Christian with a sense of fulfilment. Indeed, that is well and good, since the decision to turn away from a godless lifestyle and the receipt of salvation and new life are arguably, the greatest events in any human's life. Nonetheless, there is much more to pursue. Repentance from willful sins— "acts that lead to death" —is the beginning of the adventure of a lifetime, but life in Christ holds much, much more. Salvation is just the gate, now there is the pathway to consider.[27]

In his later years, Peter outlined the process of Christian maturity from his own experience:

Applying all diligence, in your faith supply moral excellence, and in your moral excellence, knowledge, and in your knowledge, self-control, and in your self-control, perseverance, and in your perseverance, godliness, and in your godliness,

---

[26] Wesley, "Sermon 43, The Scripture Way of Salvation , in *Works*, vol. 6: 45–46, points 4, 6, 9.
[27] Matthew (7:13–14).

brotherly kindness, and in your brotherly kindness, love. For if these qualities are yours and are increasing, they render you neither useless nor unfruitful in the true knowledge of our Lord Jesus Christ. For he who lacks these qualities is blind or short-sighted, having forgotten his purification from his former sins.[28]

Peter's brief outline is loaded with meaning, carrying the believer from initial conversion to perfect love:

- You have saving faith, now pursue moral integrity. Repentance and saving faith result in good intentions, a willingness to know and follow God's ways.

- As you develop moral integrity, grow in the knowledge of God. Good intentions are given focus by learning God's ways, mostly through exposure to the Bible and other believers.

- As your knowledge increases, control yourself accordingly. With good intentions and an accurate understanding of God's ways, we learn to discipline ourselves to follow Christ more consistently.

- As your self-control is strengthened, learn to be consistently self-controlled. Consistent godly behavior, even in times of trial, develops perseverance, which is the capacity to keep pressing forward without faltering.

- As your perseverance increases, you increasingly reflect the image of Jesus Christ.

- As you grow in godliness, be sure to exercise love for those around you. Godliness is not simply a matter of self-discipline. The motivation for godliness comes from the love of Christ; it flows from the heart (Matthew 15:19). At first it is easier to show love to those to whom we are most easily attracted (*fileo* or brotherly love).

- As you learn to show brotherly love, learn also to love those you do not like: In time, as the Spirit of God works within us, we learn to show unconditional love (*agape* love), even to those for whom there is no easy affection.

---

[28] 2 Peter 1:5–9.

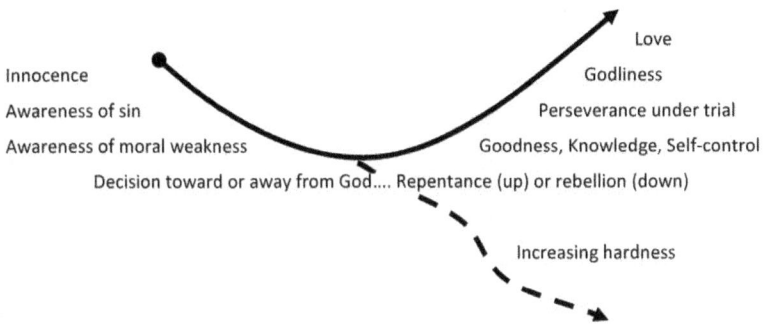

Although Peter described these stages of Christian development in a way that suggests a continuum, his statement that these are to be possessed "in increasing measure" shows that believers are growing in their capacity at all levels throughout their life. This is an important distinction because it allows that we never have perfect knowledge or perfect self-control in this life, and it allows that the progress of love is concurrent to the progress of knowledge and application. Brotherly and unconditional love are achieved while knowledge, self-control and perseverance are being learned. Furthermore, at no time on this earth does God fill us up with perfect faith, goodness, knowledge, self-control, perseverance or godliness, but he does fill us up with love. The result is that it is possible to be much further advanced in love than in actions. You might mean well but perform poorly. In theological terms we speak of entire sanctification (holiness, perfect love) occurring in a specific moment in time, but progressive sanctification (growing maturity) as an ongoing process until glorification. There is a turning point, and there is subsequent growth.

Therefore, Christian maturity should not be confused with perfect love, although the two may sound like the same thing. A believer may have the best of intentions (love) but an undeveloped capacity for self-control (immaturity). As we know, humans look on the outward appearance, but God looks on the heart.

Paul wrote to the church at Philippi:

> ... that I may know Him and the power of His resurrection and the fellowship of His sufferings, being conformed to His death; in order that I may attain to the resurrection from the dead. Not that I have already obtained it or have already become **perfect**, but I press on so that I may lay hold of that for which also I was laid hold of by Christ Jesus. Brethren, I do not regard myself as having laid hold of it yet; but one thing I do: forgetting what lies

behind and reaching forward to what lies ahead, I press on toward the goal for the prize of the upward call of God in Christ Jesus. Let us therefore, as many as are **perfect**, have this attitude. emphasis mine][29]

This passage can be confusing because Paul claims that he is not perfect in verse twelve, while in verse fifteen he is amongst several who are already perfect. The bible student is now confronted with the truth that there is a form of perfection that *is not possible* and there is a form of perfection that *is possible* in this life. Unfortunately, in many bible versions the translators take the liberty of rendering this second occurrence (v. 15) of the Greek word *teleioi* as "mature," while they have translated the same root word in verse twelve as "been made perfect." Both verses contain conjugations of the same Greek word that should properly be translated as a form of "perfect". In Paul's letter to the Ephesians the same root word is often paraphrased as maturity,[30] even though the meaning is defined as "the measure of the stature which belongs to the fullness of Christ." This unwarranted variation by translators imposes a particular theological interpretation upon the Word of God and supposes that *maturity* and *perfection* can be used interchangeably. On the contrary, being perfected in love is a work of the Spirit that runs parallel to growing in spiritual maturity. This deep truth can be lost when the translation does not make the reader aware that a word has been substituted.

There is a perfection available to the believer in this world, if that statement can be accepted while knowing that there is no time when the blood of Jesus is not required. Perfection is an attitude of love, an undivided heart. Maturity, however, includes knowledge and behavioral capacity, which are never perfect. In the following verses, Paul and James were speaking of a form of perfection that is available in this lifetime:

> Epaphras, who is one of your number, a bondslave of Jesus Christ, sends you his greetings, always laboring earnestly for you in his prayers, that you may stand perfect and fully assured in all the will of God.[31]

> Consider it all joy, my brethren, when you encounter various trials, knowing that the testing of your faith produces

---

[29] Philippians 3:10–15. See also Ephesians 4:11–13.

[30] This is why we are using the New American Standard Bible, because it does not change the word "perfect to "mature when it is convenient.

[31] Colossians 4:12.

endurance. And let endurance have its perfect result, so that you may be perfect and complete, lacking in nothing.[32]

The exceptions

The experiences described above are not everyone's experiences. In fact, all Christian experience has variety. The Spirit of God is all-knowing, and he shapes our experience according to our needs. Perhaps we need more time to surrender; perhaps more time would be detrimental to us. Perhaps we need a wave of assurance on the day that we surrender to Christ; perhaps we need a very calm experience and we need to learn to trust the Bible truths. Perhaps we need to be convicted about our marital situation or perhaps addressing an issue of bitterness is more urgent. Perhaps we need victory over an addiction; perhaps we need to learn to manage our own bodies. The Spirit of God knows our needs and leads us individually toward the unwavering goal of Christlikeness and love.

Just as there are variations in the way the Spirit leads us toward Christlikeness, there are some notable exceptions to the usual process of salvation and holiness. Two examples illustrate why some may be filled with the Spirit at the time of salvation.

Some believers repent of their sin long before they are converted.[33] These ones often wrestle with their own incapacity for years before receiving the empowering presence of the Holy Spirit. This is true of many of the New Testament characters, who sought God before the Holy Spirit was generally available to all believers. It could similarly be true of some today who are seeking God through powerless religion. Those who responded to John the Baptist's baptism of repentance were likely to go through this sincere, but weakened, period of internal struggle. The new believers at Ephesus are described this way and Paul hastened to introduce them to the indwelling power of the Spirit.[34] Paul had lived this way for many years, rigorously pursuing God before he received the Spirit. It is likely that Paul was describing this period of powerless repentance in Romans 7:13-25, before he went on to describe the victory of Christian repentance in Chapter 8. John and Charles Wesley are examples of believers whose personal consecration

---

[32] James 1:2-4.

[33] That is, if you allow that in the New Testament period "conversion occurs at the time of being born again, rather than at the time of repentance and surrender.

[34] Acts 19:1-7.

and discipline brought no peace until they were saved by faith and born-again of the Spirit:

> I diligently strove against all sin. I omitted no sort of self-denial which I thought lawful: I carefully used, both in public and in private, all the means of grace at all opportunities. I omitted no occasion for doing good... Yet when, after continuing some years in this course, I apprehended myself to be near death, I could not find that all this gave me any comfort, or any assurance of acceptance with God... I dragged on heavily, finding no comfort or help... I was too learned and too wise... Yet was I "carnal, sold under sin." Before, I had willingly served sin; now it was unwillingly; but still I served it. I fell, and rose, and fell again... which had now continued above ten years... I was still "under the law," not "under grace."[35]

The Wesley brothers, who had been urgently seeking God for years, were more aware than most of their own double-mindedness. For them, conversion and an undivided heart can be found in the same instant because that moment included both repentance and consecration, new birth and fullness of the Spirit.

There is a second group who may receive the Spirit's fullness concurrent to being born-again. Whereas the previous group were people who sought God for years before receiving the Spirit, this second group includes those who have run away from God for years. Perhaps a child raised in the church or an adult living with a believing spouse might know about God and be thoroughly acquainted with biblical teachings, while living in rebellion. In fact, it may be that the very reason this person runs from faith is because they understand just how much God requires of them. A pastoral family or a missionary family might see their share of thoroughly trained, but willfully rebellious, children. For this person, surrender is the issue. Surrender and trust. When that person finally accepts Christ in faith, they may simultaneously surrender their lives and ambitions in perfect love. The Spirit knows our needs, and his invisible work can be unpredictable: "The wind blows where it wishes and you hear the sound of it, but do not know where it comes from and where it is going; so is everyone who is born of the Spirit."[36]

---

[35] Wesley, "Journal, insert in May 24, 1738 , in *Works*, vol. 1: 100–01.
[36] John 3:8.

The instantaneous experience

John Wesley described instantaneous holiness and progressive sanctification when he wrote, "I believe this perfection is always wrought in a soul by a simple act of faith; consequently, in an instant. But I believe in a gradual work, both preceding and following that instant."[37] In his *Plain Account of Christian Perfection*, Wesley responded to the suggestion that some Christians are not aware of the moment when they were made holy:

> They did not perceive the instant when holiness] was wrought. It is often difficult to perceive the instant when a man dies; yet there is an instant in which life ceases. And if ever sin ceases, there must be a last moment of its existence, and a first moment of our deliverance from it.[38]

This quote introduces the issue of freedom from sin, by describing an instant in which "sin ceases." Many find it difficult to accept that sin is removed from the heart entirely, since temptations continue throughout this life. This discussion about the removal of sin is at the interface between perfect love and godly behavior. We have stated that holiness is *primarily* a matter of perfect love, not of repentance, but it is also true that perfect love is the most effective way to achieve repentance! There is no real contradiction here, because perfect love addresses the motivations of the heart, and Jesus told us that sinful actions arise out of the heart. The motivations and the actions are two separate things, but clearly, they are vitally connected. Furthermore, addressing the motivations of the heart is the matter of greatest urgency, since removing inbred sin will also stem the flow of sins.

---

[37] Wesley, "Brief Thoughts on Christian Perfection , in *Works*, vol. 11: 446.
[38] Wesley, *A Plain Account of Christian Perfection*, sect. 26: 118.

QUESTIONS FOR REFLECTION AND DISCUSSION

1. Have you encountered teaching on the fullness of the Spirit from other sources before? Can you identify what the purpose of the Spirit's fullness was: purity of heart? power in witnessing? physical healing? something else?

2. What is your response to the author's statement, "Purity of heart *is* the power of witnessing: perfect love drives out all fear, and the effect of a godly life upon unbelievers is powerful." Have you found that your influence with unchurched people increases when you are enjoying intimate relationship with Christ?

3. In your opinion, which term is the better to describe the holiness experience: "baptism of the Spirit" or "filled with the Spirit". Is it important to differentiate? Why?

4. Was there any one concept in this chapter that best helped you to understand holiness?

5. In Romans 7, Paul wrote at length about the power of sin in the heart of a believer who is earnestly trying to follow God. Wesley is also quoted in this chapter speaking about, "the still continuing tendency of the flesh to lust against the Spirit." Have you experienced this? After reading this chapter, are you convinced that God does set us free from this power?

6. Do you understand how the imagery of the Israelites "wandering in the wilderness" can be a picture of our divided hearts between salvation and sanctification? This concept suggests that crossing the Red Sea out of Egypt is a picture of salvation and crossing the Jordan River into Canaan is a picture of sanctification. How are these concepts reflected in your own life?

7. In this chapter the author suggests that "lack of trust" was at the heart of Adam and Eve's sin. Do you have an alternative way of explaining their rebellion? Do you agree that "salvation by faith" is the remedy to the fundamental sin of distrust? Do you know anyone who appears to believe in God, but not to trust him?

8. Read 1 John 4:18. If faith is the opposite of distrust, and perfect love drives out all fear, could you argue that fear and distrust come from the same cause? What causes fear and distrust?

9. Remember a time when you meant well but performed poorly. Do you agree that a believer's love for God might be greater than their knowledge or behavior? Why?

10. Explain how the substitution of the word "mature" when translating the Greek word for "perfect" deprives the Bible reader of a biblical truth? What biblical truth does use of "perfect" highlight? Is "Christian perfection" more properly a form of maturity or of perfection.

11. This chapter suggests two reasons why a person might be saved and sanctified at the same time. Explain these in your own words. Can you think of other reasons?

12. Read Hebrews 12:14. According to this verse, what is the consequence of not being holy? Does that mean you won't get to heaven without holiness, or something different? Compare the verse with 1 John 4:12. Discuss this in your group or write down your ideas. Now, read the Beatitudes in Matthew 5:3–12. Take note of verse 8. What similarity is there between this verse and the Hebrews verse?

Read Psalm 51:10-13. Note that some versions translate this "pure heart" and others "clean heart." Is this passage speaking about heaven or life on earth? Read Psalm 24:3-4. This concept of worshiping God with a pure heart and entering his presence ("seeing God") is a recurring theme in the Bible. Read 2 Timothy 2:22 and remind yourself of 1 Timothy 1:5. Do you enjoy this intimacy with God? When are you closest to God?

Chapter 7: **INBRED SIN AND THE LAW**

In reference to your former manner of life, you lay aside the old self,
which is being corrupted in accordance with the lusts of deceit,
and that you be renewed in the spirit of your mind,
and put on the new self, which in the likeness of God has been created
in righteousness and holiness of the truth.
Ephesians 4:22–24

In this chapter we will discuss two questions that cause some confusion for the believer and for theological students. The first question is, "What happens to inbred sin within the convert and the sanctified believer?" The second question is, "What is our relationship to the Ten Commandments and other Old Testament regulations?" These can be difficult questions, but it is hoped that, building upon preceding chapters, some clarity can be achieved.

Inbred sin

We have already described inbred sin as an emptiness or absence of spiritual life. By using the analogies of a thirst or a vacuum, it can be seen that spiritual emptiness can have real physical power in this world, without being a created entity. These concepts become even more important when discussing what happens to inbred sin during conversion and holiness.

When a person is convicted of sin and humbly repents before God, they are still under the sway of inbred sin and are incapable of the consistent fidelity that they seek. This is parallel to receiving the baptism of John, rather than the baptism of the Holy Spirit.[1] The lack of moral capacity for a believer who is not indwelt by the Spirit explains why Jesus pressed Nicodemus so strongly, "You must be

---

[1] Acts 19:1–5.

born-again."[2] Consistent repentance is only possible through the indwelling power of the Spirit of God.

However, when a believer is born-again of the Spirit, they are typically still holding back some parts of their life from the Spirit's control. These reservations may not be known to the believer, but they become apparent as the believer grows in Christian experience and understanding of God's jealous requirements.[3] Because of the reservations, perfect love is not yet realized, and the presence of indwelling sin is still a reality. John Wesley described King David as an example of a man who was "born of God," and yet "still there remained in his heart that corruption of nature, which is the seed of all evil."[4] Wesley further argued:

> It is plain, in fact, that those whom we cannot deny to have been truly born of God... nevertheless, not only could, but did, commit sin, even gross, outward sin. They did transgress the plain, known laws of God, speaking or acting what they knew he had forbidden.[5]

The new believer, therefore, is torn between two worlds. They know God's loving presence and mercy but are still weakened to things of this world. As the Bible teaches, they suffer a divided heart[6] or double-mindedness.[7] The power and presence of the Spirit keeps the new believer from willful sin, as long as they cling to him, but their desires are divided, and the pathway is often troubled. Again, Wesley describes the presence of the Holy Spirit within a divided heart:

> Christ indeed cannot *reign*, where sin *reigns*; neither will he *dwell* where any sin is *allowed*. But he *is* and *dwells* in the heart of every believer, who is *fighting against* all sin; although it be not yet purified... I do not suppose any man who is justified is a slave to sin. Yet I do suppose sin remains (at least for a time) in all that are justified. emphasis Wesley's][8]

---

[2] John 3:7.
[3] See Exodus 20:5; Deuteronomy 4:24; 2 Corinthians 11:1–3.
[4] Wesley, "Sermon 19, The Great Privilege of Those that are Born of God , in *Works*, vol. 5: 230.
[5] Wesley, "Sermon 19, The Great Privilege of Those that are Born of God , in *Works*, vol. 5: 228.
[6] Ezekiel 11:19; 1 Corinthians 7:35. See also Psalm 86:11 (NIV), "Teach me your way, LORD, that I may rely on your faithfulness; give me an undivided heart, that I may fear your name.
[7] James 4:8.
[8] Wesley, "Sermon 13, Sin in Believers , in *Works*, vol. 5: 149, 154.

In this born-again, but pre-holiness state, the Bible teaches that a true Christian does not and cannot go on sinning.[9] And yet, the Bible and common experience assures us that born-again believers do, at times, sin willfully.[10] Wesley's explanation of this seeming contradiction is useful, and it helps explain Wesley's high value on the sacraments and other means of grace (to be discussed in chapter 10). Wesley taught that there is never a time in the Christian walk when the believer is incapable of willful sin if so choosing, not even in holiness, but the difference in this intermediate state is that the believer's desires are divided, which lends temptation much greater influence. Double-mindedness weakens the believer's resolve. God provides numerous support mechanisms for the diligent believer; such as the sacraments of baptism and the Lord's Supper, bible-reading, prayer, fasting, confession of sins to one another, public worship, and more.[11] When believers are drawing upon these means of grace, they can live in victory over willful sin. A glimpse of the believer's ongoing struggle with sin, and of the believer's obligation to strive, can be seen in Romans 8, "If by the Spirit you are putting to death the deeds of the body, you will live."[12] However, if the believer neglects these means of grace and surrenders to their own desires for worldly satisfactions, their desire can be acted upon as sin.[13] When the believer acts unfaithfully in this way, the Spirit of God begins to withdraw. If they repent, the Spirit re-engages in fullness, but if they continue in willful sin, ultimately the Spirit withdraws altogether. Therefore, in Wesley's explanation, it is correct to say that a true Christian cannot *continue* in willful sin because any born-again believer who intentionally continues in known sin is in the process of departing from Christ. There is still hope, but there is real danger as well. Wesley argued:

> Thus it is unquestionably true, that he who is born of God, keeping himself, doth not, cannot commit sin; and yet, if he keeps not himself, he may commit all manner of sin with greediness... For it plainly appears, God does not continue to act upon a soul, unless the soul re-acts upon God.[14]

Wesley's Arminian-based teaching that saving faith necessitates the believer "re-act upon" (respond to) God was what separated him from

---

[9] 1 John 3:9.
[10] 1 John 2:1.
[11] See 1 Corinthians 10:13.
[12] Romans 8:13.
[13] See James 1:14.
[14] Wesley, "Sermon 19, The Great Privilege of Those that are Born of God , in *Works*, vol. 5: 232–33.

his Calvinist brethren. Calvinism did, and still does, reject the concept that the believer's response is necessary for salvation, and more so, that a believer can lose their relationship with God through willful sin.[15] This teaching of Wesley's drew a dividing line between the two schools of thought.

When it is recognized that the ongoing desire for things of the world poses a real danger to the salvation of a born-again believer, then it can be seen why a further, deeper experience of the Holy Spirit is necessary to complete Christ's saving work. Born-again, but pre-holiness, believers submit to the law of Christ, even while their hearts are still attracted to ungodly desires. Such a believer has more capacity to repent than the unconverted person but is still living with a divided love and experiencing a dangerous and unfulfilling faith. Thankfully, Christ has provided for a new heart; a heart that loves the things God loves.[16]

In holiness

In holiness, inbred sin ceases to be a force in the heart of the believer. This is, perhaps, the most difficult and debated concept in the holiness doctrine, and yet it is hard to deny the simple statements in the Bible. Paul explains that there was a time when we were in rebellion and there was a subsequent time when we were committed to God's ways, but, even when we wanted to live according to God's laws, we were still in slavery to inbred sin. However, there is a final place of rest when we are no longer under the control of inbred sin.[17]

One argument has been whether inbred sin is suppressed (pushed down) or eradicated (removed altogether) at the point of holiness. The difficulty with this debate is that it might promote a perception that sin is some sort of spiritual entity, like a black cancer-shadow in an otherwise clean heart. If, however, we proceed with the understanding that sin is an emptiness, a hole left by the withdrawal of the Spirit of God in the original man and woman, then we can better

---

[15] In Chapter 3, a quote from George Whitefield illustrated that, as a Calvinist, he opposed a suggestion that believers could continue in ongoing sin as strongly as Wesley did, but the difference was that Whitefield (because of his Calvinism) considered that a person who continued in willful sin simply was not converted at all. Whitefield does not represent all Reformed theologians in this however   some would maintain the sinning saint is counted blameless through imputed righteousness.

[16] Deuteronomy 30:6.

[17] Romans 5:8, 7:25, 8:4, 9.

understand that an emptiness simply ceases to exist when the fullness of the Spirit comes. In the analogy of the sunken car, sin is air-pockets that remain for a time until they are replaced by water, as hearts are filled with the living water of God's Spirit. It is also easier to understand that, if God's leading is resisted and worldly desires are entertained, the weakness of inbred sin can be reintroduced by deliberately rejecting the Spirit. What happened to Adam and Eve can happen to any of us.

Another analogy helps explain the capacity to re-engage in willful sin even when filled with the Holy Spirit. Imagine that sin is an infection in the body, justification is pain relief and holiness is antibiotic. When we are forgiven, the crippling presence of the sinful infection is controlled as with pain-killers, but the infection remains.[18] When fullness of the Spirit comes, the infection itself is remedied, rather than merely being managed. However, freedom from infection does not imply an incapacity to be re-infected. We live in a world of sin; we are confronted by sin and temptation every day. If, in this world, we cease to bathe regularly, we disregard a healthy diet, or we place ourselves in dangerous situations, then we become susceptible to new infections. Similarly, in our faith, if we cease clinging to Christ and his Spirit, if we disregard our daily spiritual disciplines or if we allow ourselves to entertain ungodly temptations, then we are weakened and can fall into willful sin. In fact, the sanctified believer who is not making a priority of their faith has already exhibited the fruit of unfaithfulness before a willful sin is enacted. Paul said:

> So then, my beloved, just as you have always obeyed, not as in my presence only, but now much more in my absence, work out your salvation with fear and trembling; for it is God who is at work in you, both to will and to work for His good pleasure.[19]

Holiness is loving God with all your heart and soul and mind and strength. As a God-fearer (a believer who is not yet born-again) and as a born-again but pre-holiness convert, Christ's commandments are followed, at least partially, as an imposed rule upon the believer. In other words, God made the rules and I want to live with God's blessings, so I will keep the laws even if I fundamentally disagree with them. Imposed laws have an inherent weakness, in that the believer often secretly wishes they could indulge their unlawful desires. When

---

[18] This illustration is quite limited since new birth is not just a "pain killer. It is the beginning of the remedy. Nonetheless, the concept of infection helps explain how readily we can be infected again if we reject the Spirit.

[19] Philippians 2:12–13.

no witnesses are near, it is tempting to play in the sinful waters. However, when the motivations of the heart are changed, the believer's desires become the same desires that motivate God. Obedience shifts from *duty* to *personal conviction*. We abandon hatred because we truly fall in love with mercy and kindness. Our television and internet viewing changes because we find ourselves offended by the profanity, lewdness and sadness of a corrupted society. Our witness to friends becomes more vibrant as our own awareness of God is heightened. Holiness is when the believer becomes a person after God's own heart, not just a dutiful follower. This is Ezekiel's prophecy:

> I will give you a new heart and put a new spirit within you; and I will remove the heart of stone from your flesh and give you a heart of flesh. I will put My Spirit within you and cause you to walk in My statutes, and you will be careful to observe My ordinances.[20]

Inbred sin is finished while we keep ourselves immersed in God's presence and guard ourselves diligently against worldly lusts. That is to say, the believer is aware of temptations but is not seriously enticed. It is misleading to think of inbred sin having been eradicated, if that suggests that sin cannot return. Rather, the hollowness has been displaced by the joy of God's presence; loving and trusting God are the daily experience of one who has been filled with the Holy Spirit. This does not imply that troubles and suffering are finished, but the believer gladly walks with God through life's trails with a peace that "surpasses all comprehension guarding] your hearts and your minds in Christ Jesus."[21]

Greed, sensual lusts and violence are constantly pressed upon us by a world that is, not just lost in sin but, aggressively pursuing every type of sin imaginable. Knowledge of, and confidence in, the Bible (Old and New Testaments) as the revealed Word of God is essential for a godly life because, "Faith comes from hearing, and hearing by the word of Christ."[22] Growing in the knowledge and experience of God is the satisfying flavor of holiness.

---

[20] Ezekiel 36:26–27.
[21] Philippians 4:7.
[22] Romans 10:17.

No longer under the Law

The second question addressed in this chapter— "in what way are we free from the Law" —fits well in the discussion about inbred sin be[23] because "freedom from the Law" is only a promise for those who are driven by God's desires and not by inbred sin.

Four thousand years ago God established a binding agreement with the man whose descendants would become the Hebrew nation. God promised Abram blessing and protection in return for Abram's absolute loyalty. This "covenant" was first introduced while Abram was still childless.[24] Years later the covenant was sealed with blood[25] and the sign of circumcision[26] as his family began to expand. The covenant was for Abram (later Abraham) and his descendants, through the line of Isaac, Jacob and the Israelite tribes.[27] It took more than 500 years for the promise of ownership of the Canaanite lands to be fulfilled, and 2,000 years for the messianic implications to appear through the birth of the Christ.[28] At Mount Sinai, during the exodus from Egypt, comprehensive regulations of the covenant (the Law) were detailed to the tribes of Israel.[29] God spelled out his commandments, statutes and laws[30] through Moses to his chosen nation as they passed from the slavery of Egypt to the freedom of Canaan.[31]

However, with Christ's death, a new covenant was established and Abraham's covenant came to be known as the Old Covenant.[32] Two thousand years after Abraham, the ministry of Jesus Christ rendered the Old Covenant obsolete because it was flawed[33] in that, while it revealed humanity's sinful state, it did not provide any assistance to repent of sins other than the threat of punishment. In fact, Paul

---

[23] For clarity, in this publication we are using the capitalized word, "Law , to speak of God s moral and ceremonial laws of the Old Covenant. This covenant began with Abram, and so the Law includes circumcision. It was developed through several visitations to Abraham and Jacob, but especially to Moses.

[24] Genesis 12:2–3.

[25] Genesis chapt. 15.

[26] Genesis 17:11.

[27] Genesis 15:13–16; Exodus 2:24.

[28] Genesis 12:3.

[29] Galatians 3:17.

[30] Genesis 26:5; Romans 9:4.

[31] Exodus chapts. 20–23.

[32] Luke 22:20; 1 Corinthians 11:23–26; Hebrews 9:12.

[33] Hebrews 8:7.

explained that rather than help us overcome sin, the Law revealed new ways to sin.[34] The Old Covenant therefore, "killed" without offering any power for life.[35] The New Covenant, which offered the blood of Christ rather than the blood of animals, superseded the old commandments, statutes and laws because it was more effective and lasting. Moreover, the New Covenant offers regeneration through the indwelling Holy Spirit, so that it can fulfil everything that the Old Covenant failed to provide.[36]

The Old Covenant, and indeed all the Bible, reveal to us the character of God. We come to understand what things God values, what he abhors, and what his character is. God's purpose had always been to create offspring that have the same values as himself, but establishing a list of rules did not achieve that purpose. Revealing the character of God was good, so the Law was good, but legislating that people must behave in a prescribed manner resulted in rebellion and ever-deepening sinfulness. The New Covenant, therefore, set the rules aside and established a relationship based on mercy, trust and the sharing of the Spirit. Under this new system, believers are increasingly in harmony with God's values and adopt them as their own convictions, thereby fulfilling all that the Law sought. Despite abolishing former regulations, the New Covenant is more effective in fulfilling God's original purposes because it draws upon the heart-motivation of believers who are internally governed by the Spirit. Freedom from the Law is not freedom to violate God's values, it is simply achieving the same outcome that the Law sought, but now through internal motivation rather than through external threat.

---

[34] Romans 5:20; 7:7.
[35] 2 Corinthians 3:6.
[36] Matthew 5:17; Romans 3:31.

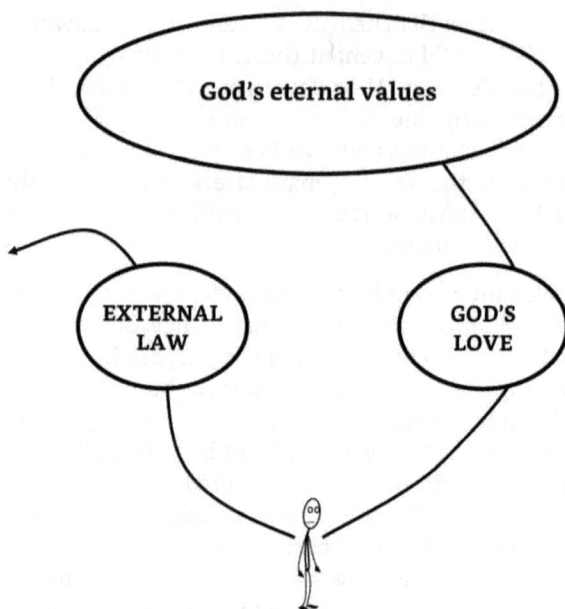

Mature believers, under the guidance of the Spirit, relate to the Old Covenant laws as an adult rather than as a child,[37] discerning not just the rule, but the eternal value from which the rule was derived. Jesus did this in the Sermon on the Mount when he expanded upon Old Testament principles:

> You have heard that the ancients were told, 'You shall not commit murder' and 'Whoever commits murder shall be liable to the court.' But I say to you that everyone who is angry with his brother shall be guilty before the court; and whoever says to his brother, 'You good-for-nothing,' shall be guilty before the supreme court; and whoever says, 'You fool,' shall be guilty enough to go into the fiery hell...

> You have heard that it was said, 'You shall not commit adultery'; but I say to you that everyone who looks at a woman with lust for her has already committed adultery with her in his heart...

> It was said, 'Whoever sends his wife away, let him give her a certificate of divorce'; but I say to you that everyone who

---

[37] Galatians 4:1–2.

divorces his wife, except for the reason of unchastity, makes her commit adultery; and whoever marries a divorced woman commits adultery...

You have heard that it was said, 'An eye for an eye, and a tooth for a tooth.' But I say to you, do not resist an evil person; but whoever slaps you on your right cheek, turn the other to him also...

You have heard that it was said, 'You shall love your neighbor and hate your enemy.' But I say to you, love your enemies and pray for those who persecute you, so that you may be sons of your Father who is in heaven...[38]

Jesus similarly spoke to the principle behind the Sabbath when he defended his disciples gathering food in the field, "The Sabbath was made for man, and not man for the Sabbath."[39] Paul did likewise when addressing the issue of religious sabbaths and holidays, "One person regards one day above another, another regards every day alike. Each person must be fully convinced in his own mind. He who observes the day, observes it for the Lord."[40] The freedom to reapply God's values was not usually expected under the Old Covenant.[41]

Hence the New Testament writers advised that Christians are no longer under law, but under the Spirit. Paul wrote, "For Christ is the end of the law for righteousness to everyone who believes."[42] Elsewhere he wrote, "But if you are led by the Spirit, you are not under the Law."[43] Note, however, the outcome of being freed from the old regulations is not license to sin; it is increased righteousness. "For I say to you that unless your righteousness surpasses that of the scribes and Pharisees, you will not enter the kingdom of heaven."[44]

---

[38] Matthew 5:21–22, 27–28, 31–32, 38–45. Note that in verses 38–45, Jesus is not just expanding upon an Old Testament regulation, but he is correcting a mis teaching of the religious leaders. In the Old Testament, "an eye for an eye" was a legal statute for public justice, while mercy was taught in relation to personal vengeance.

[39] Mark 2:27–28.

[40] Romans 14:5–6.

[41] Although, when Jesus defended David taking the consecrated bread from the house of God, he showed that even under the Old Covenant the heart of the rule was the issue. Matthew 12:3–8.

[42] Romans 10:4.

[43] Galatians 5:18.

[44] Matthew 5:20.

The born-again believer is truly free from rules and judgment, but the rules are not without value to the believer; they still provide a window into God's character, his values, and his desire for his children. This New Testament emphasis upon eternal principles existed in the Old Testament but was easily missed. The summary of Ten Commandment principles was captured in Moses' twin statements, "You shall love the Lord your God with all your heart and with all your soul and with all your might,"[45] and, "You shall love your neighbor as yourself."[46] The Prophet Micah's words similarly capture the underlying principles, "He has told you, O man, what is good; and what does the LORD require of you but to do justice, to love kindness, and to walk humbly with your God?"[47] Through the Law, God has shown us what he values, and he wants his children to share the same values, even when the cultural applications are different.

Paul wrote to his protégé, Timothy, "from childhood you have known the sacred writings which are able to give you the wisdom that leads to salvation through faith which is in Christ Jesus."[48] The New testament had not yet been written when Paul wrote this; he was referring to the Old Testament. He went further to say that all the Old Testament "is inspired by God and profitable for teaching, for reproof, for correction, for training in righteousness..."[49] If Christians disregard the former regulations of the Old Testament out of contempt or disinterest, they demonstrate that they are not led by the Spirit of God. They are, however, free to adopt different regulations in the spirit of the former regulations to suit the need of their situation— they can be trusted if they are functioning in love through the Spirit of God. The condition of this freedom from the Law is being led by the Spirit because the Spirit knows the heart of the Triune God better than could be expressed in any earthly document or upon stone tablets. In the New Covenant we are free from the Law because our hearts have been cleansed by the Spirit. For this reason and for the New Covenant to take effect, it is essential that believers must be born-again and growing in holiness.

One of the early Church leaders, Augustine of Hippo (354-430) is famously quoted for saying, "Love, and do what you want."[50] This

---

[45] Deuteronomy 6:5.

[46] Leviticus 19:18.

[47] Micah 6:8.

[48] 2 Timothy 3:15.

[49] 2 Timothy 3:16.

[50] Augustine, "Ten Sermons on 1 John: Homily 7 , in *Complete Works*, point 8, loc. 199,940.

truth reflects the biblical principle that those who love God will naturally desire the things that God desires. Paul expressed the same concept:

> But I say, walk by the Spirit, and you will not carry out the desire of the flesh. For the flesh sets its desire against the Spirit, and the Spirit against the flesh; for these are in opposition to one another, **so that you may not do the things that you please.** But if you are led by the Spirit, you are not under the Law. emphasis mine][51]

This passage speaks of an inability to do whatever you please, and in modern language that phrase is commonly used to speak of a person who wants to do something that is improper. However, in Pauline theology, this passage is parallel to Romans 7, in which Paul described the struggle when a believer wants to do *good but* is not able because of indwelling sin.

> I find then the principle that evil is present in me, the one who wants to do good. For I joyfully concur with the law of God in the inner man, but I see a different law in the members of my body, waging war against the law of my mind and making me a prisoner of the law of sin which is in my members. Wretched man that I am![52]

It is only when indwelt by the Holy Spirit, as described in Romans 8, that believers gain the liberty to do the good that they so desire, and it is only when believers are made holy that the struggle between inbred sin and the mind of the Spirit ceases. Until filled with the Spirit, the believer's desires are still taunted by the sinful nature.

The Apostle Paul's rules

Paul's two-year service in Corinth is recorded in the book of Acts and he left two lengthy letters to the Corinthian Church. These records shed light on the struggles Paul experienced when establishing Christian values in this cosmopolitan city. In those letters, Paul addressed substantive issues, such as divisions within the congregation, lawsuits between members, gross immorality, disorderly worship services, the improper use of gifts, disputes about the resurrection, disrespect for the Lord's Supper, and eating meat that had been sacrificed to idols. It would have been easy for Paul to simply

---

[51] Galatians 5:16–18.
[52] Romans 7:21–24.

announce what the rules were in these controversies, but he did not do that. Rather, he explained the deeper principles of Christian life that result in proper conclusions. Consider his response to the issue of gross immorality; "It is actually reported that there is immorality among you, and immorality of such a kind as does not exist even among the Gentiles, that someone has his father's wife."[53] The immorality of the man was not negotiated, but the willingness of the congregation to tolerate this behavior, even to congratulate themselves on their "graciousness," greatly disturbed Paul. Surely, this was a time when Paul should have quoted the Ten Commandments. This immorality violated at least two commandments, "honor your parents" and "do not commit adultery." Yet it appears that Paul never mentioned the Old Testament Law. He pressed the congregation on their shameful response to this immorality; he asked them to consider how this would permeate the whole congregation, and he reasoned that confronting sin was the only way to bring the sinning brother back to repentance and to save him from hell.

Some theologians have sought to divide the Law up into ceremonial and moral laws, to argue that the moral law continues to be binding in the New Covenant while the specifically Jewish ceremonial regulations have ceased. This has merit only if the moral law is taken to mean God's eternal values that undergird all the Old Covenant rules, but it cannot mean that the Ten Commandments are binding. This does not mean that the Ten Commandment have no moral value to us, but it is our understanding that Christ will test us according to the law of love, not the stone tablets. For example, how we apply the rule of the Sabbath may vary, but the principal of dedicated time for rest and worship is still valid. Paul illustrates this truth in his dealings with the Corinthians, and as F.F. Bruce has affirmed, the very concept of a moral law, "has to be read into Paul, for it is not a distinction that Paul makes himself."[54]

Paul's practice in addressing these Corinthian difficulties is even more extraordinary when it is recognized that he came to Corinth after the Jerusalem Council. That Council was a turning point for Jewish-Gentile relations. It had been convened because some Jews wanted to require circumcision of all Gentile believers. Both Paul and Peter opposed this requirement, and James, the half-brother of the Lord, summed up the decision that circumcision should not be required.

---

[53] 1 Corinthians 5:1.
[54] Bruce, *Paul: Apostle of the Heart Set Free*, 192–93.

However, perhaps to appease the circumcision group, James made the ruling that abstinence from food sacrificed to idols, from the blood of strangled animals, and from immorality should continue to be required of the Gentiles.[55] This was put in writing for Paul to carry to the Gentiles. The letter was taken to Antioch under supervision of some of the Council's own men, who were sent to ensure it was read publicly. On the next journey across to Europe however, Paul appears to have disregarded the Council's rules entirely. At times Paul openly contradicting the Council's regulations. In his letter to the Corinthians, Paul explained that eating meat that has been sacrificed to idols is of no real consequence:

> But food will not commend us to God; we are neither the worse if we do not eat, nor the better if we do eat. But take care that this liberty of yours does not somehow become a stumbling block to the weak. For if someone sees you, who have knowledge, dining in an idol's temple, will not his conscience, if he is weak, be strengthened to eat things sacrificed to idols? For through your knowledge he who is weak is ruined, the brother for whose sake Christ died.[56]

In this passage, Paul nominated those who were still troubled by eating such meat as being "weak" in the faith, which must include the members of the Jerusalem Council. If so, that is a surprising statement, especially when it is noted that the Jerusalem leaders were still requiring the same three regulations when Paul visited them again some five years later.[57]

One of the most obvious principles that Paul applied in the Corinthian letters was, "All things are lawful for me, but not all things are profitable. All things are lawful for me, but I will not be mastered by anything," and again, "All things are lawful, but not all things are profitable. All things are lawful, but not all things edify."[58] Paul defied Jewish traditions by teaching that believers are not under any religious law except to love God and their neighbor, and to avoid anything addictive or unedifying. His teachings still arrived at firm convictions, but not by imposing external rules.

---

[55] Acts chapt. 15.
[56] 1 Corinthians 8:8–11. See also 10:14–11:1.
[57] Acts 21:25.
[58] 1 Corinthians 6:12; 10:23.

The command to love

Throughout Paul's writings he argues that the freedom of the New Covenant must focus on how your life pleases God and impacts other people. Paul's teaching flows from Christ's "new commandment":

> A new commandment I give to you, that you love one another, even as I have loved you, that you also love one another. By this all men will know that you are My disciples, if you have love for one another.[59]

Although this commandment was directed to disciples to love other disciples, the broader requirement of loving God and all people is highlighted in Christ's teaching to "love your enemies"[60] and by John in his letters:

> If someone says, "I love God," and hates his brother, he is a liar; for the one who does not love his brother whom he has seen, cannot love God whom he has not seen. And this commandment we have from Him, that the one who loves God should love his brother also.[61]

Believers who are totally committed to God's ways, guided by the Spirit of God and seeking only good for their fellow humans, are free to conduct themselves as they see fit. There is no regulation against behaving out of, "love, joy, peace, patience, kindness, goodness, faithfulness, gentleness and] self-control."[62]

However, an incorrect understanding of love can lead believers to faulty conclusions and even to gracious tolerance of sin, as illustrated in the immoral brother in the Corinthian Church. To allow sin to continue unchallenged is to deny God's holiness and to surrender a fellow human to hell, but equally, confronting sin ruthlessly is a denial of God's love and an act of judgment. Consistently confronting sin, with neither favor nor hatred for the perpetrator, is a character trait of God, and should be so for believers. "Speaking the truth in love, we are to grow up in all aspects into Him who is the head, even Christ."[63] Again, we can cite the wisdom of Saint Augustine from his sermon on love:

---

[59] John 13:34–35. See also John 15:12.
[60] Matthew 5:44.
[61] 1 John 4:20–21. See also 1 John 2:7–11.
[62] Galatians 5:22–23.
[63] Ephesians 4:15.

We find a man may be fierce out of love; and another may be winningly gentle out of wicked intent. A father beats a boy, and a pedophile caresses. If you were to name the two things, blows and caresses, who would not choose the caresses, and decline the blows? But, if you look at the persons, it is love that beats, wickedness that caresses. See what we are insisting upon; that the deeds of men are only discerned by the motivation. For many things may be done that have a good appearance, and yet proceed not from the root of love. language modernized][64]

---

[64] Augustine, "Ten Sermons on 1 John: Homily 7 , in *Complete Works*, point 8, loc. 199, 928.

QUESTIONS FOR REFLECTION AND DISCUSSION

1. John Wesley used King David as an example of someone born-again but not filled with the Spirit. David lived one thousand years before Christ. Is it possible that David had the Spirit, given that the Spirit was only poured out at Pentecost? Read Psalm 51:10–13. Find the passages where the Holy Spirit came upon Samson or Saul. How do you understand these things?

2. This chapter, drawing upon Wesley's words, teaches that we must always be "re-acting upon" God and his Spirit. Explain that in your own words.

3. What happens if we start denying the Spirit's leading? Do you agree that inbred sin can be reintroduced? If yes, explain how this happens. If no, explain why.

4. Are there any laws of your country that you submit to, but do not agree with? If so, what? Are there any biblical regulations that you submit to, but don't understand or agree with? Which ones?

5. In your own words, describe the difference between an external law and an internal conviction.

6. What alternatives explanations have you heard to explain, "not being under the Law"?

7. Read Romans 3:20; 5:20; 7:7; Galatians 3:19–22. What was the purpose of the Law? What did the Law do? What was the Law not able to do?

8. Read Matthew 12:3–4. At one time, when David was fleeing from King Saul, David and his men were given the sacrificial bread at the Lord's Tabernacle. See 1 Samuel 21:3–6. This violated a law relating to the Tabernacle, and yet, David knew that God would not punish him for eating in a time of need. How could David and the priest have known this was acceptable. What were the principles behind the regulations at the Tabernacle? What was the lesson Jesus was trying to teach the Pharisees through this Matthew passage?

9. Read the Ten Commandments and consider why God made the rules that he made? What was the principle behind each rule?

10. One way to test whether Old Testament regulations are eternal values or cultural applications is to see if they are echoed in the New Testament. If they are repeated, there is less likelihood that they were merely cultural applications but instead a fundamental

principle. For example, Hosea 2:13 and 1 Peter 3:3. What is the eternal principle and what is the cultural application relating to wearing jewelry? Find some other passages on this topic.

11. Discuss God's view on the Sabbath, greed, alcohol, and another topic of your choosing. What Bible verses are applicable to these topics? What are the underlying principles? Do you think God is concerned about these issues? Would these practices strengthen your love for God and other people, or would they compete for your love?

Chapter 8: **THE LIES OF CULTURE**

Do not be conformed to this world,
but be transformed by the renewing of your mind,
so that you may prove what the will of God is,
that which is good and acceptable and perfect.
Romans 12:2

John Wesley's definition of willful sin has been referenced in Chapter 3— "a voluntary transgression of a known law of God"[1] — but in a less often cited work, Wesley further defines it as transgression of "the revealed, written law of God."[2] This clarification is important because our human convictions are not as pure as we might think. Our convictions come from many sources during our lives, and some of these convictions are quite unbiblical. Transgression of a "known law of God" is not specific about where that knowledge originated. When the gospel calls all believers to repentance, it is calling us to conformity to God's will as defined in the Bible. Therefore, a growing knowledge of the Bible is essential to repentance and maturity. If we are confused by our cultural values, we will find ourselves trying to repent of things for which God never voiced disapproval or accepting things that God has specifically condemned. We should not expect the indwelling Spirit to give us the moral strength for something that God never asked of us.

We are instructed that we must not add anything to the requirements of the Bible, and neither are we to take anything away from the Bible.[3] The Bible is the written Word of God, just as Jesus Christ is the living Word of God; both Jesus and the Bible have authority over creation and our lives. In our generation we are probably more aware of those who seek to explain away major biblical teachings; that is, those who want to take away from the Bible. They explain away many of the miracles,

---

[1] Wesley, "Letters to Mrs. Elizabeth Bennis , in *Works*, vol. 12: 394.

[2] Wesley, "Sermon 19, The Great Privilege of Those that are Born of God , in *Works*, vol. 5: 227.

[3] See Deuteronomy 4:2; 12:32; Proverbs 30:6; Revelation 22:18–19.

question the authenticity of whole sections, and disregard moral absolutes as out-of-date. They use unproven scientific theories to mock the inspired teachings of the Bible. This leads to liberalism and apostasy.

However, there have been times when the greater problem in the Church was with teachers who wanted to add things to the Bible. These were the ones who led believers into legalism and judgmentalism. The Pharisees were an example, but there are still people around today who seek to force their own extra-biblical convictions and their distorted interpretations upon others. In adding things to the Bible, these legalists sometimes construct fanciful interpretations of biblical passages to support their additional prohibitions. Paul was scathing in his condemnation of those who attempt to add religious practices to the doctrine of salvation by faith, "for if righteousness comes through the Law, then Christ died needlessly,"[4] and, "If any man is preaching to you a gospel contrary to what you received, he is to be accursed!"[5] It is often difficult for Christians, who are committed to repentance, to grasp how few rules God actually gave and how vigorously he opposes those who "weigh men down with burdens hard to bear."[6] Keep in mind that there were only Ten Commandments, and those were summed up in the two greatest commandments. We are inclined to err on the side of caution and sometimes bind ourselves to regulations that are not of God. Paul described it this way:

> For you were called to freedom, brethren; only do not turn your freedom into an opportunity for the flesh, but through love serve one another. For the whole Law is fulfilled in one word, in the statement, "You shall love your neighbor as yourself."[7]

Sources of our convictions

The values that we live by come from various sources, many of which are not in submission to the Bible. Non-biblical sources can include family, society, church, personal experience, personality traits, self-justification, unrealistic expectations, faulty logic, necessity and more. Satan often works through these agents to influence people away from God's values, although sometimes it is simply human

---

[4] Galatians 2:21.
[5] Galatians 1:9.
[6] Luke 11:46.
[7] Galatians 5:13–14.

willfulness that pursues wickedness. Since our consciences are shaped by these things, our innate sense of right and wrong is as unreliable as the societies in which we live. Paul described the uncorrupted remnant of our conscience as "the work of the Law written in our] hearts,"[8] but he explained in other places that the conscience, being weak, can readily be "defiled",[9] "seared"[10] and "rejected."[11] The conscience is an unreliable gauge of right and wrong until it is renewed by studying the Bible and listening to the voice of the Spirit. With constant exposure to God's ways, the conscience can be retrained "to discern good and evil."[12]

Family and society shape us from birth in worldview, values and culture. These are broad social influences, shaping every person in the collective to a common understanding of meaning and purpose, and therefore, right and wrong. They are external forces, in that they are not values that individuals arrive at themselves, although, these values can be so deeply ingrained that they feel like the only rational way to approach the world. Despite the strength of cultural values, they can shift radically in one generation, so that parents can hold substantially different values to children. Modern examples of culture shift in the Western world can be seen in attitudes to the role of the family, sexuality, modesty, discipline, greed, and more. The Bible warns emphatically:

> In the last days difficult times will come. For men will be lovers of self, lovers of money, boastful, arrogant, revilers, disobedient to parents, ungrateful, unholy, unloving, irreconcilable, malicious gossips, without self-control, brutal, haters of good, treacherous, reckless, conceited, lovers of pleasure rather than lovers of God, holding to a form of godliness, although they have denied its power.[13]

The local church, with its denominational structures, is not exempt from corruption and false teaching either.[14] Churches are often at the forefront of influencing culture in the roles of men and women and of

---

[8] Romans 2:15.
[9] 1 Corinthians 8:7.
[10] 1 Timothy 4:2.
[11] 1 Timothy 1:19.
[12] Hebrews 5:14.
[13] 2 Timothy 3:1–5.
[14] In fact, it would be reasonable to conclude that the verses quote are speaking of corruption within the Church, since it references those who "hold to a form of godliness.

laity and clergy; respect or disregard for the Bible; social abuses like slavery, drugs and domestic violence; proper or improper use of power; abstinence; modesty; social conformity and many varied rules. Even when church teachings are drawn specifically from the Bible, denominations can still hold vastly different interpretations. Churches can be misguided in their views, and church leaders can, at times, be willfully deceitful.

> There will also be false teachers among you, who will secretly introduce destructive heresies, even denying the Master who bought them, bringing swift destruction upon themselves. Many will follow their sensuality, and because of them the way of the truth will be maligned; and in their greed they will exploit you with false words.[15]

Along with these external influences, personal convictions are another powerful force in our lives, often stronger than the external forces of family, society and church. Our life-lessons, our faulty logic, and the necessities of life (such as hunger or survival) train us to accept and adopt new values. War can do this to a whole society; dividing it, encouraging violence, turning it toward or away from religion. Personality differences, our tendency to defend our own actions, and our idealistic expectations of ourselves and others all contribute to a community heaving with an ocean of differing values. The call to repentance can mean something different to every person in a congregation, although most assume that their values are not only right, but commonly agreed to.

This is the confusion that we bring into the Kingdom of God. We are not only morally weakened by inbred sin, but we are greatly confused by ungodly teachings and habits. But there is hope. The Spirit of God dwelling within, and the Bible kept infallible for millennia, can guide us back to truth. We can relocate our lives from the shifting sands of culture to the eternal truths of God.[16] Paul wrote, "Do not be conformed to this world, but be transformed by the renewing of your mind, so that you may prove what the will of God is, that which is good and acceptable and perfect."[17] Conscience can be redeemed, and as it is redeemed, we hear the voice of God more clearly speaking to our damaged souls. Our reorientation to God's values is one of the reasons why repentance is a lifelong discipline.

---

[15] 2 Peter 2:1–3. See also Matthew 24:24; 2 Timothy 4:3–4.
[16] Matthew 7:24–27.
[17] Romans 12:2. See also Ephesians 5:10, 17 and Philippians 1:9–11.

Where culture misleads

There are many examples in which culture teaches that some activities and attitudes, which are condemned in the Bible, are not only acceptable but should be celebrated and promoted. Some of these issues will be readily identifiable to the reader, such as sexuality, promiscuity and gender, greed and self-centeredness, immodesty, vengeance, personal rights, corruption and theft, disrespect for leadership, and more. Cultures shift, and each generation is confident that their values are more enlightened than those who went before. However, where there is no revival of biblical teaching, cultures inevitably descend into moral confusion. Paul described this as a symptom of the End Times:

> And just as they did not see fit to acknowledge God any longer, God gave them over to a depraved mind, to do those things which are not proper, being filled with all unrighteousness, wickedness, greed, evil; full of envy, murder, strife, deceit, malice; they are gossips. slanderers, haters of God, insolent, arrogant, boastful, inventors of evil, disobedient to parents, without understanding, untrustworthy, unloving, unmerciful; and although they know the ordinance of God, that those who practice such things are worthy of death, they not only do the same, but also give hearty approval to those who practice them.[18]

It is easier to identify the unbiblical values of a foreign culture, but more difficult to recognize the sins of one's own culture. Even when we are offended by the values promoted online, on television and in our social networks, we adjust and become numb to crude language, sexual innuendo, promiscuity, violence, blasphemy and nudity. It takes conviction and courage to resist culture. The pervasive godless culture is in front of us all day, every day. It should not surprise us then that daily prayer and bible study, regular worship and gathering with other believers is essential to spiritual understanding and growth. These means of grace are vital to ongoing holiness.

The wickedness of society becomes increasingly offensive to the believer who is under the influence of the Spirit and the Bible, but even so, there are some cultural mores that are more difficult to identify. Culture occasionally condemns some issues that God does not, and in this way, it encourages a sense of indignation or guilt that flatly contradicts God's values. Some cultures, especially Western cultures,

---

[18] Romans 1:28–32.

promote tolerance over moral absolutes, passive acceptance over anger and liberal views over conservativism. These are not values drawn from the Bible. Some exploration of specific examples will illustrate the dangers of cultural relativism.

Intolerance and anger

God has absolute values. He tolerates rebellion for a time[19] —granting the sinner opportunity to repent—but ultimately his values are unchanging, and those who violate his values without repentance will not share in the glory of eternity. Western cultures today are increasingly committed to a mantra of tolerance (although that tolerance is quite biased toward cultural liberalism and religious pluralism). It might be said that the greatest sin in modern culture is holding moral absolutes, and ironically, many point to Jesus Christ as the example of tolerant grace.[20] If tolerance means kindness and mercy, then there is truth to that suggestion. Jesus opposed the disciples' desire to rain fire down upon an inhospitable Samaritan town[21] and he reprimanded the Pharisees who wanted to stone a woman caught in adultery.[22] However, this same Jesus used physical violence to eject the money-changers and marketers from the temple:

> He found in the temple those who were selling oxen and sheep and doves, and the money changers seated at their tables. And He made a scourge of cords, and drove them all out of the temple, with the sheep and the oxen; and He poured out the coins of the money changers and overturned their tables; and to those who were selling the doves He said, "Take these things away; stop making My Father's house a place of business." His disciples remembered that it was written, "Zeal for Your house will consume me."[23]

Imagine if a young prophet came into one of our churches today and heard the preacher promoting greed and selfish ambition, so he kicked the tables over, scattered the offerings across the floor and drove the preacher and worship leaders out of the building. That is what Jesus did. Consider also, Jesus' verbal condemnation, even name-calling, of the Pharisees:

---

[19] 1 Peter 4:3; Ephesians 2:1–7.
[20] John 1:14.
[21] Luke 9:54.
[22] John 8:1–11.
[23] John 2:14–17.

> Woe to you, scribes and Pharisees, hypocrites, because you travel around on sea and land to make one proselyte; and when he becomes one, you make him twice as much a son of hell as yourselves... Woe to you, scribes and Pharisees, hypocrites! For you clean the outside of the cup and of the dish, but inside they are full of robbery and self-indulgence... Woe to you, scribes and Pharisees, hypocrites! For you are like whitewashed tombs which on the outside appear beautiful, but inside they are full of dead men's bones and all uncleanness... You serpents, you brood of vipers, how will you escape the sentence of hell?[24]

A proper understanding of Jesus' character must include a blend of "grace and truth."[25] Jesus was patient with people, but that should not be confused with tolerance. He loved people too much to allow them to continue in their sin. Truth without grace is harshness, but grace without truth is deceit. Christ's grace is truth clothed in mercy, and it always points toward godliness, "For the grace of God has appeared, bringing salvation to all men, instructing us to deny ungodliness and worldly desires and to live sensibly, righteously and godly in the present age."[26] It is not gracious to gloss over sin, lulling sinners into a sense of false security and delivering them into the hands of the devil. God's patience is not tolerance; it is always, only so that "the kindness of God leads you to repentance."[27] "For certain persons have crept in unnoticed, those who were long beforehand marked out for this condemnation, ungodly persons who turn the grace of our God into licentiousness and deny our only Master and Lord, Jesus Christ."[28]

God (and Jesus) is patient with sinners, but he is never tolerant of sin. Sin is destructive. It has gruesome consequences that destroy families and send people to eternal suffering. God would be inconsistent if he wavered on the truth that sin is the enemy of every human soul. Jesus response to the woman caught in adultery illustrates his response to sinners, "I do not condemn you, either. Go. From now on sin no more."[29] God is patient with sinners, but he holds the consequences of sin up for all to see and he does not shy from tough discipline. "Do not regard lightly the discipline of the LORD, nor faint when you are

---

[24] Matthew 23:13–33.
[25] John 1:14, 17.
[26] Titus 2:11–12.
[27] Romans 2:4.
[28] Jude v. 4.
[29] John 8:11.

reproved by Him; for those whom the LORD loves He disciplines, and He scourges every son whom He receives."[30] Jesus was literally "scourging" in the temple.

The early church swung between pharisaic legalism and excessive tolerance, and much of the New Testament Epistles is given to correcting one extreme or the other. Training the young church to properly interpret grace as a balance of truth and mercy was a constant struggle, and that struggle continues today. The Corinthian congregation considered it a sign of grace not to confront sin in their midst, but Paul wrote, "You have become arrogant and have not mourned instead, so that the one who had done this deed would be removed from your midst."[31] Paul wrestled against those in Corinth who would use God's grace to excuse ongoing sin,[32] while he rebuked the church in Galatia for its propensity to revert to Jewish legalism at the expense of their freedom in Christ.

Anger is closely associated with intolerance, and indeed it can be the cause of ungracious attack. However, anger is one aspect of our creation in the image of God. Anger is not a sin, and, in fact, if you aren't stirred to anger by some things, something is very wrong. The Italian priest, Thomas Aquinas (1225–74), famously noted, "Lack of the passion of anger is also a vice."[33] Injustice and godlessness should rightly make us angry, but we are warned, "Be angry, and yet do not sin; do not let the sun go down on your anger."[34] Anger that is out-of-control lacks grace, and anger that is sustained for days or weeks becomes the sin of unforgiveness. However, anger in itself is not sin, and neither is an abiding opposition to sinful behavior. Maintaining a constant objection to some people of destructive behavior is consistent with Christ's command to love our neighbor, as seen with the brother who refuses correction[35] and Christ's correction of the "blind" Pharisees.[36]

If we believe that an expression of anger or intolerance is a sin, then we are subject to unbiblical convictions and our conscience will lead us away from the love of Christ. It is unlikely that the Spirit of God is

---

[30] Hebrews 12:5–6; Proverbs 3:11–12.
[31] 1 Corinthians 5:1–5.
[32] Romans 6:1–2.
[33] Aquinas, *Summa Theologica*, vol. 4, part 3, sect. 1: 1838.
[34] Ephesians 4:26.
[35] Matthew 18:17.
[36] Matthew 15:12–14.

AN UNDIVIDED HEART

going to grant freedom from a virtue that God has planted in the human heart.

Religious regulations

Paul addressed the issue of eating food that had been sacrificed to idols in two substantial sections,[37] and in another place he addressed observance of certain religious festivals and the Hebrew ritual of circumcision.[38] He argued that these religious regulations are of no value to Christians, but they are "weak and worthless elemental things."[39] Neither circumcision nor uncircumcision, eating nor abstaining have any power over the Christian. Through our religious background we may feel guilty for violating similar regulations. The short-term solution provided in the Bible is to be careful of each other's sensitive (weak) consciences; which means, go along with their reservations out of love for Christ. The long-term solution is to train each other in the truth of freedom. Paul did just that for his disciple, Timothy. Paul defied godless teachings that required celibacy and abstinence from certain foods, instructing Timothy to publicly oppose these "doctrines of demons," saying:

> In pointing out these things to the brethren, you will be a good servant of Christ Jesus, constantly nourished on the words of the faith and of the sound doctrine which you have been following. But have nothing to do with worldly fables fit only for old women. On the other hand, discipline yourself for the purpose of godliness.[40]

In more recent centuries the Church and culture have been more fixated on smoking cigarettes and drinking alcohol than on food sacrificed to idols. Again, maturity requires carefully weighing the biblical instructions that impact upon these issues. Drunkenness is condemned in the Bible,[41] but drinking alcohol is not. Believers are free to drink alcohol,[42] but if their partaking causes them, or someone else, to violate their conscience or stumble into drunkenness, then they

---

[37] 1 Corinthians 8:1–13; 10:14–33.
[38] Galatians 4:8–11; 5:1–6.
[39] Galatians 4:9.
[40] 1 Timothy 4:1–7.
[41] 1 Corinthians 5:9–13; 6:9 11; Galatians 5:19–21; 1 Peter 4:3; Romans 13:11–14; Ephesians 5:18.
[42] See the example of Jesus; Luke 7:33–34; John 2:1–11. Also 1 Timothy 5:23.

have sinned against Christ.[43] What is the best example in the culture; is it moderation or abstinence? Is moderation with cigarettes even a possibility? How is the consumption of alcohol and the use of tobacco impacted by the biblical teachings of stewardship,[44] addiction,[45] and the body being the temple of the Holy Spirit?[46] Paul strenuously taught believers not to be bound by religious rules, but he also called us to not be addicted to anything and to carefully consider the most loving behavior in our own culture. Congregations and denominations often adopt their own understanding of best-practice in these matters, and that is acceptable, provided the denominational regulation is not associated with being saved. To conclude that a person is not justified in Christ because of their convictions on social issues is entering into the Galatian heresy. The freedom of Christ allows each Spirit-led believer to form their own convictions in such matters.

Biblical values

It is revealing to summarize the issues commonly named in the New Testament as sinful and, therefore, attitudes or actions that will keep a person out of heaven. It is instructive to see what is not mentioned as much as what is repeatedly named. The table below compares nine lists found in the New Testament. Seven of the nine are from Paul's writings.

---

[43] 1 Corinthians 8:9–13.
[44] Luke 16:11; Titus 1:7.
[45] 1 Corinthians 6:12.
[46] 1 Corinthians 6:19–20.

Jesus	Paul					Peter
Matthew 15:19	Romans 1:26–32	1 Corinthians 5:9–10; 6:9–10	Galatians 5:19–21	Ephesians 5:3–6; Colossians 3:5–9	1 Timothy 1:10	1 Peter 4:3
Evil thoughts				Evil desire, Passion		
Murder	Murder				Murder	
Adultery		Adultery				
Fornication		Immorality, Fornicating	Immorality, Impurity, Sensuality, Carousing	Immorality, Impurity	Immorality	Sensuality, Lust
Theft		Swindling, Theft				
Slander	Slander			Slander		
False witness	Deceit			Lying	Lying, Perjury	
		Coveting		Coveting		
		Idolatry	Idolatry	Idolatry		Idolatry
		Drunkenness	Drunkenness			Drunkenness, Orgies
		Effeminate (by perversion)				
	Homosexual	Homosexual			Homosexual	
			Sorcery			
		Reviling	Enmity, Strife, Disputes, Dissentions, Factions, Angry outbursts	Anger, Wrath, Malice, Abusive speech	Strife, Malice	
			Jealousy			
	Envious		Envy			
	Disobedient to parents				Parent killer	
					Kidnappers	
	Greed			Greed		
	Gossip					
	Hater of God					
	Insolent					
	Arrogant					
	Boastful					
	Untrustworthy					
	Unloving					
	Unmerciful					
				Filthy talk, Coarse jokes		

In Ephesians 5, greed is described as a form of coveting, and in Colossians 3, greed is described as idolatry. Sometimes our focus falls more easily on sexual immorality in these lists, but the Church would be well advised to study the teachings on greed, slander, coarse joking and arrogance, without neglecting the biblical teachings on immorality.

Sometimes the things which generate a sense of guilt in our minds are not even named in the Bible. They are cultural taboos, not biblical teachings. For example, culture tells us that we must be slim or muscular, while the Bible is clearly more interested in inward beauty than outward appearances. Culture trains us to live for the moment and to look after our own interests first. We are told that we should accumulate wealth or pamper ourselves "because we are worth it." Jesus, however, told us to find true fulfillment by "dying to ourselves." Some live under a cloud of shame or inferiority because they do not share family or group traits. But God does not condemn personality types, and he has specifically told us that we should not all be alike.[47] God made each of us, and he has a role for the quiet people and the loud people, the introverts and the extroverts, the ones for whom confrontation comes naturally and the ones for whom confrontation is painfully difficult. He loves the behind-the-scenes people and the leadership people—he loves them both equally. He made the bold, sometimes rash, adventurers and the steady long-haul, sometimes controlling, administrators. God made the variety, and he has a role for every personality. However, all people are ruled by the law of love. Every personality has unpleasant extremes and can demonstrate ungodly responses when feeling attacked. Some are prone to anger, while others are prone to passive-aggressive vengeance or capitulation. There is no place for unkindness in the life of a Christian believer who is living in repentance and grace. There can be tough love, but there is no room for demolition of people.

In these examples (anger, smoking, drinking, personalities, etc.) we have tried to illustrate how convictions and freedom come from a better understanding of the Bible and a sensitivity to the Spirit's leading. There are many other issues, of course. In fact, any activity or neglect can be sin if undertaken in defiance of the Spirit's leading. The focus here has been that, in repentance, there is a danger of false guilt. We should not be afraid to proclaim that, as a disciple, "you will know the truth, and the truth will make you free."[48] The truthful message differentiates between freedom-to-love and freedom-to-sin, and the witness of the sanctified believer should illustrate the same principles.

---

[47] 1 Corinthians 12:12–26.
[48] John 8:32.

The yoke of Christ

The gospel of Jesus Christ includes freedom from the Old Covenant Law, but it does not mean that we are under no obligation at all. Jesus offers to exchange the unbearable burden of law for the easy burden of love:

> Come to Me, all who are weary and heavy-laden, and I will give you rest. Take My yoke upon you and learn from Me, for I am gentle and humble in heart, and you will find rest for your souls. For My yoke is easy and My burden is light.[49]

There is a "yoke" in the gospel, but it is an easy yoke. Imagine that a person had to go and work in the field to earn money to eat. That person hated working in the dusty field under the hot sun but was forced to work by the threat of starvation. That is the burden of law—to do what is right, even though we dislike doing it. Now imagine a person who loves working with the soil, away from noisy crowds, feeling the cool breeze and the warm sun, watching the crops grow and drawing the greatest satisfaction in life from achieving something worthwhile. That is love. Imagine this second person was forced to go to university in the city and could not walk in the fields for an entire three years. Oh, the joy of returning to the farm and the eager anticipation of planting a new crop. That is the yoke of Jesus—it is hardly a yoke at all to spend your whole life doing that which you intrinsically love.

Now, note the logical necessities. To be eligible for the easy yoke of Christ, we must inherently love the things that Jesus loves. If not, we will not find Jesus commandments easy at all; they will be just another burden and a heavy yoke. To love as Jesus loves, we must have the indwelling presence of the Holy Spirit. We cannot love properly without the Spirit.[50] We must be justified by Christ to wear his yoke and to be free from the Law, we must be born-again to experience the easing of the burden, and we must be filled with the Spirit to draw full pleasure from the love of God. A person without Christ is still under the Law, and a person with a divided heart is still likely to find their new yoke uncomfortable and unachievable.

Furthermore, to say that we love as Christ loved, or that we love with Christ's love, but not to spend time in the Bible and prayer contradicts our claim. The Bible and prayer are the primary ways that we learn

---

[49] Matthew 11:28–30.
[50] 1 John 4:13–18.

Christ's values. To say we love Christ's values, while showing that we don't care to learn about Christ's values, reveals a deep inconsistency. We may even convince ourselves that we love God and our neighbor with all our heart, but if we are not constantly training our heart and mind in the ways of God, we are engaged in self-deception. The freedom that Christians enjoy is a life-long occupation that is a source of joy and relief, with the most pleasant obligations:

> So then, brethren, we are under obligation, not to the flesh, to live according to the flesh—for if you are living according to the flesh, you must die; but if by the Spirit you are putting to death the deeds of the body, you will live. For all who are being led by the Spirit of God, these are sons of God. For you have not received a spirit of slavery leading to fear again, but you have received a spirit of adoption as sons by which we cry out, "Abba! Father!" The Spirit Himself testifies with our spirit that we are children of God, and if children, heirs also, heirs of God and fellow heirs with Christ, if indeed we suffer with Him so that we may also be glorified with Him.[51]

Addictions

Before we conclude this chapter on cultural lies and freedom from the Law, we must consider the power of addictions in believers. In this section we are using a broad definition for addictions, that of "any compulsive, habitual behavior that limits the freedom of human desire... because] attachment of desire is the underlying process that results in addictive behavior."[52]

It is a mistake to think that inbred sin and the Spirit of God are the only forces at work within believers. There are also habits, addictions, memories, peer pressure and other common desires. These pressures continue to influence the behavior of believers when justified and sanctified. This is understandable because many believers have spent decades delving into unhealthy practices before repenting and accepting Christ. It can take years to break free from some addictions, and others must simply be managed for the duration of this earthly life. A chemical or emotional compulsion, a deeply ingrained habit, or a long-established relationship impacts the process of repentance. Spiritual forces are not the only forces at play.

---

[51] Romans 8:12–17.
[52] May, *Addiction and Grace*, 24.

It would be pleasant if God simply removed our addictions when regenerating us with the indwelling Spirit, but usually he does not. This is because of the ultimate purpose that God has for his earthly children. He wants us to develop character, and character requires self-discipline and perseverance. If God simply deleted the believer's nicotine or methamphetamine addiction, then the believer's growth would be impoverished because they never learned to manage themselves. If he merely dissolved each new convert's cultivated sexual proclivities, their gambling addiction, or their life-time practice of gossiping, lying, ranting, coveting, distrust, laziness, filthy language, cursing, slandering or greed, then converts would miss the discipline most necessary for their own character development. There is value in working through the painful process of breaking free, learning what small indiscretions inevitably lead to catastrophic moral failure, practicing self-control and confessing burdens with others who are likewise struggling. Occasionally God does indeed, simply release us from addictions, but often he does not. God knows what is best for each one of us and he knows what purpose he has in our struggles.

The difficult theological question is whether addictive behavior is willful sin. Of course, if the sin is freely embraced, then it is willful, but if it is resisted to the best of the believer's capacity, then it is unwelcome and there is the hope of ultimate victory. To know of one's own weakness is a torment, but it is not necessarily willful. We have already noted John Wesley's comments on this matter of unwelcomed sin, arguing that the Spirit "dwells in the heart of every believer, who is fighting against all sin; although it be not yet purified."[53] Only God truly knows the motivations of the heart, but the presence of grief over sin suggests that the Spirit is still active and guiding the believer toward stronger character. A hard-won victory is a precious gift and ultimately worth the struggle.

Search for the triggers that result in sinful defeat and learn to avoid those temptations before they even arrive. Examine your own heart to see whether your regret is caused by grieving the Father's heart or by a personal hatred of being weak—the first is repentance but the second is self-righteousness. Self-righteousness is a sin with devasting consequences, and it can disguise itself as purity of heart. Christians of many years can be most susceptible to self-righteousness. Ask yourself, would you go to an altar for prayer at the front of the

---

[53] Wesley, "Sermon 13, Sin in Believers , in *Works*, vol. 5: 149, 154.

congregation, or would you confess your sin to another with whom you have a trusting relationship?

In discussing addictions, it is worth noting that every human is crippled by sin in one way or another. Every human is dysfunctional. Some are converted while physically incarcerated and others are converted while chemically addicted. Some carry the consequences of generational abuse or character deformities that are not immediately evident. Most believers will become increasingly aware of their own failures, even addictions, after years of walking with Christ.

Forgiveness for sin does not mean release from the consequences of sinful behavior. Addiction is one of the consequences. All are damaged and in need of the blood of the Lamb and the Spirit of God. Our first and foremost obligation is to confess our need and surrender ourselves to the power of God, and from there to work out our salvation under the Spirit's leading, "For it is God who is at work in you, both to will and to work for His good pleasure."[54]

Memories

For the believer who is trying to break free from a history of sinful behavior, memories can be a powerful and abiding source of temptation. Equally, the believer who has lived through abuse can struggle with bitterness or unforgiveness. The human capacity to remember past events is not a result of Adam's sin, it is not sinful, and it is not suspended once inbred sin is evicted. In truth, not being able to remember is a symptom of physical, mental or emotional trauma and dysfunction. Memories can carry a sanctified believer back to an earlier time and taunt them with past pleasures, forbidden thrills or crippling hurts.[55] However, the power of memories can be overcome by the renewed heart. In the "heart of flesh," that is, the cleansed and renewed heart, we are regenerated to love as God loves. His love is placed within us,[56] and in that love our convictions are brought into line with God's values. Those memories that once brought pleasure and thrill, now bring shame and grief. Memories of abuse can be healed, the pain released, and anger can be replaced by forgiveness and even sympathy. Memories can remind you of a time when you treated God with contempt and people as disposable objects. Memories, which

---

[54] Philippians 2:13.
[55] Numbers 11:4–6.
[56] 1 John 4:16–18.

can be such a force of temptation, can be turned into a motivator for repentance and godliness through the fullness of the Spirit.

There are many forces at work in this world, external influences and internal desires, that seek to draw us away from God's values into ever-increasing sin. And yet, the power of God is overwhelmingly greater than anything in this created realm. He is *El Shaddai*, God Almighty. For those who seek God with all their heart, there is nothing that can separate us from the love of God:

> In all these things we overwhelmingly conquer through Him who loved us. For I am convinced that neither death, nor life, nor angels, nor principalities, nor things present, nor things to come, nor powers, nor height, nor depth, nor any other created thing, will be able to separate us from the love of God, which is in Christ Jesus our Lord.[57]

---

[57] Romans 8:37–39.

QUESTIONS FOR REFLECTION AND DISCUSSION

1. Read Revelation 22:18. Give examples, in your opinion, of where we add to the Bible and where we take away from the Bible. What is the consequence for doing either?

2. How trustworthy is a person's conscience? Some people seem to have little conscience, and some have an overly-active conscience. How can that be? Read Romans 2:15; 1 Corinthians 8:7; 1 Timothy 4:2 and 1 Timothy 1:19. Has this chapter challenged your conscience? Read Hebrews 5:14 and Romans 12:2. Do these two verses have a bearing upon the conscience?

3. Read 2 Timothy 3:1–5 and Romans 1:28–32. Do you see these traits in your own generation? Do you find yourself increasingly offended by these things, or are you becoming desensitized? What does this teach you about yourself?

4. Name some issues and attitudes that culture approves, but the Bible condemns? Does that create a divide between Christians and secular culture, or does culture permeate the Church? What issues do you find most difficult to resist?

5. Discuss intolerance. When is *tolerance* offensive to God and when is *intolerance* offensive to God? Explain how Jesus is patient with people but not tolerant of sins?

6. Read Mark 3:1–6. How do you explain verse 5, Jesus looked "around at them with anger"? Was Jesus angry? Was he wrong to be angry? Explain your perspective on this.

7. How do you explain the difference between Jesus' response to the woman caught in adultery in John 8:1–11 and the Pharisees in Mark 3:1–6? How might James 3:1 bear upon this passage in Mark 3?

8. Read Galatians 4:8–10. Can you think of a regulation in your church that is based on an Old Testament teaching? Do you believe that regulation has been reaffirmed in the New Testament, or is it one that has been set aside in the transition from Old to New Covenant? Can you name a non-church issue for which we feel guilty, even though it is not named in the Bible?

9. Discuss the difference between matters of conscience and law. Name some civil laws that you obey but do not like or agree with. Name something that you have never engaged in because of

personal conviction. Read Hebrews 8:10 and discuss how this passage impacts matters of law and conscience.

10. Do you agree that, "To know of one's own weakness is a torment, but it is not necessarily willful." Where is the line between knowing your own weaknesses and accepting your own weaknesses?

11. Consider the problem of self-righteousness. How is it that can sometimes repent more because of our own pride and less because we hate the sin? Is this more likely to be a problem for new Christians or long-time Christians? Why?

12. Have a group individually rate the following actions on a scale from 1 to 3. Keep the responses unseen and anonymous. Have the responses collated and present the summary to the group for discussion.

	1 Always Sin	2 Sometimes Sin	3 Never Sin		I'm Not Sure
Murder					
Killing in a war					
Homosexual practice					
Homosexual feelings					
Theft					
Invitro-fertilization					
Adultery					
Sex before marriage					
Relaxation					
Smoking					
Anger					
Drunkenness					
Drinking alcohol					
Missing church for sport					
Over-eating					

Chapter 9: **PERSEVERANCE**

*Do not be deceived, God is not mocked; for whatever a man sows,
this he will also reap. For the one who sows to his own flesh will from
the flesh reap corruption, but the one who sows to the Spirit will
from the Spirit reap eternal life.*
Galatians 6:7–8

The gospel of Jesus Christ is not a means of escaping the seemingly impossible demands of God's righteousness. It is, rather, a more effective way of achieving those very same demands. In place of the Mosaic Law,[1] the gospel is a means of syncing with the mind of God and his values, for "having been freed from sin, you became slaves of righteousness."[2] The gospel achieves the righteousness that the Law failed to achieve. The goal of righteous living and the penalty for unrighteous living remains, but the means of achieving the goal has been redefined. Jesus said emphatically:

> Do not think that I came to abolish the Law or the Prophets; I did not come to abolish but to fulfill. For truly I say to you, until heaven and earth pass away, not the smallest letter or stroke shall pass from the Law until all is accomplished.[3]

The Law sought to direct people to righteousness by announcing the regulations and the punishment for failure. This had some success in outward conformity, but it generally failed to change heart motivations. In the New Covenant, Christ offers a better salvation in which he redeems us from our guilt, restores relationship, fills us with new moral strength, and reboots our internal motivations to love the

---

[1] Law (with a capital) refers to the Law of Moses or the Jewish Torah. It includes the five books of the Pentateuch. The "Law and the Prophets therefore, refers to the writings of Moses and the other Old Testament prophets. Jesus separated the Psalms from the Law and the Prophets. See Luke 24:44.

[2] Romans 6:18.

[3] Matthew 5:17–18.

things that God loves. Our motivation to fulfil the demands of the Law are now internal love rather than external threat of punishment. Having an undivided heart does not mean that believers have perfect knowledge, flawless interaction with people, or freedom from struggles with worldliness. What it does mean is that they have a clear conscience before God because they have ceased willfully defying him. They trust him, know him, and follow him because they heartily welcome his moral absolutes.

In Chapter 1 we touched upon John Fletcher's teaching of the second justification by works. We have suggested that, although this has some biblical basis, it was an unwise term because it suggested that salvation by faith is superseded in the day of judgment. However, Fletcher had good reason for speaking this way; he was magnifying a truth that is specifically stated in the Bible. James had written, "You see that a man is justified by works and not by faith alone."[4] What Fletcher meant by this term is solidly biblical, and he spent some effort clarifying his teaching. He insisted that he was speaking of the "evidence of works", not the "merit of works".[5] Good works are the evidence of a living faith, and therefore they are examined in the Judgment. As we have said earlier, good works *follow after* saving faith, they do not *come before*.

The 1770 Methodist Conference was that which stirred up opposition from Rev. Shirley and some of the Calvinist leadership. This in turn, led to the publication of Fletcher's *Checks to Antinomianism*. The final sentence from the 1770 Conference Minutes affirmed, "We are every hour and every moment pleasing or displeasing to God, according to our works; according to the whole of our inward tempers, and our outward behavior." It seems that in this furor, Wesley, Fletcher and the Methodist preachers recognized that they were too easily misunderstood. In something of a truce between Shirley and the Methodist leadership, the 1771 Conference agreed to modify their statement, publishing:

We abhor the doctrine of "justification by works", as a most perilous and abominable doctrine. And as the said Minutes are not sufficiently guarded in the way they are expressed, we hereby solemnly declare, in the sight of God, that we have no trust or confidence but in the alone *merit* of our Lord and Savior Jesus Christ for justification or salvation, either in life, death, or

---

[4] James 2:24.
[5] Fletcher, *Checks to Antinomianism*, "Second Justification, letter 1, loc. 1713.

the day of judgment. And though no one is a real Christian believer (and consequently cannot be saved) who doeth not good works, where there is time and opportunity; yet our works have no part in meriting or purchasing our justification, from first to last, either in whole or in part.

Signed by the Rev. Mr. Wesley and fifty-three Preachers emphasis in the 1771 statement][6]

The final part of this statement reaffirms the Methodist doctrine that a person cannot be saved who does not continue in good works as fruit (or evidence) of their salvation by faith. This is a teaching commonly promoted in the New Testament, though rarely mentioned in Methodist circles today.

The teaching of Jesus

John the Baptist was sent to prepare the way for the Christ. He did this primarily by baptizing people for the repentance of sins, creating a heightened sensitivity to things of God in his generation. He also served by identifying the Christ to his disciples, some of whom turned and followed Jesus as a result.[7] John knew the message that the Christ would teach and predicted the work of the Holy Spirit's ministry which would flow out of the ministry of Jesus. When John saw many Pharisees and Sadducees coming, he said to them:

You brood of vipers, who warned you to flee from the wrath to come? Therefore bear fruit in keeping with repentance; and do not suppose that you can say to yourselves, 'We have Abraham for our father'; for I say to you that from these stones God is able to raise up children to Abraham. The axe is already laid at the root of the trees; therefore every tree that does not bear good fruit is cut down and thrown into the fire.[8]

John pre-empted Christ's teaching that anyone who claims to be a believer but does not bear the fruit of repentance will be sent to hell. Jesus repeated this theme many times during his earthly teaching. In the parable of the Ten Virgins, Jesus described ten "betrothed" who awaited the return of the Lord. Five of the ten did not keep their lights burning; that is, they failed to persevere, and they were rejected from

---

[6] Watson, *The Life of John Wesley*, 255–256. These sentiments are also expressed in Wesley, *Notes on the New Testament*, Titus 3:5, 559.

[7] John 1:35–50.

[8] Matthew 3:7–10.

entry into heaven.[9] It is astounding that Jesus would nominate as many as 50% of the Church who could be rejected from eternal glory with the words, "I do not know you." In another parable, Jesus stated that believers "light" shines through good works, "Let your light shine before men in such a way that they may see your good works, and glorify your Father who is in heaven."[10]

The parable of the tares (or weeds) describes the great division in Church at the Judgment. These "tares" are people who have been in the Church for many years but are doing the works of the devil rather than works of repentance.

> The Son of Man will send forth His angels, and they will gather out of His kingdom all stumbling blocks, and those who commit lawlessness, and will throw them into the furnace of fire; in that place there will be weeping and gnashing of teeth. Then the righteous will shine forth as the sun in the kingdom of their Father. He who has ears, let him hear.[11]

He who can hear this message, should take note. Before we look around the congregation, we should examine our own lives. It is not only actions that will be examined for evidence of a living faith, however. Careless, hurtful words are also a violation of the command to love one's neighbor, and if practiced without repentance, they shall be enough to bring a verdict of "I do not know you!" and "No living faith!" Jesus said, "But I tell you that every careless word that people speak, they shall give an accounting for it in the day of judgment. For by your words you will be justified, and by your words you will be condemned."[12]

Public ministry is no protection from the Judgment. People's praise can be its own reward for those who seek recognition. Just as the Pharisees were condemned for their self-serving performances,[13] Christian ministers who have dynamic ministries and hidden sin will be cast out.

> Not everyone who says to Me, 'Lord, Lord,' will enter the kingdom of heaven, but he who does the will of My Father who is in heaven will enter. Many will say to Me on that day, 'Lord, Lord, did we not prophesy in Your name, and in Your name cast

---

[9] Matthew 25:1–13.
[10] Matthew 5:16.
[11] Matthew 13:41–43.
[12] Matthew 12:36–37.
[13] Matthew 6:5.

out demons, and in Your name perform many miracles?' And then I will declare to them, 'I never knew you; depart from Me, you who practice lawlessness.[14]

Paul echoed Christ's teaching when he wrote to Titus, "They profess to know God, but by their deeds they deny Him, being detestable and disobedient and worthless for any good deed."[15] It is a tragic error to think that Paul's teaching against *works of the Law*[16] implies a denial of *works of faith*. Paul, Jesus and James are in agreement; if there are no works of faith, there is no saving faith.

Jesus compared the Kingdom of Heaven to a fishing net that gathers up all sorts of people. In the Judgment the "righteous" people will be kept but the "wicked" will be thrown "into the furnace of fire; in that place there will be weeping and gnashing of teeth."[17] This is not a description of judgment of the world, but of the Kingdom, of the Church Universal. True followers of Jesus must die to their worldly ambitions and comforts. If they refuse to die to themselves, they will die eternally. Death to self is demonstrated through good works. "For the Son of Man is going to come in the glory of His Father with His angels, and will then repay every man according to his deeds," and truly, some followers of Jesus "will not taste death until they see the Son of Man coming in His kingdom."[18] Many in the Church are going to be shocked to find that they never actually knew Christ.

When we understand that saving faith *must* be evidenced by good works, or it is not living faith at all, then we can properly understand other teachings of Christ. In some teachings about the Day of Judgment, Christ speaks of the general separation of the entire population (not only within the Church). At other times he speaks of judging the Church, at which time he separates some to heaven and some to hell. What is striking is that in these cases he does not test their "faith", he tests their "works". This does have the appearance of salvation by works, unless our theology recognizes that there simply is no real living faith without real evidence in works. There are three possibilities: those who rejected Christ and were never capable of consistent good works; those who received Christ and his Spirit and were capable of consistent good works; and those who initially accepted Christ and his Spirit but were unprepared for perseverance

---

[14] Matthew 7:21–23.
[15] Titus 1:16.
[16] See Galatians 2:16 and later in this chapter.
[17] Matthew 13:47–50.
[18] Matthew 16:24–28.

and did not consistently produce good works. Therefore, a judgment of "works" is in reality a judgment of "faith". Pretense and half-hearted faith do not qualify for eternal glory. Here are Christ's words:

> Then He will also say to those on His left, "Depart from Me, accursed ones, into the eternal fire which has been prepared for the devil and his angels; for I was hungry, and you gave Me nothing to eat; I was thirsty, and you gave Me nothing to drink; I was a stranger, and you did not invite Me in; naked, and you did not clothe Me; sick, and in prison, and you did not visit Me." Then they themselves also will answer, "Lord, when did we see You hungry, or thirsty, or a stranger, or naked, or sick, or in prison, and did not take care of You?" Then He will answer them, "Truly I say to you, to the extent that you did not do it to one of the least of these, you did not do it to Me." These will go away into eternal punishment, but the righteous into eternal life.[19]

Salvation is by faith—only, always—but faith is not genuine unless it is confirmed by works. However, in saying this, we know that the most righteous person on earth will still not be sufficiently righteous for heaven. All have sinned and fall short of God's glory. We have past sins, ongoing failings, and occasional stumblings. If works of faith must be perfect works, then nothing has changed—none of us will enter heaven. Therefore, works only confirm whether the believer was truly motivated by the Spirit of God and had died to the desires of this world, even though his or her works were always weak and flawed. God knows that we are broken vessels in process of renewal, so he looks for symptoms of new life rather than perfection.

As Jesus said, "If you know these things, you are blessed if you do them."[20] Unfortunately, our capacity for rationalizing truth, leads us to conclude the very opposite of Christ's teachings. Some conclude that they were saved some years ago, and that behavior now has no bearing upon eternal destiny.

Rejected at Judgment

There are several parallel discussions in the New Testament, some that discuss rewards in heaven, some that deal with the danger of falling away from faith, and some that address exclusion from eternal

---

[19] Matthew 25:41–46.
[20] John 13:17.

life. In this section we shall touch upon the apostolic writings (and those of James) that deal with exclusion from heaven. The matter of rewards in heaven is a different discussion and is taken up separately.

James, the half-brother of Jesus, is the author most often referenced when discussing the role of works in salvation. Martin Luther is famously known to have, at least for a time, resisted the inclusion of the book of James in the New Testament canon because of the seeming denial of the central Protestant tenet of salvation by faith. James wrote:

> What use is it, my brethren, if someone says he has faith but he has no works? Can that faith save him? ... Faith, if it has no works, is dead, being by itself. But someone may well say, "You have faith and I have works; show me your faith without the works, and I will show you my faith by my works." You believe that God is one. You do well; the demons also believe, and shudder. But are you willing to recognize, you foolish fellow, that faith without works is useless? Was not Abraham our father justified by works when he offered up Isaac his son on the altar? You see that faith was working with his works, and as a result of the works, faith was perfected... You see that a man is justified by works and not by faith alone... For just as the body without the spirit is dead, so also faith without works is dead.[21]

The statement that "a man is justified by works and not by faith alone" appears, at first glance, to contradict the doctrine of salvation by faith. But part of the confusion is the word *justified*. We have already shown that we are saved by faith, while our works will be weighed in the Judgment as proof of a living faith. The word *justified* can be used when discussing the day of saving faith or the Day of Judgment. Believers are shown to be blameless (justified) when they turn to Christ in faith and again when their works illustrate their living faith. A believer's works prove their saving faith, and so they are received into heaven. Therefore, Jesus similarly said "By your words you will be justified, and by your words you will be condemned."[22] In another chapter, James again pressed his reader to good works, "But prove yourselves doers of the word, and not merely hearers who delude themselves."[23]

---

[21] James 2:14–26.
[22] Matthew 12:37.
[23] James 1:22.

Paul, the great defender of salvation by faith,[24] similarly insisted on good works flowing out of true faith. "For we must all appear before the judgment seat of Christ, so that each one may be recompensed for his deeds in the body, according to what he has done, whether good or bad."[25] Paul understood that salvation by faith must produce good works if it is alive. He wrote, "In Christ Jesus neither circumcision nor uncircumcision means anything, but faith working through love."[26]

As Jesus taught that the ungodly words of our mouths can result in judgment, Paul taught that the godly words from our mouths result in salvation:

> If you confess with your mouth Jesus as Lord, and believe in your heart that God raised Him from the dead, you will be saved; for with the heart a person believes, resulting in righteousness, and with the mouth he confesses, resulting in salvation.[27]

The implication here is that confessing Christ, a good work, is a necessary response of the believer for salvation. This is in agreement with the words of Jesus, "Whoever is ashamed of Me and My words, the Son of Man will be ashamed of him when He comes in His glory, and the glory of the Father and of the holy angels."[28]

Paul expressed his confidence that we shall all give account for our lives at the Judgment, "So then each one of us in the Church] will give an account of himself to God,"[29] meaning our works shall be reviewed. This knowledge is summed up in Paul's own life goal:

> I run in such a way, as not without aim; I box in such a way, as not beating the air; but I discipline my body and make it my slave, so that, after I have preached to others, I myself will not be disqualified.[30]

Peter and John also affirmed that entrance into heaven is dependent upon the believer's actions. Peter wrote:

---

[24] Ephesians 2:8–9.
[25] 2 Corinthians 5:10.
[26] Galatians 5:6.
[27] Romans 10:9–10.
[28] Luke 9:26.
[29] Romans 14:10–12.
[30] 1 Corinthians 9:26–27.

Therefore, brethren, be all the more diligent to make certain about His calling and choosing you; for as long as you practice these things, you will never stumble; for in this way the entrance into the eternal kingdom of our Lord and Savior Jesus Christ will be abundantly supplied to you.[31]

John highlighted the truth that keeping the commandments and having faith in Jesus are interwoven, forming the foundations of perseverance:

Here is the perseverance of the saints who keep the commandments of God and their faith in Jesus. And I heard a voice from heaven, saying, "Write, 'Blessed are the dead who die in the Lord from now on!'" "Yes," says the Spirit, "so that they may rest from their labors, for their deeds follow with them."[32]

Paul explained that if a so-called Christian claims to be a believer but practices sin, that person should be shunned.[33] Such behavior should have ceased when the believer was cleansed, sanctified and justified.[34] Similarly, John confirmed that sinning under the Blood of the Lamb shall exclude the half-hearted from access to heaven:

Blessed are those who wash their robes, so that they may have the right to the tree of life, and may enter by the gates into the city. Outside are the dogs and the sorcerers and the immoral persons and the murderers and the idolaters, and everyone who loves and practices lying.[35]

This is a very threatening concept, that Christ is going to weigh my claims of being a true follower against my actions in the world. Who can stand under that scrutiny? Who of us does not fail Jesus every day in some way or another? Fortunately, we are still covered by the blood of the Lamb, even in our efforts to be true to Christ's commandments. We are not condemned for imperfect performance, but our efforts and intentions speak to the vitality of our faith, and for that we are judged. Think of faithfulness this way: How can you show unwarranted kindness to someone this week? Make a conscious decision. How can you give up some of your own time, your own money, your own rights, to pour out love upon someone else this week, and in so doing, show your love for God? Can you help a neighbor clean up their yard, can you

---

[31] 2 Peter 1:10–11.
[32] Revelation 14:12–13.
[33] 1 Corinthians 5:9–10.
[34] 1 Corinthians 6:11.
[35] Revelation 22:14–15.

write a letter of friendship to someone, can you teach in Sunday School, can you phone or visit someone? One unwarranted, unexpected action this week, and then one more next week, and another and another, building a lifetime habit. This is faith in action; faith and works reflecting each other.

Jesus told of a man who had his unclean spirit removed, but then failed to fill up his cleansed life with good activities. The demon returned to the empty house and brought seven other demons with it, so that, "the last state of that man becomes worse than the first. That is the way it will also be with this evil generation."[36] Working out your salvation "with fear and trembling"[37] includes filling your life up with good priorities. This is pleasing to the Lord.

Two types of Works

This chapter is speaking to the topic that divided the early Evangelicals. John Wesley's teachings contradicted the widely accepted Calvinism of the day and appeared to promote salvation by works. Thus far we have referenced some of the passages that support salvation by faith as evidenced through works, but there is good reason to tread carefully in this matter. Paul urgently argued that, "If salvation] is by grace, it is no longer on the basis of works, otherwise grace is no longer grace."[38] Again, he pressed:

> Knowing that a man is not justified by the works of the Law but through faith in Christ Jesus, even we have believed in Christ Jesus, so that we may be justified by faith in Christ and not by the works of the Law; since by the works of the Law no flesh will be justified.[39]

How can we reconcile Paul's insistence that believers are not justified by works with other passages where he said, "For we are His workmanship, created in Christ Jesus for good works, which God prepared beforehand so that we would walk in them"?[40] A key to this potential confusion is found here in the Galatians reference, where Paul rejects any possibility of salvation by *works of the Law*. Seven times in the books of Romans and Galatians, Paul uses the phrase *works*

---

[36] Matthew 12:43–45.
[37] Philippians 2:12.
[38] Romans 11:6.
[39] Galatians 2:16.
[40] Ephesians 2:10.

of the Law.[41] Works of the Law are good works done in an effort to earn salvation, and Paul strongly rejected salvation by these works. In 1 Thessalonians, however, he commends "your work of faith and labor of love and steadfastness of hope in our Lord Jesus Christ."[42] These are the works that flow out of living faith. So, it is obvious that these are two different types of works: works of law and works of faith. In fact, there are more than just two types of works. The book of Hebrews describes "dead works" as a descriptor of sins[43] and the works of Jesus were his miraculous signs and wonders.[44] The difference between works of law and works of faith is clearly shown in Paul's letters to Timothy, in which Timothy's congregations are instructed that salvation cannot be earned by works[45] but that those who are saved should be "rich in good works."[46]

Salvation by the Law involved works that preceded salvation; works that resulted in salvation. However, this pathway to salvation was impossible because of our fallen nature, so that no one was ever saved by works of the Law.[47] Works of faith, however, come after salvation. They are the result of salvation, not the source of it. Good works can never result in salvation, but salvation must always result in good works. Everyone who has been justified by the grace of Jesus Christ and regenerated by the indwelling Spirit is capable of, and compelled to, works of faith and therefore, outward works of faith are a reliable indicator of inward grace. In our hopelessness, we were saved through the mercy of Jesus, and we are filled with thankfulness. Works of faith are works of thankfulness, and there is no self-righteousness in them.

Now if, after being saved by grace, we revert to self-righteous works of the Law, then we are following the error of the Galatian Church. We are falling back into justifying ourselves through good works. These efforts are often religious regulations or ministry, and they are to be greatly feared. Through religious self-righteousness, the blood of Christ is rendered useless to us.[48] One person might adopt a lifestyle of abstinence out of love for Christ and another might adopt the same lifestyle as a show of self-righteousness. There is real danger in this,

---

[41] Romans 3:20, 28; Galatians 2:16 (x3), 3:2, 5.
[42] 1 Thessalonians 1:3.
[43] Hebrews 6:1; 9:14.
[44] John 5:36.
[45] 2 Timothy 1:9.
[46] 1 Timothy 6:18; see also 1 Timothy 2:10.
[47] Romans 3:20.
[48] Galatians 5:2.

because even those who enter a pathway of love can become caught up in human praise and self-righteousness.

Rewards

Jesus introduced the concept of rewards and treasures in heaven for those who remain faithful in this world. The apostles also offered occasional mention of rewards in heaven, and although the Bible does not offer a thorough teaching on heavenly rewards, there are numerous glimpses into this truth. It is good to consider the truths of heaven, for after all, it is difficult to store your treasures somewhere that you never think about.[49]

The greatest treasure that awaits us corporately in heaven is our relationship with the triune God and sharing in his glory. "For now we see in a mirror dimly, but then face to face; now I know in part, but then I will know fully just as I also have been fully known."[50] We shall see the Father, the Son and the Spirit. We shall walk with the angels and reflect upon their care during our earthly trials. We shall be known as children of the Most High[51] and we shall be free from all sin, death and suffering.[52] We shall receive a crown of life,[53] of righteousness[54] and of glory.[55] We shall be rewarded with eternal life,[56] access to the tree of life and unhindered entrance into the City of God.[57]

There are rewards specific to individuals as well. We shall be rewarded according to our efforts upon the earth.[58] Perhaps the greatest personal reward will be in the words of Jesus, "Well done, good and faithful slave."[59] Those whom we have brought to Christ shall be, "our hope or joy or crown of exultation,"[60] and we shall be given responsibilities in the future work of God according to our faithfulness

---

[49] Matthew 6:19–21.
[50] 1 Corinthians 13:12.
[51] Luke 6:35.
[52] 1 Corinthians 15:26; Revelation 21:1–4, 27.
[53] James 1:12; Revelation 2:10.
[54] 2 Timothy 4:8.
[55] 1 Peter 5:4.
[56] Romans 2:7.
[57] Revelation 22:14.
[58] 1 Corinthians 3:8; 2 Corinthians 5:10.
[59] Matthew 25:23. NASB uses the word "slave while others use "servant .
[60] 1 Thessalonians 2:19.

on earth.[61] We shall be reunited with friends and family who died in Christ, and together we shall live with Christ.[62] However, since God is just, some will be in heaven, but as if "through fire," which is to say, they will be present but shall have sent little or no rewards ahead of them into heaven.[63]

There is much we do not know about heaven, and perhaps that is part of the joy—seeing, knowing and understanding for the first time. Our "momentary, light affliction is producing for us an eternal weight of glory far beyond all comparison."[64]

> Beloved, now we are children of God, and it has not appeared as yet what we will be. We know that when He appears, we will be like Him, because we will see Him just as He is. And everyone who has this hope fixed on Him purifies himself, just as He is pure.[65]

The hope of heaven is, therefore, an important motivating factor for earthly perseverance.

---

[61] Luke 19:17.
[62] 1 Thessalonians 4:13–18.
[63] 1 Corinthians 3:15.
[64] 2 Corinthians 4:17.
[65] 1 John 3:2–3.

QUESTIONS FOR REFLECTION AND DISCUSSION

1. This chapter begins with the concept that God's righteous demands did not change in the transition from law to faith. Read Matthew 5:17–20. Do you accept that, through the Spirit, it is possible to be more righteous than the Pharisees? Use these verses to show that Jesus was speaking about *imparted* righteousness, not *imputed* righteousness. If you don't know those terms, find a definition.

2. Do you agree with the author's concerns about the phrase, "a second justification by works"? Read James 2:22. How does James express the concept of being justified by works? What terminology would you use to describe this principle?

3. In your own words, explain the distinction between "the evidence of works" and "the merit of works". Which of the two did the Methodist conference "abhor"?

4. Read Matthew 13:41–43. Restate this in your own words. Find three other passages in which Jesus or Paul explicitly speaks about the evidence of works.

5. Did you find the concept of a judgment of works threatening? Why? Explain the concept that Jesus will look for as, "symptoms of new life rather than perfection."

6. Read James 1:12. How does this passage impact you and your personal faith. Is "trial" therefore, a necessary component of salvation? Explain your conclusion.

7. Read 1 Timothy 4:16. How does this verse go beyond your own personal faith to impact what you teach others. Consider the responsibility that any teacher or preacher carries when explaining the urgency of perseverance. Read 1 Timothy 4:6 and 2 Timothy 4:1–5 and write your own summary of this teaching.

8. Read Romans 3:20, 28; Galatians 2:16 and 3:2, 5. Mark the phrase "works of the Law". Now, read Romans 9:30–33; read it in several versions if you can. Did the Gentiles find personal righteousness, or merely imputed righteousness—that is to say, does this passage teach that the Gentiles came to live holy lives or were they merely forgiven for their sins? Remember, what the Gentiles found was the same thing that the Jews were pursuing through the Law.

9. What do you know about heaven? What do you know about our resurrected bodies? Read Mark 12:18–27. This passage teaches that

we will not have married partners in heaven, but what else does it suggest? Read Revelation 2:7 and 22:1-5. Why is the tree of life in heaven? Does this suggest that our resurrected bodies will still be able to eat, and perhaps even require the fruit for eternal life? Read Revelation 21:21-27. What does this tell us about heaven?

10. Read Matthew 25:31-46. Consider the glory of the first two verses. What an extraordinary day this will be. Every one of us will be there, but for some, this is not a time of glory! Consider Christ's separation of the "sheep" from the "goats". Can you explain why he made no reference to salvation by faith or to the Book of Life?[66] Explain your understanding of this.

11. Once you have given thought to this, consider one key to understanding this passage. Note that Jesus (the King) had already separated the two groups before he spoke to them of their good works or lack thereof. In effect, the judgment had already been made, but now he was explaining to them why he judged the way he did, and there appears to be many people who are surprised by his judgment. Some thought they should be sheep but have been put with the goats, and others feel like goats and are amazed that they are placed with the sheep. This is a shocking time of realization and of paralyzing fear. Explain how this is consistent with our gospel of salvation by faith.

---

[66] Philippians 4:3; Revelation 3:5; 20:12; 21:27.

Chapter 10: **MEANS OF GRACE**

[14] Since we have a great high priest who has passed through the heavens, Jesus the Son of God, let us hold fast our confession... Let us draw near with confidence to the throne of grace, so that we may receive mercy and find grace to help in time of need.
Hebrews 4:14, 16

Means of grace are disciplines or activities that provide opportunity for, and heighten our experience of, God's grace. John Wesley defined them as "outward signs, words, or actions, ordained of God, and appointed for this end, to be the ordinary channels whereby he might convey to men, preventing, justifying, or sanctifying grace."[1] Means of grace is a larger grouping that includes the sacraments (baptism and the Lord's Supper), the ordinances of the Church (such as public worship, corporate prayer, organized fasting and other ministries),[2] and individual spiritual exercises. These are means to strengthen believers in the grace of God. They are approved in the Bible and were the "ordinary channels" used by God to touch his people, which is to say, God is in no way limited to working through the means of grace—he is equally able to achieve his work with or without means of grace[3] —but these are the normal ways that he works. The most prominent means of grace in Wesley's writings were the Lord's Supper, prayer and bible study; a principle that can be illustrated in the early Church when the believers, were devoting "themselves to the apostles' teaching and to fellowship, to the breaking of bread and to prayer."[4] However, in differing contexts Wesley spoke of numerous other activities including giving alms (helping the poor), listening to sermons, singing praises, and good works in their various forms.

---

[1] Wesley, "Sermon 16, The Means of Grace", in *Works*, vol. 5: 187.
[2] Wesley, "General Rules of United Societies", in *Works*, vol. 8: 270.
[3] Wesley, "Sermon 16, The Means of Grace", in *Works*, vol. 5: 188–89.
[4] Acts 2:42.

There is no miraculous power in means of grace, but rather, they are activities, rituals and disciplines that stimulate the believer's faith. The death of the Lamb of God and the ongoing miraculous working of the Spirit; these alone are the power of salvation. Means of grace, however, serve to remind believers of spiritual realities, they provide opportunities for confession and consecration, and they strengthen the believer's resolve to remain true. Wesley was quite determined to deny any inherent power to means of grace for the simple reason that people were so very prone to conclude that going to church and taking the Lord's Supper would somehow make them Christians. "Whosoever, therefore, imagines there is any intrinsic power in any Means of Grace] whatsoever, does greatly err, not knowing the Scriptures, neither the power of God."[5] In the same way, no means of grace can ever atone for sin or render the believer pleasing to God. They are simply a means of focusing upon the saving power of Christ and the Spirit.

Wesley had much to say about means of grace, although sometimes his discussion was dominated by the conflict that he and Charles had with the Moravian missionary, Philip Molther, in 1740. Molther was teaching that all means of grace were sinful before conversion because they became a form of salvation by works. A glimpse of this developing theological rift can be seen in November 1739, as the society gathered at Fetter Lane under Molther's new teaching:

> We sat an hour without speaking. The rest of the time was spent in dispute; one having proposed a question concerning the Lord's Supper, which many warmly affirmed none ought to receive, till he had "the full assurance of faith."[6]

The Wesley brothers, together with George Whitefield and the other British Evangelicals, rejected Molther's view,[7] and subsequently, the value of means of grace *before* salvation remained a recurring topic for Wesley. More importantly for us however, Wesley taught that the ordinances of God and the means of grace were essential to an ongoing life of holiness.[8] Believers must avoid the two extremes of either neglecting the means of grace or overstating the power of religious rituals.[9]

---

[5] Wesley, "Sermon 16, The Means of Grace , in *Works*, vol. 5: 188–89.
[6] Wesley, "Journal, November 7, 1739 , in *Works*, vol. 1: 248.
[7] Tyerman, *Life and Times of John Wesley*, chapt. 7, loc. 4774.
[8] Wesley, *A Plain Account of Christian Perfection*, sect. 15: 34.
[9] Wesley, "Journal, November 12, 1739 , in *Works*, vol. 1: 249.

The Wesley brothers, George Whitefield and John Fletcher all remained Anglican priests until death, so not surprisingly, they maintained a common value upon the means of grace, notwithstanding their theological differences. Fletcher wrote, "Now, if your Master Jesus] was tempted and assaulted to the last; if to the last He watched and prayed, using all means of grace Himself... think not yourselves above Him, but go and do likewise."[10] Whitefield wrote, "I have seen too many fatal instances of the inexpressible danger and sad consequences of leaving off any one means of grace, not to encourage her] to persevere in the good way she has begun."[11] Again, he wrote:

> Have we received the Holy Ghost since we believed? Are we new creatures in Christ, or no?... Do we constantly and conscientiously use all the means of grace required thereto? Do we fast, watch and pray? Do we, not lazily seek, but laboriously strive to enter in at the strait gate? In short, do we renounce our own righteousness, take up our crosses and follow Christ? If so, we are in that narrow way which leads to life; the good seed is sown in our hearts, and will, if duly watered and nourished by a regular persevering use of all the means of grace, grow up to eternal life.[12]

If we have the Blood and the Spirit and are ready to "strive" to enter by the narrow gate, we can discuss the biblical evidence for means of grace.

Baptism

Wesley did not usually include baptism in his lists of ordinances or means of grace, but this appears not to be out of disregard for baptism, but rather because his normal focus was upon recurring means of grace that strengthened believers in their daily and weekly diligence. Baptism is the only Means that is intended to be received just once in a lifetime. The other Means are regularly practiced. Nonetheless, baptism is certainly a means of strengthening the believer's resolve.

Wesley was at pains to emphasize that baptism is only a symbol of the deeper spiritual experience of justification and regeneration. He argued that, "If either he or you die without new birth], your baptism

---

[10] Fletcher, *On Christian Perfection*, sect. 3, loc. 811.
[11] Whitefield, "Letter 18 , in *Works*, vol. 1: 22.
[12] Whitefield, "Sermon 49, On Regeneration , in *Works*, vol. 6: 269.

will be so far from profiting you, that it will greatly increase your damnation,"[13] meaning, if you were baptized but found unfaithful, your baptism will speak against you at the Judgment since you obviously knew about Christ's sacrifice. Referencing the Anglican Catechism, Wesley taught:

> Baptism is not the new birth: They are not one and the same thing... Baptism is a sacrament, wherein Christ hath ordained the washing with water, to be a sign and seal of regeneration by his Spirit...I mean an outward and visible sign of an inward and spiritual grace... Baptism is not the new birth.[14]

The biblical mandate for baptism is obvious in the Gospels and the book of Acts. Jesus instructed his disciples:

> Go therefore and make disciples of all the nations, baptizing them in the name of the Father and the Son and the Holy Spirit, teaching them to observe all that I commanded you; and lo, I am with you always, even to the end of the age.[15]

The words of Peter indicate that baptism was to be part of the gospel message throughout the world:

> Repent, and each of you be baptized in the name of Jesus Christ for the forgiveness of your sins; and you will receive the gift of the Holy Spirit. For the promise is for you and your children and for all who are far off, as many as the Lord our God will call to Himself.[16]

The concept of baptism has two applications in the New testament: baptism with water and baptism with the Spirit, just as John baptized with water but Christ baptized with the Holy Spirit. References to baptism or washing in the Epistles, therefore, must be weighed as to whether the author is speaking of the symbolic water-baptism or the spiritual reality. Some passages are clearly speaking of spiritual baptism— "For by one Spirit we were all baptized into one body,

---

[13] Wesley, "A farther Appeal to Men of Reason and Religion", in *Works*, vol. 8: 48–49. It is noteworthy that in this quote it is clear that Wesley considered a person who is not born again is not forgiven either. This reflects his view that justification and new birth are necessarily concurrent (Chapter 5).

[14] Wesley, "Thoughts Upon Methodism", in *Works*, vol. 6: 73.

[15] Matthew 28:19–20. See also John 4:1–2.

[16] Acts 2:38–39. See also Acts 8:12–17; 9:18.

whether Jews or Greeks, whether slaves or free, and we were all made to drink of one Spirit,"[17] —while others are less obvious.[18]

Jesus was himself baptized with water, "to fulfill all righteousness,"[19] and believers are instructed to publicly declare their faith in Jesus Christ by receiving water baptism. As a means of God's grace, baptism tests the sincerity of the believer and strengthens their resolve to follow Christ faithfully. It provides a public testimony and a natural opportunity to be distanced from former corrupting influences.

The Lord's Supper

The Lord's Supper is also named Communion, Holy Communion, or the Eucharist (a distinctly Catholic term). Holy Communion has an historical connection to the Catholic and Anglican Churches, while The Lord's Supper has been often used in Reformed and Evangelical circles.[20] Wesley and his Methodists used the term *Lord's Supper*, although as an Anglican, Wesley had used the term *Holy Communion*[21] until he met the Moravians and adopted the new terminology.[22] The Lord's Supper references the Last Supper (Passover) of Jesus and his disciples, while Communion references the fellowship that the believers have with Christ and each other through the sacrament, as rendered in the King James Bible, "The cup of blessing which we bless, is it not the communion of the blood of Christ? The bread which we break, is it not the communion of the body of Christ?" (KJV)[23]

The Lord's Supper was instituted by Jesus Christ as a remembrance of his sacrificial death,[24] and given as a continuing sacrament until he returns: "For as often as you eat this bread and drink the cup, you

---

[17] 1 Corinthians 12:13; Galatians 3:27–28; Titus 3:5–6.

[18] Romans 6:1–4; Colossians 2:12.

[19] Matthew 3:15.

[20] We are not suggesting that Reformed are not Evangelical or vice versa, merely that *all* Reformed are not Evangelical and *all* Evangelical are not Reformed.

[21] At about 20 years of age, John Wesley was taking, "the holy communion, which I was obliged to receive thrice a year. As his zeal for God increased, he adopted the habit of "communicating every week. Wesley, "Journal, Insert in May 1738 , in *Works*, vol. 1: 98.

[22] First appearance in Wesley s Journal is in October 1735 as Wesley sailed to America with the Moravian missionaries, (*Works*, vol. 1: 19) and continues in connection with the Moravians until it became Methodist terminology.

[23] 1 Corinthians 10:16–17 (KJV).

[24] Matthew 26:26–29.

proclaim the Lord's death until He comes."[25] Participation in this sacrament was an essential support to repentance and the maintenance of an undivided heart for the Methodists; it included solemn self-examination, with the threat of sickness, death or judgment for failing to do so:

> For he who eats and drinks, eats and drinks judgment to himself if he does not judge the body rightly. For this reason many among you are weak and sick, and a number sleep. But if we judged ourselves rightly, we would not be judged. But when we are judged, we are disciplined by the Lord so that we will not be condemned along with the world.[26]

The disciplines of regular self-examination, repentance and gratefulness remain essential for vibrant faith. Some denominations (even some of Methodist heritage) have not continued the sacrament of the Lord's Supper today, and others are uncomfortable with the sense of ritual. One way or another, these disciplines of thanksgiving, introspection and renewed consecration should be built into the life of believers who take seriously the Lord's commandments, and if not through this sacrament, then how?

Prayer

Corporate and private prayer are both a privilege and an obligation for followers of Christ. Jesus taught this by example and precept. He prayed alone all night before making important decisions, such as the appointment of the twelve apostles.[27] He prayed before his trial and crucifixion,[28] he prayed alone after an exhausting day of ministry,[29] and he prayed *with* his followers and *for* his followers.[30] He prayed in the evening and early in the morning,[31] he prayed alone, and he prayed in company.[32] His habit of prayer was well known.[33]

---

[25] 1 Corinthians 11:22–26.
[26] 1 Corinthians 11:29–32.
[27] Luke 6:12 16.
[28] Matthew 26:36–42.
[29] Matthew 14:23.
[30] John chapt. 17.
[31] Matthew 14:23; Mark 1:35.
[32] Luke 5:16; 9:18, 28.
[33] Luke 5:16.

We are instructed to pray for our enemies,[34] pray in secret,[35] pray together,[36] pray for each other,[37] pray intelligently,[38] pray without ceasing,[39] pray against temptation,[40] pray for healing,[41] and pray especially in the End Times.[42] We are to be "devoted to prayer."[43] "By prayer and supplication with thanksgiving," we are to let our "requests be made known to God,"[44] never giving up on prayer,[45] trusting in God's goodness.[46]

John Wesley wrote of his love for prayer and prayer meetings.[47] His commitment to prayer and its priority as a means of grace are evident in his explanation of Matthew 7:7–8:

> First, all who desire the grace of God are to wait for it in the way of prayer. This is the express direction of our Lord himself. In his Sermon upon the Mount... Here we are in the plainest manner directed to ask, in order to, or as a means of, receiving; to seek, in order to find, the grace of God, the pearl of great price; and to knock, to continue asking and seeking, if we would enter into his kingdom.[48]

Prayer is of great value to the believer. It teaches believers to look to God rather than trust in wealth or human help,[49] it requires that hurts are forgiven,[50] and it encourages us to reverence the Lord.[51]

---

[34] Matthew 5:44, Luke 6:28.
[35] Matthew 6:6.
[36] Acts 1:14.
[37] Acts 20:36; Ephesians 1:16–18; Colossians 1:3, 9.
[38] Matthew 6:7; 1 Corinthians 14:15.
[39] Ephesians 6:18; 2 Timothy 1:3; 1 Thessalonians 5:17.
[40] Matthew 6:9; 26:41.
[41] James 5:14–15, 1 Peter 3:12.
[42] 1 Peter 4:7.
[43] Romans 12:12; Colossians 4:2; 1 Corinthians 7:5.
[44] Philippians 4:6.
[45] Luke 18:10.
[46] Matthew 7:7–11.
[47] Wesley, "Several Conversations , in *Works*, vol. 8: 328 and "Letter 459, December 1772 , in *Works*, vol. 12: 417.
[48] Wesley, "Sermon 16, The Means of Grace , in *Works*, vol. 5: 190.
[49] Matthew 21:21–22; Mark 11:24; 1 Timothy 6:17.
[50] Mark 11:25.
[51] Ecclesiastes 5:2–3; Mark 12:40; Luke 18:13.

Bible study

The Bible is one of the chief means through which God speaks to the world, and for this reason it is the Word (Communication) of God. It stands alongside Jesus, the living Word/Communication of God, and the message of true prophets, the spoken Word/Communication of God. Since the Word originates from God, it is without error and we can trust it for guidance. The Word is the Sword of the Spirit,[52] with the capacity to pierce "as far as the division of soul and spirit, of both joints and marrow, and able to judge the thoughts and intentions of the heart."[53] This work of the Bible is useful "for teaching, for reproof, for correction, for training in righteousness."[54] The Bible provides powerful means of grace for the believer's spiritual development.

The connection between confidence in the inerrancy of the Bible and its effectiveness as the Sword of the Spirit is clear; if we lack confidence in the truthfulness of the Bible, we do not necessarily accept what we read, and the Sword is blunted. Wesley echoed this confidence in the truths of the Bible:

> "All Scripture is given by inspiration of God;" consequently, all Scripture is infallibly true; "and is profitable for doctrine, for reproof, for correction, for instruction in righteousness;" to the end "that the man of God may be perfect, thoroughly furnished unto all good works."[55]

Daily bible study is a vital means of growth for believers. "Be diligent to present yourself approved to God as a workman who does not need to be ashamed, accurately handling the word of truth."[56] Ezra, an Old Testament leader was a good example to us, "For Ezra had set his heart to study the law of the Lord and to practice it, and to teach His statutes and ordinances in Israel."[57]

Wesley expressed the priority of bible study with these words, "All who desire the grace of God are to wait for it in searching the Scriptures."[58] He advised that bible study should begin with "serious and earnest prayer... seeing 'Scripture can only be understood through

---

[52] Ephesians 6:17.
[53] Hebrews 4:12.
[54] 2 Timothy 3:16.
[55] Wesley, "Sermon 16, The Means of Grace , in *Works*, vol. 5: 193.
[56] 2 Timothy 2:15.
[57] Ezra 7:10.
[58] Wesley, "Sermon 16, The Means of Grace , in *Works*, vol. 5: 192.

the same Spirit whereby it was given'."[59] Study should be in a quiet place, away from distraction, and should draw upon larger sections of the text, ideally one chapter from each of the New and the Old Testaments. It is not adequate for a believer to merely listen to other people's sermons or to read theological or devotional books. Preachers do not, in any way, share God's infallibility. There is no substitute for reading an accurate translation of the Bible under the guidance of the Holy Spirit.

Fasting and abstinence

Temporarily fasting from food or some other form of abstinence has long been practiced in the Church and ancient Israelite society. Jesus left instructions about how to fast and how not to fast,[60] indicating his expectation that his followers would continue to have times of fasting. Fasting is a response to some distress or deep concern; it is a way of casting oneself upon the Lord, setting aside one's needs and acknowledging that unless God intervenes there is no hope. Fasting is a conscious decision to enter a period of deprivation to focus one's attention in prayer. Fasting mirrors those times when one might forget to eat in times of emotional distress. When Saul (Paul) was blinded on the road to Damascus, he was so shaken that he went three days without food or drink.[61] When his ship was wrecked at Malta, the sailors had gone fourteen days in the storm without food.[62] Fasting may be organized by the Church for some abiding need or it may be a personal response to an urgent situation, but it always has a focus and a desired outcome.

Fasting may be a heart-felt need to be free from worldliness, so that denying oneself of food is repentance from overindulgence and a personal reminder that one "does not live by bread alone."[63] It may be an appeal to God to turn his wrath away.[64] It may be to seek relief in a time of loss or grief,[65] or it may be to seek a blessing or some other miraculous intervention.[66] It may be to find an answer and

---

[59] Wesley, "Preface to Explanatory Notes upon the Old Testament , in *Works*, vol. 14: 253.

[60] Matthew 6:16–18.

[61] Acts 9:9.

[62] Acts 27:33.

[63] Deuteronomy 8:3; Matthew 4:4.

[64] Joel 2:12–17; 2 Chronicles 7:13–18.

[65] Matthew 9:15.

[66] Acts 13:1–3.

guidance.[67] Fasting reminds us that the Kingdom of God is real, but the pressures of this world are fleeting. Through fasting we draw near to God to humbly state our case and to learn from him.

Wesley warned of a risk of self-righteousness in fasting:

> Let us beware of fancying we *merit* anything of God by our fasting... Fasting is only a way which God hath ordained, wherein we wait for his unmerited mercy; and wherein, without any desert of ours, he has promised freely to give us his blessing.[68]

Wesley had his Methodists fast each week, from Thursday evening until 3pm on Friday, in keeping with the practice of the Early Church. He recognized that the failure to fast regularly was closely associated with powerlessness in the church. He wrote of the great difficulty of "Christian self-denial." "I fear there are now thousands of Methodists who] have entirely left off fasting."[69]

> Do you know the obligation and benefit of fasting? How often do you practice it? The neglect of this alone is sufficient to account for our feebleness and faintness of spirit. We are continually grieving the Holy Spirit of God by the habitual neglect of plain duty! Let us amend from this hour.[70]

Confession

Protestants do not practice confession to a priest, but that should not exclude confession to each other. James instructed, "Therefore, confess your sins to one another, and pray for one another so that you may be healed."[71] The absence of any system for confession in evangelical churches today is a substantial deviation from biblical teaching and one cause for ineffectiveness. The early Methodists were strongly committed to mutual confession within the weekly class meetings. The conduct of classes was summarized by John Wesley:

> Each society is divided into smaller companies, called *classes*, according to their respective places of abode. There are about twelve persons in every class; one of whom is styled *the leader*...

[67] Daniel 9:3.
[68] Wesley, "Sermon 27, Sermon on the Mount 7 , in *Works*, vol. 5: 358.
[69] Wesley, "Sermon 116, Causes of the Inefficacy of Christianity , in *Works*, vol. 7: 288.
[70] Wesley, "Minutes of Several Conversations , in *Works*, vol. 8: 316.
[71] James 5:16.

There is only one condition previously required in those who desire admission into these societies, —a desire "to flee from the wrath to come, to be saved from their sins:" But, wherever this is really fixed in the soul, it will be shown by its fruit...[72]

The design of our meeting is, to obey that command of God, "Confess your faults to one another..." To this end, we intend, —1. To meet once a week, at the least... 4. To speak each of us in order, freely and plainly, the true state of our souls, with the faults we have committed in thought, word, or deed, and the temptations we have felt, since our last meeting. 5. To end every meeting with prayer, suited to the state of each person present...[73]

The results of the Methodist class meetings were immediately seen, so that "It can scarce be conceived what advantages have been reaped from this little prudential regulation."[74] Members held each other accountable, supported each other in prayer, experienced a deeper walk with Christ, "and 'speaking the truth in love, they grew up into Him in all things, who is the Head, even Christ.'"

In the second half of the nineteenth century, Methodist conferences around the globe voted to discontinue the previous membership requirement of class attendance, and from the early twentieth century many saw the rapid decline of Methodism and the loss of holiness revivals. Wesley's words of praise for class meetings and the result that followed when class meetings were dismantled, both point to the conclusion that intimate sharing in a small group on a weekly basis is one of the most effective means of grace available to sincere believers.

For those who shy from the terminology used by Wesley, modern variations might be tried. However, the essence of confession of sins to one another and prayerful support must be central to whatever format is adopted. Jon Weist's publication, *Banding Together: A Practical Guide for Disciple Makers* (2018), is recommended as a suitable modern application of these timeless biblical principles.

---

[72] Wesley, "General Rules of the United Societies", in *Works*, vol. 8: 269–70.

[73] Wesley, "Rules of the Band Societies", in *Works*, vol. 8: 272.

[74] Wesley, "A Plain Account of the People Called Methodists", in *Works*, vol. 8: 254.

Giving

Opportunities to give out of our own resources are a means of grace to us, although because of greed, we often view requests for money to be an ugly imposition upon our faith. The threat that wealth and greed pose for the believer is hard to overstate, and those who cannot disengage from the pursuit of financial security *will* have their faith damaged. Jesus solemnly warned that if we love money, we will hate God, for "You cannot serve God and wealth."[75] Again, he said, "Beware, and be on your guard against every form of greed; for not even when one has an abundance does his life consist of his possessions."[76] Paul warned us that, "the love of money is a root of all sorts of evil, and some by longing for it have wandered away from the faith and pierced themselves with many griefs."[77] In another place he described greed as a form of idolatry[78] and in numerous places greed is named as a sin that would keep us out of heaven.[79] The warnings of James are especially relevant to us today:

> Come now, you rich, weep and howl for your miseries which are coming upon you. Your riches have rotted and your garments have become moth-eaten. Your gold and your silver have rusted; and their rust will be a witness against you and will consume your flesh like fire. It is in the last days that you have stored up your treasure! Behold, the pay of the laborers who mowed your fields, and which has been withheld by you, cries out against you; and the outcry of those who did the harvesting has reached the ears of the Lord of Sabaoth. You have lived luxuriously on the earth and led a life of wanton pleasure; you have fattened your hearts in a day of slaughter.[80]

John Wesley named the accumulation of wealth as one of the greatest threats to true religion, stating, "I fear, wherever riches have increased, (exceeding few are the exceptions,) the essence of religion, the mind that was in Christ, has decreased in the same proportion."[81]

> Those who calmly desire and deliberately seek to attain riches], whether they do, in fact, gain the world or no, do infallibly lose

---

[73] Matthew 6:24.
[76] Luke 12:15.
[77] 1 Timothy 6:10.
[78] Colossians 3:5.
[79] See Chapter 8.
[80] James 5:1–5.
[81] Wesley, "Thoughts Upon Methodism", in *Works*, vol. 13: 260.

their souls. These are they that sell Him who bought them with his blood, for a few pieces of gold or silver... How then is it possible for a rich man to grow richer, without denying the Lord that bought him?[82]

Wesley's solution to the increase of wealth was to "gain all you can", "save all you can", and "give all you can". He instructed his followers to live plainly, "Despise delicacy and variety, and be content with what plain nature requires."[83] Wesley's teaching on riches is not easily passed over. He maintained that "rich people" are not only people of immense wealth, but:

One that has food and raiment sufficient for himself and his family, and something over, is rich... and] It is absolutely impossible, except by the power of God], that a rich man should be a Christian; to have the mind that was in Christ, and to walk as Christ walked: Such are the hindrances to holiness, as well as the temptations to sin, which surround him on every side.[84]

With this in mind, we can begin to comprehend how necessary is the grace of God in our efforts to stay free from bondage to greed. Three types of giving from the Bible—tithing, offerings and faith promises— illustrate how giving is a means of grace and serves to strengthen our knowledge of, and commitment to, Christ.

Tithing is a concept that first appeared in the Bible when Abraham acknowledged God's protection by giving one tenth of the spoils of war to the priest, Melchizedek.[85] This principle of giving the first tenth of crops, income or spoils was re-applied centuries later in the Israelite duties to the Levitical priesthood.[86] The practice of tithing was continued throughout the Old Testament, with stern warnings about the failure to honor God through tithes.[87] In the New Testament era, under the New Covenant, believers who are led by the Spirit are no longer subject to Old Testament laws, but the principles of the Law are carried through in the twin commandments to love God and your neighbor.

---

[82] Wesley, "Sermon 28, Sermon on the Mount 7 , in *Works*, vol. 5: 369, 373.
[83] Wesley, "Sermon 50, The Use of Money , in *Works*, vol. 6: 124–36, in particular: 131, 133.
[84] Wesley, "Sermon 108, On Riches , in *Works*, vol. 7: 215.
[85] Genesis 14:20.
[86] Leviticus 27:30 and Numbers 18:21–26.
[87] Malachi 3:8.

Jesus told the Pharisees that, in as much as they were following the Mosaic Law, they should be diligent to pay their tithes.[88] Some have used this to argue that, since Christians are no longer under the Law, they are no longer required to tithe. There are two reasons why this argument fails. The first is that God's eternal principles are still required, and one of those principles is gratefulness to God for his saving grace. The second reason is that tithing predates the Mosaic Law, initially appearing in Abram's relating to Melchizedek. Moses' Law then re-applied that Melchizedekian principle of gratefulness to the Israelites who had recently been rescued from Egypt, showing that tithing is worthy of consideration as an abiding principle of gratefulness.

It is impossible to love God or to show proper concern for our neighbors if we are slaves to greed. The purpose of tithing was to acknowledge God's care and provision. Without God, Abraham would not have survived the war in Canaan and the Israelites would have been destroyed many times over. Tithing was an expression of thanksgiving for salvation and a way of acknowledging dependence upon God. These same purposes are still relevant today; tithing helps the believer to repent of their own self-sufficiency and it acknowledges that our own works will only lead to death. Tithing is a practical action, a means of grace, that expresses our total dependence upon God. It is a joyful celebration and an act of worship. It is given freely to the local church and is accompanied by God's promise that he will provide for the giver in ways beyond the believer's own capacity.[89]

Tithing is an expression of thanks for personal salvation and it is given to the local ministry, but free-will offerings[90] are given in a variety of ways and situations. They are not prescribed, but instead are voluntary acts of the believer who desires to participate in God's work in addition to their tithe. They can be for building programs, outreach, or for ministries beyond the local church and around the globe. Free-will offerings support missionary activity, community development and relief for the poor and oppressed. Free-will offerings are sacrificial and unheralded. They originate in love for God and find fulfillment in love for humanity. Free-will offerings are a means of grace for believers to demonstrate love and to send their treasures ahead to heaven.

---

[88] Matthew 23:23
[89] Malachi 3:10–11.
[90] Exodus 36:3; Numbers 29:39; Psalm 119:108.

In the second letter to the Corinthian Church, Paul hints at a third type of giving that has commonly become known as faith promise giving. Paul encouraged the Corinthians to emulate the "abundance of joy" of the members of the Macedonian Church, who had given "according to their ability, and beyond their ability" to the need of the mother-church in Jerusalem.[91] Giving according to one's abilities is free-will giving but giving beyond one's abilities must be miraculous. It is based on the discovery that God cares about human suffering and church expansion more than we do. Free-will giving is developing one's own love for the world, but faith-promise giving is connecting with God's concern for the world, with the promise of providing more than believers could realistically do themselves. It requires prayer, perseverance and faith. It is asking God to send unexpected resources, above and beyond current possibilities, and then, as God sends unexpected resource, forwarding the entire amount to the ministry of focus. Faith promise giving taps into the heart of God and enables us to enter into a miraculous dimension of faith.

Good works

Previously we have discussed good works as evidence of our faith, but good works can also be a means of strengthening our faith. Wesley had much to say about the essential discipline of good works. For Wesley, good works are part of repentance and "necessary for complete sanctification."[92] Good works include feeding the hungry, clothing the naked, caring for the stranger, visiting those in prison, sick, or otherwise afflicted, and instructing or encouraging people in their Christian faith. As a means of grace, good works are of great benefit to the practitioner. For example:

> If you do not visit the sick], you lose a means of grace; you lose an excellent means of increasing your thankfulness to God, who saves you from pain and sickness, and continues your health and strength; as well as of increasing your sympathy with the afflicted, your benevolence, and all social affections. One great reason why the rich, in general, have so little sympathy for the poor, is, because they so seldom visit them...[93]

In the last decades of the nineteenth century, the rise of liberal theology ushered in a teaching that came to be known as "social

---

[91] 2 Corinthians 8:1–4.

[92] Wesley, "Sermon 43, The Scripture Way of Salvation , in *Works*, vol. 6: 51.

[93] Wesley, "Sermon 98, On Visiting the Sick , in *Works*, vol. 8: 119.

gospel". In its extremes, social gospel taught that the personal born-again conversion is replaced by a humanistic concept of converting communities and influencing people toward God. It isolated the supernatural intervention of God from the Christian faith, in keeping with the foundations of liberal theology, and it promoted good works as a form of social renewal. This teaching reversed Evangelicalism by claiming that Christian faith results out of civilized societies, rather than renewed societies being the consequence of individual believers being regenerated by the indwelling Spirit of God. This false gospel so distorted the purpose of good works and community action, that Evangelicals began to distance themselves from any activity that might be mistaken for social gospel.[94] The evangelical body's withdrawal from good works damaged generations of believers and disempowered the gospel.

Let us allow Christ to guide us in the matter of good works: "Let your light shine before men in such a way that they may see your good works, and glorify your Father who is in heaven."[95] Again, Jesus taught:

> Then He the Son of God, the King] will also say to those on His left, "Depart from Me, accursed ones, into the eternal fire which has been prepared for the devil and his angels; for I was hungry, and you gave Me nothing to eat; I was thirsty, and you gave Me nothing to drink; I was a stranger, and you did not invite Me in; naked, and you did not clothe Me; sick, and in prison, and you did not visit Me."[96]

As a means of grace, good works are particularly effective. It is through works that faith is enriched, for "faith was working with his works, and as a result of the works, faith was perfected."[97] Indeed, there is greater blessing for those who give than those who receive.[98]

Church attendance

Faithful attendance in a local congregation is one of the most obvious and beneficial means of developing Christian character. The Bible

[94] For more on this discussion, see Cameron, *Methodism Reborn*, 85–106; Piggin, *Spirit, Word and World*, chapt. 4, loc. 1996; and Rauschenbusch, *A Theology for the Social Gospel*.
[95] Matthew 5:16.
[96] Matthew 25:41–43.
[97] James 2:22.
[98] Acts 20:35.

instructs us, "Let us consider how to stimulate one another to love and good deeds, not forsaking our own assembling together, as is the habit of some, but encouraging one another; and all the more as you see the day drawing near."[99] A local congregation provides opportunities to engage in the other means of grace and it teaches consistency and perseverance. Participation will help you to grow in your faith, and you will help others to grow in their faith.

The Church of course, is the gathering of believers; it is not a building. Some believers do not have a building, and some live in a situation where public worship would draw violent persecution. Neither the venue nor the timing of the gathering is prescribed but gathering with other believers where you are known and can serve is important for spiritual growth.

Not another law

Means of grace are not simply more rules by which believers must abide. As Paul explained to the Galatians, faith is not controlled by religious regulations. We must be careful not to allow these good activities to become law-by-stealth. Means of grace are a source of support for believers, not a burden. They might be compared to the Sabbath, which was provided for humanity, not humanity for the Sabbath. The Sabbath is important, and a believer should give due consideration to the principles of rest and worship enthroned in one day off in seven, but the Sabbath is not a requirement for salvation. Neither are means of grace required for salvation. However, living above habitual willful sin is required for salvation, and means of grace provide a proven mechanism for appropriating God's grace.

---

[99] Hebrews 10:24–25.

QUESTIONS FOR REFLECTION AND DISCUSSION

1. List the means of grace named in this chapter. Have you been baptized? Which of the other means of grace do you regularly participate in? Which ones have you never participated in? Do you feel that the means of grace assist you in your faith?

2. Are there other means of grace? For example, how could ministry involvement impact your faith? Would teaching a Sunday School class or preparing a bible study lesson strengthen your faith? Have you been part of a ministry team to another country? What activities make your faith feel more alive to God? Ministries of service benefit us as much as they help others. As a result of this chapter, what might you do differently this next week? Read Acts 20:35. In light of our discussion, what did Paul and Jesus mean?

3. Read Matthew 12:43–45. We touched upon this passage in a previous chapter. What is the danger of leaving your life "empty"? This parable is not limited to the return of demons. It might refer to the return of sinful behavior, destructive thoughts or bad company. Read 2 Thessalonians 3:11–13. Rephrase this in your own words. Read Proverbs 18:9. Explain this proverb. Can you find other bible passages that reference the dangers of idleness, laziness or slackness?

4. John Fletcher is quoted as saying, "Now, if your Master Jesus] was tempted and assaulted to the last; if to the last He watched and prayed, using all means of grace Himself... think not yourselves above Him, but go and do likewise." Had you ever thought of Jesus being "tempted and assaulted to the last" and "using all means of grace Himself"? Read about Christ's own baptism. Explain how these thoughts impact your faith and practice.

5. Read 1 Corinthians 11:17–34. What self-examination does Paul require before participation in the Lord's Supper? What has been your experience and understanding of the Lord's Supper?

6. Read Matthew 14: 23; 26:36–42; Mark 1:35; Luke 5:16; 6:12–16; 9:18, 28 and John 17:1–21. How important is prayer for believers? Do our prayers inform God? Do our prayers change God's mind? How do our prayers affect us?

7. Read Ephesians 6:17 and 2 Timothy 3:16. How does denial of the inerrancy of the Bible render the Sword of the Spirit "blunted"? Discuss this and explain your own understanding of the accuracy

of the Bible. Is it accurate in matters of faith? Is it accurate in matters of science and history?

8. Fasting most often is abstaining from food for a predetermined period and praying in place of meals. Have you been encouraged to fast in your Christian experience? Could you commit yourself to the Methodist weekly fast? If you were fasting, what would you be appealing to God for? Discuss how it would impact your faith if something seemingly impossible happened after fasting.

9. How do you feel about the concept of confessing your sins and needs to each other? What conditions would you require from your Christian friend or your small group before you would do that?

10. Discuss your experiences of blessing when you have given unexpectedly to someone in need? How is that a means of grace? Have you been taught the difference between "tithes" and "free-will offerings" before? If you agreed to sponsor a child through a charitable agency, which type of giving would that be? Have you engaged in faith-promise giving before? If yes, describe your experiences.

11. How are people hurting or needy in your community? What community good works could you or your group undertake to address these needs? Is loneliness a need in your community? Is poverty a need? Is isolation a need? What else can you name?

12. Explain at least three ways that means of grace are different to religious laws?

Chapter 11: **GOD'S TESTING**

My son, do not regard lightly the discipline of the Lord, nor faint
when you are reproved by Him; for those whom the Lord loves He
disciplines, and He scourges every son whom He receives.
Hebrews 12:5–6; see Proverbs 3:11–12

There is a vast difference between being tempted and being tested. Testing is designed to strengthen; tempting is designed to weaken. God does not tempt anyone, not the godly nor the ungodly.[1] We invite sinful temptation into our own hearts when we entertain thoughts of self-gratification that are not consistent with our Christian faith, whether pursuits of bitterness, revenge, lust, wealth, laziness, or other worldly desires.[2] The Christian's responsibility is to discipline themselves and follow Christ's example, to take "every thought captive to the obedience of Christ."[3] This is one of the reasons why an undivided heart is so important: it requires vigilance to maintain Christian integrity, and it is doubly hard if we are battling against our own selfish desires as well as against the uninvited temptations. Temptation may be sent by evil forces, but it may also be manufactured out of our own hearts, so that we are often our own tempter.

Testing is different. It is often associated with trials, but testing can also come through good times or in the form of a difficult decision. Testing may be sent from God or it may be sent by other forces and permitted by God. It reveals what lies in the heart, for the purpose of character growth. Therefore, testing is for our benefit, so that we might develop some previously untapped strength or correct some abiding weakness. It is for our good, and God does not allow temptation in our lives beyond what we are able to bear.[4]

---

[1] James 1:13.
[2] James 1:14–15.
[3] 2 Corinthians 10:5.
[4] 1 Corinthians 10:13.

When the Israelites came out of the desert after forty years of testing, Moses revealed to them God's purposes:

> You shall remember all the way which the LORD your God has led you in the wilderness these forty years, that He might humble you, **testing you, to know what was in your heart**, whether you would keep His commandments or not. He humbled you and let you be hungry, and fed you with manna which you did not know, nor did your fathers know, that He might make you understand that man does not live by bread alone, but man lives by everything that proceeds out of the mouth of the LORD. Your clothing did not wear out on you, nor did your foot swell these forty years. Thus you are to know in your heart that **the LORD your God was disciplining you just as a man disciplines his son**. emphasis mine][5]

We can hear how similar these words are to the New Testament teaching:

> You have forgotten the exhortation which is addressed to you as sons, "My son, do not regard lightly the discipline of the LORD, nor faint when you are reproved by Him; for those whom the LORD loves He disciplines, and He scourges every son whom He receives."[6]

How easily this sits within the holiness emphasis. God looks upon the heart and he tests and trains us as beloved children. These emphases continue throughout the book of Deuteronomy.

Testing in hard times

Forty years in the wilderness was a difficult test. For the adults who came out of Egypt, the remainder of their lives were spent in desolation and frugality, in apparent aimless wandering. Their trial was the consequence of their own unfaithfulness, of course, and for almost all the adults it was a life sentence. In some ways, the wandering Israelites might be compared to refugees and immigrants today, who settle in foreign countries, living in self-imposed deprivation so that their children have an education and new opportunity. However, for the wilderness adults, their deprivation was the consequence of their distrust of God. They were being

---

[5] Deuteronomy 8:2–5.
[6] Hebrews 12:5–6.

disciplined, for the salvation of their souls and the souls of the next generation.

As believers today, we are tested through sickness and injury, financial troubles, relationship problems, concerns for our children, workplace disputes, local church upsets, persecutions, and numerous other struggles. Our faith is tested and the weakness in our hearts is exposed in the process. God wants us to know ourselves better, to learn to draw upon his strength, and to cultivate habits of self-discipline. God's purpose is to train us for our royal duties in eternity, and it is God himself who allows the testing. He wants us to learn integrity, consistency, perseverance, patience, kindness and love. Of course, God is all-powerful and all-loving; he could intervene and change our situation at any time. He could have changed Jesus' situation in the Garden of Gethsemane too, but he had a higher purpose. To curtail the test midway would be to defeat his own higher priorities of character development and vibrant testimony in a hurting world. *Salvation* comes through faith in God but, *walking with God* also requires faith. When we have walked through impossible situations under the care of God, we become different people. The young Jewish exiles in Babylon had learned these lessons. When confronted with a brutal death, Shadrach, Meshach and Abednego boldly responded to Nebuchadnezzar:

> Our God whom we serve is able to deliver us from the furnace of blazing fire; and He will deliver us out of your hand, O king. But even if He does not, let it be known to you, O king, that we are not going to serve your gods or worship the golden image that you have set up.[7]

Perhaps more confronting is the biblical teaching that Jesus himself was perfected through suffering. The Bible tells us that, "although Jesus] was a Son, He learned obedience from the things which He suffered. And having been made perfect, He became to all those who obey Him the source of eternal salvation."[8] God made Jesus, "perfect through suffering."[9] Jesus' "perfection" was through practiced obedience, and this perfection occurred before his death. Even the sinless Son of God was enriched when he persevered through suffering. Being perfected is not only a matter of overcoming sin, it is the development of character. It is not a sin to lack courage or conviction, but both of these are strengthened through testing.

---

[7] Daniel 3:17–18.
[8] Hebrews 5:8–9.
[9] Hebrews 2:10.

One way to understand this teaching is to compare Christ to the Apostle Peter. Both Jesus and Peter had the intention of remaining faithful through the looming trial of the crucifixion. Christ prayed in the Garden for deliverance, if it was possible, while Peter boldly proclaimed, "Even though all may fall away because of You, I will never fall away."[10] Peter started out well, attempting to defend Jesus with the sword in Gethsemane, but he failed badly when the challenge was made during the Sanhedrin trial. Jesus, however, faced cruel beatings and death by crucifixion with unwavering grace and determination. Peter was subsequently restored by Jesus, and tradition informs us that he freely gave his life for Christ in Rome decades later. Peter was tested and initially failed, but through further testing and perseverance he learned to remain faithful. Jesus Christ was also tested, and he was found faithful throughout his earthly life. Christ's internal resolve to remain faithful enabled him to endure the cross and remain merciful to the end.

It is often unjust accusations and personal attacks that hurt us most. However, it is in these times of persecution that we have the clearest opportunity to respond as Jesus responded. We can be like Jesus, showing grace and kindness. With this understanding, we can grasp the truth of James:

> Consider it all joy, my brethren, when you encounter various trials, knowing that the testing of your faith produces endurance. And let endurance have its perfect result, so that you may be perfect and complete, lacking in nothing.[11]

Once tested and trained by difficulties, we may be again sent into difficult situations or to stand alongside others who are going through hardship. At that point it ceases to be testing, but rather it is an assignment from God precisely because you have proved yourself true. God desires his representatives to stand for him in the deepest valleys of this world. Christ comforts us through suffering and then sends us to comfort others who are undergoing their own time of difficulty:

> Blessed be the God and Father of our Lord Jesus Christ, the Father of mercies and God of all comfort, who comforts us in all our affliction so that we will be able to comfort those who are in any affliction with the comfort with which we ourselves are comforted by God. For just as the sufferings of Christ are ours in

---

[10] Matthew 26:33–35.
[11] James 1:2–4.

abundance, so also our comfort is abundant through Christ. But if we are afflicted, it is for your comfort and salvation; or if we are comforted, it is for your comfort, which is effective in the patient enduring of the same sufferings which we also suffer; and our hope for you is firmly grounded, knowing that as you are sharers of our sufferings, so also you are sharers of our comfort.[12]

Testing in good times

In the parable of the sower, Jesus described four responses to the gospel: rejecting the message, accepting but withering because of hardship, accepting but dying because of wealth, and accepting and flourishing.[13] As difficult as persecution and sufferings are, this parable of the sower illustrates the truth that there is a second form of testing under which Christians seem even more vulnerable to failure. The person who suffered hardship withered, but the person deceived by wealth died altogether. This should be most alarming to those who live in relative affluence. The test of prosperity is highlighted in Deuteronomy:

> When you have eaten and are satisfied, and have built good houses and lived in them, and when your herds and your flocks multiply, and your silver and gold multiply, and all that you have multiplies, then your heart will become proud and you will forget the LORD your God who brought you out from the land of Egypt, out of the house of slavery... Otherwise, you may say in your heart, "My power and the strength of my hand made me this wealth."[14]

Logic would suggest that when believers are abundantly blessed by God, they should be most grateful and gladly faithful. But this is often not so. When we are not driven to God by difficult circumstances, when we are not humbled by impossibilities, when we are not confronted by our own weakness, we quickly forget our first love. Where there is greater wealth and opportunity there is greater temptation and our eyes wander. Throughout the books of Judges, Kings and Chronicles, the nation of Israel exemplified this cycle of suffering, repentance, rising prosperity, wandering from God, oppression, and a return to suffering. The nations of the West are

---

[12] 2 Corinthians 1:3–7.
[13] Matthew 13:18–23.
[14] Deuteronomy 8:11–14, 17.

largely following that same process of godliness-rise-ungodliness-decline today. Nations which were formerly leaders in Christendom are now leaders in immorality, while other more-recently evangelized nations are known for their flourishing Christianity and rising prosperity.

This critical danger of affluence is not new. Jesus taught that pursuing wealth, or even worrying about the future, undermines the believer's faith in God:

> No one can serve two masters; for either he will hate the one and love the other, or he will be devoted to one and despise the other. You cannot serve God and wealth... Do not worry then, saying, "What will we eat?" or "What will we drink?" or "What will we wear for clothing?" For the Gentiles eagerly seek all these things; for your heavenly Father knows that you need all these things. But seek first His kingdom and His righteousness, and all these things will be added to you.[15]

For most people, wealth ties us to this world. It is possible to have wealth and not be devoted to it, but it is very difficult. "It is hard for a rich man to enter the kingdom of heaven... it is easier for a camel to go through the eye of a needle, than for a rich man to enter the kingdom of God."[16] It is not impossible, but it certainly requires surrendering everything to the work of God.[17]

The deceitfulness of wealth and its corrosive effect upon living faith were of great concern to John Wesley. In his "Thoughts Upon Methodism", Wesley wrote:

> I fear, wherever riches have increased, (exceeding few are the exceptions,) the essence of religion, the mind that was in Christ, has decreased in the same proportion. Therefore, I do not see how it is possible, in the nature of things, for any revival of true religion to continue long. For religion must necessarily produce both industry and frugality; and these cannot but produce riches. But as riches increase, so will pride, anger, and love of the world in all its branches... So, although the form of religion remains, the spirit is swiftly vanishing away.[18]

---

[15] Matthew 6:24, 31–33.
[16] Matthew 19:23–24.
[17] Matthew 19:21.
[18] Wesley, "Thoughts Upon Methodism , in *Works*, vol. 13: 260.

Francis Asbury, the first Methodist bishop in America, identified the same dynamic draining the life out of the American Church in the late eighteenth century, "We are losing the spirit of missionaries and martyrs, we are slothful... Our *ease in Zion* makes me feel awful... Ah, poor dead Methodists!... How shall preachers who are well provided for maintain the spirit of religion!" italics Asbury's][19]

The Bible teaches that the pursuit of wealth will increase in the End Times, to the destruction of many.[20] If wealth was a problem in Palestine during Christ's time on earth and in Britain during Wesley's time, how much more will it become a preoccupation in the End. Christians who seek a deeper walk with Christ should be very cautious of any teaching that promotes prosperity, who confuse "godliness" with "financial gain":

> Those] who suppose that godliness is a means of gain... But those who want to get rich fall into temptation and a snare and many foolish and harmful desires which plunge men into ruin and destruction. For the love of money is a root of all sorts of evil, and some by longing for it have wandered away from the faith and pierced themselves with many griefs. But flee from these things, you man of God, and pursue righteousness, godliness, faith, love, perseverance and gentleness.[21]

Faithful, generous, regular giving is one protection against the sins of greed and worldliness, provided the giver is not motivated by greed for greater financial return from God. Give generously, expecting nothing in return.[22] When a believer, who has known the kindness and mercy of God, is blessed with wealth and does not share their wealth generously and selflessly, their sin is worse than unbelief.[23]

Testing in confusing times

Moses referenced a third type of testing in the book of Deuteronomy, one which may be even more difficult than suffering or prosperity. Sometimes God will ask us to do something that seems unnecessary or confusing and we treat his command as trivial. He says to speak to a

---

[19] Asbury as quoted in Wigger, *American Saint*, 367.
[20] 2 Timothy 3:1–5.
[21] 1 Timothy 6:5, 9–11.
[22] Luke 6:35.
[23] 1 Timothy 5:8; Philippians 2:4; Galatians 6:10.

rock,[24] or to strike a handful of arrows on the ground,[25] or to go home a different way than you came and not to eat anything along the way.[26] Often God tests us this way, and the purpose is more to do with our obedience than any other outcome, although, time will show that there was a reason for his strange instruction. Imagine the arrogance of the creature questioning the Creator.

Moses described a very confusing situation in Deuteronomy:

> If a prophet or a dreamer of dreams arises among you and gives you a sign or a wonder, and the sign or the wonder comes true, concerning which he spoke to you, saying, "Let us go after other gods (whom you have not known) and let us serve them," you shall not listen to the words of that prophet or that dreamer of dreams; for the LORD your God is testing you to find out if you love the LORD your God with all your heart and with all your soul. You shall follow the LORD your God and fear Him; and you shall keep His commandments, listen to His voice, serve Him, and cling to Him.[27]

One immediate question prompted by this passage is, "How do we know if a prophet is truly from God?" The answer most commonly provided is that, if their prophecy comes true, they are from God, since Moses had instructed the Israelites that if the prophecy does not come true, then they have "spoken presumptuously."[28] The Old Testament regulation is that such a false prophet should be stoned to death. However, what if they prophesied a miracle and it did occur, as in the Deuteronomy 13 hypothetical? That would be confusing! They seem to have an anointing from God, but what they are teaching becomes increasingly heretical. This is not merely an ancient problem—this could very easily happen to us in the Church today. So, how would a person with an undivided heart discern what is right in this test of confusion?

The first thing to be sure of is that there is only one Lord of the Church and he alone—Jesus Christ—is infallible and without shadow. No human being is to be followed without reservation. When conflicting messages are heard, turn to prayer and to the Bible. The same Spirit of God who whispers assurance of salvation and peace that passes

---

[24] Numbers 20:8.
[25] 2 Kings 13:18.
[26] 1 Kings 13:17.
[27] Deuteronomy 13:1–4.
[28] Deuteronomy 18:22.

understanding, can also speak caution to your soul. Ask God for wisdom, "But if any of you lacks wisdom, let him ask of God, who gives to all generously and without reproach, and it will be given to him."[29] Check everything against your Bible. The Bible is the infallible Word of God, without error, delivered to us from God.[30] "Do not quench the Spirit; do not despise prophetic utterances. But examine everything carefully; hold fast to that which is good; abstain from every form of evil."[31]

In the Deuteronomy case, the passage that tells us how to test the prophets should be studied more closely. Deuteronomy 18 does not say that the prophet can be trusted emphatically if their prophecy does come true. It simply provides one preliminary test—if the prophecy does *not* come true, they were *not* speaking on behalf of God. However, since the devil can also perform miracles,[32] then some other tests are required when dealing with a positive outcome.

The performance of miracles sometimes generates self-centeredness rather than a deeper hunger for Christ. At least twice Jesus refused to perform miracles for the Pharisees because to do so merely encouraged their "evil and adulterous" ways.[33] If our relationship with God is likewise a means of receiving assistance for our own self-centered plans, then there is a serious problem. Our Christian priority is to seek God's ways and to be pleasing to him. Our priority is not to have him please us. The irony is that signs and wonders can encourage a selfish faith, which is the very opposite of an undivided heart. Do we pray to worship God, do we pray to discover God's purpose and his wisdom, or do we pray primarily to seek God's blessing upon our own world of cares? When John advised us to test the spirits, saying "every spirit that confesses that Jesus Christ has come in the flesh is from God,"[34] he was not merely saying that using the name of Jesus is proof. Test whether the prophet is teaching the message of Christ, and in particular his command, "If anyone wishes to come after Me, he must deny himself, and take up his cross and follow Me. For whoever wishes to save his life will lose it; but whoever loses his life for My sake will find it."[35]

---

[29] James 1:5.
[30] 2 Peter 1:20; 2 Timothy 3:16.
[31] 1 Thessalonians 5:19–22.
[32] 2 Thessalonians 2:9; Matthew 24:24.
[33] Matthew 12:38–39; 16:1–4.
[34] 1 John 4:1–3.
[35] Matthew 16:24–25.

Every believer has periods of confusion, when God does not answer prayers as expected, when evil seems to prosper, when previously-godly leaders bring disgrace upon the name of Christ, when disturbed about a teaching but unable to identify the error, and so on. Sometimes we take advantage of the confusion to act out our secret desires, by abusing someone, following another into sin, or giving up on the truth. God is testing you, "to find out if you love the LORD your God with all your heart and with all your soul... Listen to His voice, serve Him, and cling to Him."[36]

Testing the heart

There is a deeper discussion to be had in this matter of testing, and the Deuteronomy 13 confusion points us toward the source of many of our spiritual struggles. Suppose a miracle-worker visited our community—would we not be inclined to see it as an opportunity to have our personal needs met? Any time our faith is focused on what we can get out of our relationship with God, we are moving toward idolatry. If faith in God is reduced to merely a source of protection, wealth, healing or relief, then God ceases to be the Living God whose wisdom and plans infinitely exceed our own small minds. Our goal is to seek his purposes rather than to draw him into our purposes. Our focus is to share the heart of God through the blood of Jesus and the indwelling Spirit. While it is good to present our needs to God, and we are urged to do so, it is a danger if our needs and plans become the focus of our worship or prayers. Letting our "requests be made known to God,"[37] is to release our concerns into the loving care of the Father, not to become consumed by them.

In the Old Testament period, adherence to a god was a means of survival in a dangerous earthly existence. Warfare and sickness killed whole populations in brutal, unpoliced, societies with primitive medical care. Little was known about life after death, so the focus of worship was on protection and provision in this world. This reality can be seen in Abraham's blessing, "I will make you a great nation, and I will bless you, and make your name great; and so you shall be a blessing."[38] Jacob, likewise, was promised temporal blessings:

> The land on which you lie, I will give it to you and to your descendants. Your descendants will also be like the dust of the

---

[36] Deuteronomy 13:1–4.
[37] Philippians 4:6.
[38] Genesis 12:2.

earth, and you will spread out to the west and to the east and to the north and to the south; and in you and in your descendants shall all the families of the earth be blessed. Behold, I am with you and will keep you wherever you go, and will bring you back to this land; for I will not leave you until I have done what I have promised you.[39]

The concept of an after-life was present, but it was not clearly understood. Believers placed their hope in the love of God, although they showed no understanding of what God might do:

For we will surely die and are like water spilled on the ground which cannot be gathered up again. Yet God does not take away life, but plans ways so that the banished one will not be cast out from him.[40]

Job similarly provided a glimpse of a rudimentary faith in life after death, since he was a man who knew temporal blessings but put greater store in, someday, rising from the grave: "You will call, and I will answer You from Sheol]; You will long for the work of Your hands."[41] However, even the book of Daniel, which is so essential to New Testament eschatology, is focused almost entirely upon God's dealing with earthly nations. By the time of the Roman Empire, the Jewish religious leaders were still divided over the very possibility of life after death,[42] so that Christ's teachings about the Kingdom of God were consistently misinterpreted as a worldly kingdom.[43]

In contrast, however, Christ's teaching was focused on the spiritual kingdom of heaven (now and future) and the reality of eternal suffering (including teachings on hell, the Judgment, weeping and gnashing of teeth, fire, and being shut out of heaven).[44] Whole chapters of the Bible are given to Christ's teaching on the Second Coming and the eternal separation that is to follow.[45] Christ, the One who came from heaven, had authority to speak of heavenly things, although many of his hearers were slow to learn.[46] The apostles added

[39] Genesis 28:13–15.
[40] 2 Samuel 14:14.
[41] Job 14:13–15; also 1:21.
[42] Acts 23:5–8; Matthew 22:23–33.
[43] John 6:14–15; 18:36–37.
[44] In the book of Matthew alone, see 5:21–22; 5:27–30; 7:21–23; 8:10–13; 10:11–15; 10:26–28; 11:22–24; 12:36; 12:39–42; 13:40–43; 13:47–50; 18:7–9; 22:1–14; 23:33; 24:36–51; 25:1–13; 25:14–30; 25:31–46.
[45] Matthew chapts. 24–25.
[46] John 3:12–13.

more to our understanding of the end of this world and the separation in the next world, especially through the revelations of Paul and John. With this shift in theological priority, Paul was able to write that our faith and godliness are specifically related to "the hope of eternal life."[47] This was not nearly as clear in the Old Testament.

Therefore, today, when the gospel is presented, the major focus is generally upon eternal salvation rather than temporal needs, although the balance varies from group to group. Christ's teaching changed the way that faith in God was viewed, and with Christ's emphasis on eternal rewards and punishments, came the outpouring of the Holy Spirit. It is not a surprise then, that holiness teaching has most often been associated with an emphasis on the Second Coming, judgment and eternal life. From the early origins of Methodism, John Wesley's followers gathered together to "flee the wrath to come."[48] He preached:

> O who shall warn this generation of vipers to flee from the wrath to come!... But if there be a Christian upon the earth, if there be a man who hath overcome the world, who desires nothing but God, and fears none but Him that is able to destroy both body and soul in hell; thou, O man of God, speak, and spare not; lift up thy voice like a trumpet![49]

Judgment and eternal destiny were strong themes for John Fletcher, who warned would-be Christians of the danger of arriving at the Judgment to hear Christ say:

> Depart from me, ye that work iniquity! ... Depart, ye that made the doctrine of my atonement a cloak for your sins, or sewed it as a "pillow under the arms of my people," to make them sleep in carnal security, when they should have "worked out their salvation with fear and trembling."[50]

In the latter parts of the nineteenth century, in the wake of the American Civil War, camp meetings and holiness revivals caused a resurgence of the holiness message across the United States and Canada, which then flowed back to Britain. This was accompanied by the widespread shift from postmillennialism to premillennialism, as American fundamentalists lost confidence in the future of their

[47] Titus 1:2.
[48] Wesley, "A Plain Account of the People Called Methodist , in *Works*, vol. 8: 250.
[49] Wesley, "Sermon 28, Sermon on the Mount 8 , in *Works*, vol. 5: 369.
[50] Fletcher, *Checks to Antinomianism*, Second Check, Letter 1, loc. 1414.

nation under God.[51] Teachings of divine healing and the imminent return of Jesus were mingled with the core message of "a pure heart".[52]

A connection can be seen between the preaching of holiness and a focus upon End Times and Judgment because eternal glory and/or damnation are strong motivators for personal purity. If we are not just trying to survive in this hostile world, but we are expecting to give account before the throne of God in due time, then the message of heart holiness is essential.

Storing up "treasures in heaven"[53] is more meaningful when awareness of heaven and Christ's imminent return are encouraged. Christ taught:

> He who loves father or mother more than Me is not worthy of Me; and he who loves son or daughter more than Me is not worthy of Me. And he who does not take his cross and follow after Me is not worthy of Me. He who has found his life will lose it, and he who has lost his life for My sake will find it.[54]

Self-denial in this world and taking up our cross daily are heavily influenced by the knowledge of the resurrection. The sacrifice of the Lamb of God preceded the resurrection, which preceded the outpouring of the Spirit of God and fulfillment of the prophecy of undivided love. All these world-changing events were grounded in the earthly teachings of Jesus Christ. Jesus ushered in a vital change in both motivation and power for holy living. He forewarned us that we would give account of our lives at Judgment and he provided unheard-of grace through his Spirit so that we might be faithful. Christ was building a spiritual kingdom, a holy nation, a royal priesthood, "so that you may proclaim the excellencies of Him who has called you out of darkness into His marvelous light."[55] Armed with a thorough understanding of the call to self-denial, a believer is better enabled to judge whether the prophet of miracles is fulfilling the greater calling of promoting holiness. Learn through your trials, practice your faith, rejoice that you are following in the footsteps of Jesus, develop a character fit for a royal priesthood.

---

[51] Marsden, *Fundamentalism and American Culture*, chapt. 2.
[52] As shown in the history of the International Holiness Union and Prayer League, which later formed into the Pilgrim Holiness Church. Thomas and Thomas, *Days of Our Pilgrimage*, 16.
[53] Matthew 6:20.
[54] Matthew 10:37–39.
[55] 1 Peter 2:9.

QUESTIONS FOR REFLECTION AND DISCUSSION

1. Read James 1:12–18. Consider verse 12 carefully. According to this verse, who will go to heaven? What do you think is the connection between trials and loving God? From this passage, how can a believer be tempted and fall into sin? In your own words, what is the process?

2. Name the three categories of testing from this chapter. Describe how you have experienced testing in each category. Which have you found most difficult?

3. Read Matthew 13:18–23. Describe who the hard soil represents in your community. Who are the hardest people? What can be done for hard people to soften them up?

   Describe what sort of person the rocky soil represents. What causes the seedling in the rocky soil to wither? Does the rocky-soil person lose faith altogether? Read verse 6.

   Describe what sort of person the thorny soil represents. What causes the seedling in the thorny soil to choke? Does the thorny-soil person lose faith altogether? Read verse 7.

   Consider the good-soil people. What was it about them that was "good"? How do you think some were able to produce more than others—30, 60 or 100-fold?

4. Do you agree with the author's statement, "The performance of miracles sometimes generates self-centeredness rather than deeper hunger for Christ." Explain your response. Can you illustrate that principle from the Gospels? How can we protect ourselves from falling into a self-serving faith?

5. In your Christian experience, is salvation more often directed toward blessings in this world or eternal life in heaven? Discuss the benefits of teaching both and the dangers of overstating each one.

6. How do you think the Church of Jesus Christ is viewed in secular society today? What major scandals have impacted the credibility of Christianity? Do you think that bringing shame on the Church is a violation of the third Commandment—read Deuteronomy 5:11. Name a high-profile Christian who served for many years without moral failure.

7. Read 2 Corinthians 5:1–10. Note how Paul's heavenly expectation motivated his earthly behavior. Which of these verses speak most

clearly to Paul's pursuit of holiness? Read 1 Peter 1:3–5, 13–16. Peter speaks of the day when Jesus is revealed. When is that? How did this motivate Peter?

8. Look up a definition for postmillennialism and premillennialism and discuss the differences. How would each of these views motivate your faith. Can you see any parallel between these two eschatological views and the concepts of Old Testament worldly blessing and New testament heavenly salvation?

9. Read Luke 9:23–27. Explain this passage in your own words. Is this passage for every Christian believer, or only for ministers? What does Jesus ask of those who seek to follow him? What does it mean to "take up your cross"? What does it mean to do this "daily"? How well is this teaching applied in the Christian community today? Is Christ asking you to give your life up, and if so, what is he asking of you?

Chapter 12: **BRINGING BALANCE**

The one on whom seed was sown on the good soil,
this is the man who hears the word and understands it;
who indeed bears fruit and brings forth,
some a hundredfold, some sixty, and some thirty.
Matthew 13:23

The evangelical revivals changed cultures wherever they flowed. Individuals were regenerated, and societies revitalized. This revival power was the same, regardless whether it shone through the lenses of Calvinism or Arminianism; it was intense enough to draw sinners to salvation and sanctification despite human theological interpretations. Surely God does not change, and his message still has the same power today. If we fail to see evangelical power in our ministries, it is possible that we have forgotten how to teach the evangelical truth. We have deceived ourselves that the gospel cannot mean freedom from willful sin, and in doing so, we have neglected weighty portions of the sacred text. Both John Wesley and George Whitefield proclaimed that the indwelling Spirit required an end to ongoing willful sin. Whitefield reasoned that a person who continued to sin willfully was never truly saved, while Wesley taught that they may have been saved at one time but were no longer. Regardless of their differences, they both believed that the gospel achieved what it promised—an end to the devil's work. John the Baptist, Whitefield and Wesley celebrated the coming of the baptism of the Spirit and victory over sin.

Salvation has only ever been by faith. Conscience, circumcision and the Mosaic Law were never pathways to salvation.[1] The best that the regulations of the Law could achieve was to awaken a person's conscience to God's values, but because of the tyranny of inbred sin, any such awakening invariably led to greater depths of depravity.[2] Paul confirmed that the Law was given to prepare the Jewish nation

---

[1] Galatians 3:11.
[2] Romans 3:20; 5:20.

(and every other hearer) for the coming of Christ;[3] in that, it exposed humanity's incapacity to live righteously and brought the humbling that is a prerequisite to the gospel. Without awareness of sin and repentance, salvation cannot be received by faith, because salvation is the gift of God's grace to those who acknowledge their own unworthiness. No one was ever saved by the self-righteousness of the Mosaic Law or any other form of legalism—salvation was only ever found by trusting the God of heaven and taking hold of his mercy and loving-kindness.

Even so, the New Covenant brought a radical reformation to salvation by faith. We are told that salvation by faith extends from Abraham to the Final Judgment, and by examining such ancients as Noah, Enoch and Abel, it is seen to have been the same all the way back to Adam himself:

> Now faith is the assurance of things hoped for, the conviction of things not seen. For by it the men of old gained approval. By faith we understand that the worlds were prepared by the word of God, so that what is seen was not made out of things which are visible. By faith Abel offered to God a better sacrifice than Cain, through which he obtained the testimony that he was righteous, God testifying about his gifts, and through faith, though he is dead, he still speaks. By faith Enoch was taken up so that he would not see death; and he was not found because God took him up; for he obtained the witness that before his being taken up he was pleasing to God. And without faith it is impossible to please Him, for he who comes to God must believe that He is and that He is a rewarder of those who seek Him. By faith Noah, being warned by God about things not yet seen, in reverence prepared an ark for the salvation of his household, by which he condemned the world, and became an heir of the righteousness which is according to faith.[4]

After Christ's resurrection, however, the indwelling Holy Spirit was added to the general benefits of salvation by faith.[5] This new birth introduced unprecedented power over sin in the life of every Spirit-led believer. That Spirit-power is the same strength of God that raised

---

[3] Galatians 3:24.

[4] Hebrews 11:1–7.

[5] Notwithstanding our contention that some who are justified may not have received the Spirit because of lack of proper training, or that the Holy Spirit was clearly available to some individuals in the Old Testament.

Jesus from the dead,[6] sweeping aside every device of the devil. The same person who could not help sliding progressively deeper into sin when following religious laws, cannot now help but be reformed into the image of Christ once saved by faith and surrendered to Christ's Spirit.[7] Works that were futile under law, are now the norm for Christians. Good works arising out of self-righteousness never brought anyone closer to God, but good works flowing from a justified and regenerated heart are essential evidence of salvation by faith. The condition of this new heart is being surrendered to the Spirit of Christ, while the evidence is good works flowing out of love.

Christ's parable of ten virgins betrothed to the Bridegroom (Christ) concluded that, regardless of their betrothal, only five of the ten were eventually granted entry, while the other five were rejected. These ten were all in the Church and all had the oil of the Holy Spirit, but one-half of their number ran dry before the Bridegroom returned, and they were eternally condemned. This parable sits amidst other End Times teachings, reflecting a tragic era when a large percentage of the Visible Church will be apostate and will not enter heaven. Later in the same chapter, Christ told a parable of the separation of the nations into sheep and goats.[8] Some from the nations will go to heaven and some to hell. However, it must be noted that this separation was not conducted according to who had "given their heart to the Lord", but by their actions. Some who thought they were going to heaven were destined for hell, regardless of their claims to faith. Their actions (or their inaction) were judged as evidence of their faith. Did they feed the hungry, give water to the thirsty, host the stranger, clothe the naked or visit the prisoners? Jesus revealed the truth that, when kindness is shown to a fellow human, it is received as a kindness to Christ himself. Believers cannot claim to love Jesus while refusing to help others in need. To ignore those who suffer while living in comfort is a denial of the faith.

Nonetheless, believers are not to be judged the same as heathens. For those who do not accept Christ, no amount of good works will suffice for entry into heaven. Faith in Christ is the only "gate" to heaven. Believers, on the other hand, are judged according to the evidence of their works, not the perfection of their works. Despite ongoing failings, believers' good works will be assessed to evaluate whether they indicate growing faith and love for God and neighbors.

---

[6] Ephesians 3:19–20.
[7] Ephesians 2:8–10; Titus 3:5, 8.
[8] Matthew 25:31–46.

The gateway to eternal suffering is very wide, but "the gate is small and the way is narrow that leads to life, and there are few who find it."[9] The message of holiness has always been unpopular in the world, but Jesus warned us that in the End Times it would be increasingly unpopular to preach self-denial and holiness within the Church, not just in the World. In the book of Daniel it is recorded that an angelic being who looked like a man (perhaps Christ) gave the same warning of separation at the Judgment:

> Many of those who sleep in the dust of the ground will awake, these to everlasting life, but the others to disgrace *and* everlasting contempt. Those who have insight will shine brightly like the brightness of the expanse of heaven, and those who lead the many to righteousness, like the stars forever and ever.[10]

The truths we have been considering in this book remind us of God's eternal purpose in claiming a people after his own heart and refining them for the glory of heaven. The gospel is not simply a message of those Jesus saves from past sins, but those Jesus restores after his own likeness. We have entered the kingdom of heaven by the mercy of God and the blood of the Lamb, we have been empowered by the indwelling Spirit and we have been taught God's holy ways. Now it is our responsibility to work out our salvation, with whole-heartedness and sincerity,[11] with joy, earnestness, care, caution, diligence and speed,[12] knowing that those who serve faithfully will share in the glory to come.

> This day the Lord your God commands you to do these statutes and ordinances. You shall therefore be careful to do them with all your heart and with all your soul. You have today declared the Lord to be your God, and that you would walk in His ways and keep His statutes, His commandments and His ordinances, and listen to His voice. The Lord has today declared you to be His people, a treasured possession, as He promised you, and that you should keep all His commandments; and that He will set you high above all nations which He has made, for

---

[9] Matthew 7:13–14.
[10] Daniel 12:2–3.
[11] Ephesians 6:6–7.
[12] Wesley, "Sermon 85, Working Out Your Own Salvation , in *Works*, vol. 6: 510.

praise, fame, and honor; and that you shall be a consecrated people to the Lord your God, as He has spoken.[13]

Christian differences

Two sanctified believers can have very different understandings of the Christian faith. The Calvinists and the Arminians did, and God worked through them both. Even those who have repented, been forgiven and born-again, and who have the fullness and freedom of an undivided heart, can disagree with each other. They may each love God with all their heart and soul and mind and strength, and yet their social conditioning brings them to different interpretations of the Bible. One is shaped by personality, religious training and experiences to favor a strict application of biblical commands. Another is predisposed toward patience and flexibility. Both can be sincerely applying biblical teachings and the Spirit's leading to the best of their understanding, and both can be misguided nonetheless.[14] All believers interpret the Bible for themselves under the Spirit's guidance and should be extended respectful courtesy. Disagreeing with both vigor and respect is a challenge, but it can be respectful and healthy. In disagreeing, the goal is not to destroy an adversary, but to correct false teachings and to facilitate redemption.

It is possible to be sincerely and dangerously wrong. Inbred sin is not our only impediment to clear thinking. Those who are freed from the self-centeredness of inbred sin can still be susceptible to self-deception and self-justification. The willfulness of sin may be gone, and with it the hard edge of malicious intent, but there are some factors in self-deception that naturally remain. To illustrate this concept, imagine a courtroom jury that is swayed toward a guilty or innocent verdict by the evidence presented to it. If the jury only receives part of the evidence, the verdict will be compromised. In the same way, even well-intentioned believers are influenced by their own incomplete perspectives. We do not know all the factors at work in another person's life, and our understanding of God's values may yet be incomplete. Sometimes, years later, we recognize the other person's point of view or we see the unfortunate consequences of our own narrow decisions. We may disagree with each other as faithful believers, but we must remain mindful that we too are still in the process of becoming like Christ.

---

[13] Deuteronomy 26:16–19.
[14] James 3:2.

It should be humbling for each of us. Often, the longer believers walk with Jesus, the more they become aware of their own failings and their need for God's mercy. Although we are rendered outwardly righteous by the blood of the Lamb and inwardly free from willful sin, the Spirit still works away at our imperfections. We continue to stand against old and new temptations throughout this life. Therefore, believers should live blamelessly—living without willful sin while abounding in mercy and kindness.[15] Paul wrote:

> And this I pray, that your love may abound still more and more in real knowledge and all discernment, so that you may approve the things that are excellent, in order to be sincere and blameless until the day of Christ; having been filled with the fruit of righteousness which comes through Jesus Christ, to the glory and praise of God.[16]

Peter agreed that we should, "be diligent to be found by Him in peace, spotless and blameless, and regard the patience of our Lord as salvation."[17]

Finding balance

Balance is required in our relationships with others and in our personal conduct before God.

We come into God's presence with boldness,[18] and at the same time, with humility. The "boldness" described by Paul is not haughtiness, but rather the confidence of knowing that we are truly welcome into the presence of God. We are children of the King, and doors are open to us. We are humbled because we know that he is still working on our character, and we are confident because we know that he cares deeply about us. We are not to come rudely or in a demanding manner, but reverently as those, who through high privilege, are in the presence of the Almighty.

> Guard your steps as you go to the house of God and draw near to listen rather than to offer the sacrifice of fools; for they do not

---

[15] Deuteronomy 18:13; Proverbs 11:20; Luke 1:6; Acts 24:16; 1 Corinthians 1:8; Ephesians 1:4; 1 Thessalonians 2:10.
[16] Philippians 1:9–11.
[17] 2 Peter 3:14–15.
[18] Ephesians 3:12; Hebrews 10:19–22.

know they are doing evil. Do not be hasty in word or impulsive in thought to bring up a matter in the presence of God.[19]

We do not hide from God's presence, as Adam and Eve did in their guilt.[20] We have no secrets to hide from God because we have confessed our sins and many failings, to the best of our understanding. God knows these things and claims us as his own regardless. He remembers that we are but dust[21] and that our spirit is willing even when our flesh is weak.[22] By the mercy of Jesus, we are given the time we need to grow and mature. So, it is good to approach God and other believers with a balance of humility and quiet confidence.[23]

Faith is a balance between "fear and trembling" and "assurance", "hope" and "peace that passes understanding". The "fear" that Paul describes is fear of sin, not fear of God. Be very careful of sin; run from it in fear because it is much stronger than it looks. Be confident though that, if we reject sin, God will wrap his love around us. "Submit therefore to God. Resist the devil and he will flee from you."[24] We are wretchedly weak and damaged, but Christ is spectacularly merciful and more powerful than sin and the devil. The prophet correctly said, "The fear of the Lord is *the beginning* of wisdom," emphasis mine][25] but the apostle added that the love of the Lord is *the end* of fear.[26] Those who love God with all their heart should not be afraid of the Judgment. If you have lived as a follower of Christ, you will be received as a follower of Christ. As John said:

> By this, love is perfected with us, so that we may have confidence in the day of judgment; because as He is, so also are we in this world. There is no fear in love; but perfect love casts out fear, because fear involves punishment, and the one who fears is not perfected in love.[27]

Christian faith is not only what we stop doing, it is also what we start doing; not what we put down but what we take up. Repentance is essential to salvation but taking on the life of Christ (consecration) is

---

[19] Ecclesiastes 5:1–2.
[20] Genesis 3:8.
[21] Psalm 103:14.
[22] Matthew 26:41.
[23] Micah 6:8; Matthew 6:12; Romans 14:4, 10; James 4:6; 1 Peter 5:5.
[24] James 4:7.
[25] Proverbs 9:10.
[26] 1 Timothy 1:5.
[27] 1 John 4:17–18.

the fullness of salvation. What we stop doing is addressed in the Law; what we start doing is a result of love. Repentance is just a doorway to faith... a narrow doorway, but only a doorway. Fill your life up with actions and words of love. Go to your neighbor, to your suburb or to a foreign land to share the love of Christ. Diligently seek opportunities to be the hands of Christ in this world. Those are the works that Christ will be testing at judgment time. "If you know these things, you are blessed if you do them."[28]

Holiness statements

1. The primary argument presented in this publication is that holiness centers upon undivided love and commitment to God, and it cannot humanly be assessed in terms of performance. Holiness is trust and unreserved consecration offered by the believer and made possible by the indwelling Spirit of God. Holiness (purity of intention) precedes maturity (right thinking and behavior), and the potential for maturity will be hindered by resistance to total surrender.

2. Inasmuch as inbred sin is fundamentally a lack of trust in God and is epitomized by self-will, it is correct to say that inbred sin is completely removed from the heart of a sanctified believer. That is, when the Spirit of God is welcomed into every part of a believer's life, self-will is necessarily driven out. Though crippled by human frailty and abiding weakness, the sanctified believer is thereafter driven by an abiding desire to please God and is free from the stifling power of indwelling sin. This does not negate the truth that, just as Adam and Eve opted to sin in their primitive holiness, so too, any sanctified believer can be so enamored by sin that they neglect their first love and fall away from holiness.

3. To believe that sin continues to reign in the life of a sanctified believer is to defy the prophecies and promises of God. The coming of the Spirit of Christ has brought the era of "undivided hearts", of "hearts of flesh", a time of "God's Spirit within you" when you are "careful to observe his ordinances".[29] We are confident that "the Son of God appeared for this purpose, to destroy the works of the devil. No one who is born of God practices sin, because His seed His Spirit] abides in him."[30] Christian teachers may violently misconstrue the truth of holiness, and believers may come to reject the resulting

---

[28] John 13:17.
[29] Ezekiel 36:26–28.
[30] I John 3:8–9.

overstatements, but we cannot deny that we are living in the promised time of an undivided heart. If we do not experience this abiding love for God, then our faith is compromised and cheapened.

4. This abiding desire to please God in all things must not, however, be confused with perfect behavior. Even when inbred sin is exiled from a believer's life, many powerful forces remain that must be systematically resisted and overcome by the believer. These forces can include such powerful drives as addictions, habitual behaviors, sinful or abusive memories, emotional and personality needs, self-protection drives, fear, faulty understanding of God's values, destructive cultural values, self-deceit, and so on. Neglecting to acknowledge the ongoing presence of powerful temptations to sin is arguably the greatest flaw of holiness teaching over the past three centuries. It is a grave error—quite faith-destroying—to think that having one's heart cleansed of inbred sin is the end of the struggle with sin. We live in a corrupted world, we have inherited a corrupted humanity, and we have personally delved into corrupting behaviors. God gives us new spiritual life, but he expects us to develop our new strength and train ourselves for obedience.

5. God could, of course, remove every remnant of past compromise and weakness, but he does not. God's purpose is that his children develop character, and character must include the capacity to self-regulate. God provides the miraculous power that the descendants of Adam cannot achieve themselves—he provides forgiveness, new hope, and a new moral capacity to consistently choose good over bad—but God expects his children to wield that new-found freedom for themselves. This is the bond between Heavenly Father and earthly child: he lifts us up and rejoices as we learn to walk. A child that is carried everywhere does not learn to walk, and risks having stunted growth through an over-protective parent. A stunted child is not the eternal plan of Almighty God. Holiness is the perfect partnership between the miraculous, liberating power of God and the striving, relentless passion of Spirit-filled humanity. Relentless striving does not mean never failing, but it does mean pressing "forward toward the goal for the prize of the upward call of God in Christ Jesus."[31]

6. In the Final Judgment, Christ will himself judge every purported believer to see whether their actions support their claims of faith, and he will separate the sheep from the goats, the wheat from the tares. He will not be searching for perfect performance, but he will be looking

---

[31] Philippians 3:14.

for proof of spiritual life. Nonetheless, fear of the Judgment is not the driving force of the Christian faith. Those who love with their whole heart have already moved beyond fear and judgment, because their lives are driven by love, and love cannot sit idly by while fellow humans are suffering.

Conclusions

We have argued that both Arminians and Calvinists have drifted from their early evangelical message and integrity. In some instances, they have each surrendered some of their own emphases; Arminians having lost their priority on personal striving for Christian perfection and the Calvinists having accommodated a variation of the holiness message. Furthermore, since the mid-1800s, too many from both parties have abandoned commonly-held fundamental evangelical doctrines; distancing themselves from Wesley's and Whitefield's insistence that born-again believers cannot continue in willful sin, rejecting the truths of biblical inerrancy and the miraculous working of the Spirit of God, and surrendering the priority of community action to the godless Social Gospel.

In the nineteenth century, as these changes penetrated Methodism, Anglicanism, Presbyterianism and Congregationalism, these world-changing denominations lost their vitality and their capacity to overcome hostile cultures. That loss of discipline and the decline of effectiveness are directly connected. It is no surprise that we lost our power, once we lost our first love. We long for revival, but we do not return to the original evangelical doctrines and disciplines. If this is true, then the reason why revival evades us is not because the world is too strong, but because the Church is too weak. In effect, we in the Church are the cause of rising secularism and moral confusion because we have failed to proclaim eternal truths through our own lives.

However, hope can be found in the knowledge that God has long worked through small remnants of his people. In a similar vein, Wesley said:

> Give me one hundred preachers who fear nothing but sin and desire nothing but God, and I care not a straw whether they be

clergymen or laymen, such alone will shake the gates of hell and set up the kingdom of heaven upon earth.[32]

Nothing has changed since Wesley's day. If a remnant would turn their backs on the accumulation of wealth and on worldly ambition, and would rise again to discipline their lives in obedience to the Scriptures through the power of the Spirit, God might again surge through his Church and into our cultures.

Perhaps you are one of God's remnant! Perhaps you will turn your back on worldly ambition and follow Christ in this world. If that is you, then an identity as a Calvinist, Arminian, Pentecostal or Catholic is truly not as important as a life of purity and consecrated service.

Do not be deceived, this call to holy, diligent consecration is not an impossibility and neither is it an enormous sacrifice. The blessing of an undivided heart is one of God's most precious gifts to his children. For thousands of years prophets and believers cried out for release from the tyranny of a sinful heart and a guilty conscience, and in the fullness of time, Jesus Christ came to us as the perfect sacrifice and the doorway to a cleansed heart.[33] His salvation is not just a promise for heaven but an unprecedented liberation in this world. Why would we cling to the rags of this world? God's plan for us is whole-hearted love, confidence in humility, increased spiritual growth, and joy in the face of worldly troubles. This was God's plan since before the Creation,[34] and it is still where we find God's power and presence today.

On his deathbed John Wesley is quoted as saying, "The best of all, God is with us."[35] That is still true today. God is still with his disciples, and the Gates of Hades cannot stand against those who walk according to the Spirit. The question that remains then is:

"Are we with God?!"

---

[32] John Wesley, "Letter to Alexander Mather, August 6, 1777 , *Wesley Center Online,* http://wesley.nnu.edu/john wesley/the letters of john wesley/ wesleys letters 1777/, accessed July 25, 2018.

[33] Galatians 4:4–7.

[34] Ephesians 1:4–6.

[35] Rigg, *The Living Wesley,* 214.

QUESTIONS FOR REFLECTION AND DISCUSSION

1. Have you been troubled by the lack of power of the Church? What is most disturbing: our incapacity to stand against rampant humanism in our societies, the corruption of church leaders, the divisions in the Church that stop us from taking a united stand on any moral issue, something else? Or, has your experience been abundantly positive, as you've been welcomed, befriended and nurtured into e group of fellow-believers? Discuss the concept that the Church bear some blame for moral confusion in modern society.

2. How is it possible for two Spirit-led believers to arrive at different interpretations of the same Bible passage? What are some differences of interpretation that you have seen between well-intentioned Christians?

3. Explain the balance between coming into God's presence with boldness and coming with humility and silence. How does a Christian "listen" during times of prayer? How much time should be spent in listening and how much in praise, intercession and making requests?

4. Explain the difference between assurance of salvation and working out salvation with fear and trembling. What did the Apostle John mean when he wrote that, "there is no fear in love"?

5. If full salvation includes both repentance from dead acts and consecration to a new life, how can that be seen in your life? What good works could a believer do alone and what good works would be better undertaken with the congregation?

6. Do you have an abiding sense of loving God with all your capacity? What struggles do you still have? Struggles are opportunities for growth, but they can be discouraging at times. Read James 1:2–4 and give thanks for your struggles.

7. John Wesley asked for one hundred sanctified workers. What would it cost to be one of those few? What would be the rewards of being one consecrated and serving God? What motivates you most—the concept of rewards or the knowledge that Jesus is watching you and me, looking for evidence of life and signs of love.

APPENDIX A

John Wesley's record of Count Zinzendorf's sermon

preached at the Runneberg Castle near Marienborn, Germany, July 9, 1738.[1]

Can a man be justified and not know it? The Count spoke largely and scripturally upon it, to this effect: —

1. Justification is the forgiveness of sins.

2. The moment a man flies to Christ he is justified;

3. And has peace with God; but not always joy:

4. Nor perhaps may he know he is justified, till long after.

5. For the assurance of it is distinct from justification itself.

6. But others may know he is justified by his power over sin, by his seriousness, his love of the brethren, and his "hunger and thirst after righteousness," which alone prove the spiritual life to be begun.

7. To be justified is the same thing as to be born of God. (Not so.)

8. When a man is awakened, he is begotten of God, and his fear and sorrow, and the sense of the wrath of God, are the pangs of the new birth.

---

[1] Wesley, "Journal, July 9, 1739 , in *Works*, vol. 1: 110–111.

AN UNDIVIDED HEART

APPENDIX B

Minutes of the 1770 Wesleyan Methodist Conference,[1]

relating to the question:

We said, in 1744, "We have leaned too much toward Calvinism." Wherein?

1. With regard to *man's faithfulness*. Our Lord Himself taught to use the expression. And we ought never to be ashamed of it. We ought steadily to assert, on His authority, that if a man is not "faithful in the unrighteous mammon," God will not give him the true riches.

2. With regard to *working for life*. This also our Lord has expressly commanded us. "Labor" — ἐργάζεσθε, literally "work" — "for the meat that endures to everlasting life." And, in fact, every believer, till he comes to glory, works *for* as well as *from* life.

3. We have received it as a maxim, that "a man is to do nothing in order to justification." Nothing can be more false. Whoever desires to find favor with God should "cease from evil, and learn to do well." Whoever repents should do "works meet for repentance." And if this is not in order to find favor, what does he do them for?

Review the whole affair.

1. Who of us is *now* accepted of God? He that now believes in Christ, with a loving, obedient heart.

2. But who among those that never heard of Christ? He that fears God, and worketh righteousness, according to the light he has.

3. Is this the same with "he that is sincere?" Nearly, if not quite.

4. Is not this "salvation by works?" Not by the *merit* of works, but by works as a *condition*.

---

[1] Wesleyan Methodist Conference, *Minutes of the Methodist Conferences*, 95–96. italics in the Minutes]

5. What have we then been disputing about for these thirty years? I am afraid, about words.

6. As to *merit* itself, of which we have been so dreadfully afraid: we are rewarded "*according to our works*," yea, "because of our works." How does this differ from *for the sake of our works?* And how differs this from *secundum merita operum*, —as our works *deserve?* Can you split this hair? I doubt I cannot.

7. The grand objection to one of the preceding propositions is drawn from matter of fact. God does in fact justify those who, by their own confession, neither feared God nor wrought righteousness. Is this an exception to the general rule? It is a doubt, God makes any exception at all. But how are we sure that the person in question never did fear God and work righteousness? His own saying so is not proof: for we know how all that are convinced of sin undervalue themselves in every respect.

8. Does not talking of a justified or a sanctified state tend to mislead men? almost naturally leading them to trust in what was done in one moment? Whereas, we are every hour and every moment pleasing or displeasing to God, according to our works; according to the whole of our inward tempers, and our outward behavior.

BIBLIOGRAPHY

Aquinas, Thomas. *Summa Theologica*, 5 volumes, Trans. Fathers of the English Dominican Province. New York: Cosimo, 2007.

Augustine of Hippo, *The Complete Works of Saint Augustine*, editor Philip Schaff, trans. Marcus Dods, Rose Elizabeth Cleveland and J.F. Shaw. Kindle edition, 2013.

Bebbington, David W. *Evangelicalism in Modern Britain: A History from the 1730s to the 1980s*. Abingdon, UK: Routledge, 2002.

Bruce, F.F. *Paul: Apostle of the Heart Set Free*. Grand Rapids: Eerdmans, 1998.

Cameron, Lindsay. *Methodism Reborn: The Wesleyan Methodist Church in the South Pacific*. Australia: Cypress Project, 2017.

_____. *Getting Right with God*. Mackay, Australia: Self published, 1993.

Carter, R. Kelso. *The Atonement for Sin and Sickness or, Full Salvation for Soul and Body*. Philadelphia: Willard Tract Repository, 1884.

Cartwright, Peter. *Autobiography of Peter Cartwright: The Backwoods Preacher*, editor W.P Strickland. Cincinnati: Swormstedt and Poe, 1859.

Dayton, Donald W. *Theological Roots of Pentecostalism*. Grand Rapids: Baker, 1987.

Dunn, James D. G. *Baptism in the Holy Spirit: A Re examination of the New Testament Teaching on the Gift of the Spirit in Relation to Pentecostalism Today*, second edition. London: SCM Press, 2010.

Edwards, Jonathan. *A Faithful Narrative of the Surprising Work of God*, 1737. Countedfaithful.org: Kindle edition, 2012.

Finney, Charles G. *The Autobiography of Charles G. Finney: The Life Story of America's Greatest Evangelist In His Own Words*, 1876. Condensed and Edited by Helen Wessel. Bloomington MN: Bethany Kindle edition 2012.

Fletcher, John. *Five Checks to Antinomianism*, 1770–71. Amazon.com: Kindle edition, 2014.

_____. *Fletcher on Christian Perfection*. Amazon.com: Kindle edition, 2014.

Gibson, Edmund. *Observations Upon the Conduct and Behavior of a Certain Sect, Usually Distinguished by the Name of Methodists*, c. 1740. Reprinted in USA by ECCO Print Editions, 2010.

Hempton, David. *Methodism: Empire of the Spirit*. London: Yale: University Press, Kindle edition, 2005.

Marsden, George M. *Fundamentalism and American Culture*, 2nd edition. Oxford: University, Kindle edition, 2006.

May, Gerald G. *Addiction and Grace: Love and Spirituality in the Healing of Addictions*, 2007. USA: HarperCollins, Kindle edition.

Palmer, Phoebe. *The Way of Holiness*, 1845. Kindle edition, 2011.

Petty, John. *The History of the Primitive Methodist Connexion from its Origin to the Conference of 1860*. London: Primitive Methodist Conference, 1864.

Piggin, Stuart. *Spirit, Word and World: Evangelical Christianity in Australia*. Brunswick, VIC: Acorn, Kindle edition, 2012.

Rauschenbusch, Walter. *A Theology for the Social Gospel*. New York: MacMillan, 1917.

Ridgway, Kingsley M. *In Search of God: An Account of Ministerial Labors in Australia and the Islands of the Sea*, 1937. Republished in *Pioneer with a Passion*, 2nd edition, ed. Lindsay Cameron. Australia: Wesleyan Methodist Church, 2011.

Rigg, James H. *The Living Wesley*. London: Charles H Kelly, 1891.

Synan, Vinson. *The Holiness Pentecostal Tradition: Charismatic Movements in the Twentieth Century*. Grand Rapids: Eerdmans Publishing, Kindle edition, 1997.

Thomas, Paul Westphal and Paul William Thomas. *The Days of Our Pilgrimage: History of the Pilgrim Holiness Church*. Marion IN: Wesley Press, 1976.

Tyerman, Luke. *The Life and Times of Rev. John Wesley M.A.: Founder of the Methodists*, three vols., 1870. Revival Library Series, Kindle edition, 2013.

Ward, W.R. *The Protestant Evangelical Awakening*. Cambridge: University Press, 1992.

Watson, Richard. *The Life of the Rev. John Wesley, A.M.: Sometime Fellow of Lincoln College, Oxford, and Founder of the Methodist Societies*. London: John Mason, 1831.

Weist, Jon. *Banding Together: A Practical Guide for Disciple Makers*. Indianapolis: Wesley Press, 2018.

Wesley, John. *A Plain Account of Christian Perfection*. Peabody, M.A.: Hendrickson, 2007.

_____. *Explanatory Notes upon the New Testament*, twelfth edition. New York: Carlton & Porter, c. 1856.

_____. *The Works of John Wesley*, fourteen volumes, 3rd edition. Grand Rapids: Baker, 2007.

Wesley Center Online. http://wesley.nnu.edu.

Wesleyan Methodist Conference. *Minutes of the Methodist Conferences, from the First in the Year 1744*, vol. 1. London: John Mason, 1862.

Whitefield, George. *The Works of the Reverend George Whitefield, M.A.,* 6 volumes. London: Dilly, Kincaid and Creech, 1771.

Wigger, John. *American Saint: Francis Asbury and the Methodists.* Oxford: University Press, 2012.

Wood, Laurence W. *The Meaning of Pentecost in Early Methodism: Rediscovering John Fletcher as John Wesley's Vindicator and Designated Successor,* 2002. Amazon.com: Kindle edition, 2012.

AN UNDIVIDED HEART

INDEX OF BIBLE TEXTS

www.ingramcontent.com/pod-product-compliance
Lightning Source LLC
Chambersburg PA
CBHW071526040426
42452CB00008B/903